Mentoring New Parents

Investing in your returning talent

Becoming a parent is life changing. Our experience as employers, practitioners, researchers and working parents tells us this is a critical time for offering support to new parents as they navigate the transition, plan for their return and re-engage with work and career. At an organisational level, there are huge costs associated with losing experienced and talented employees when they start a family and, in the interest of building a more diverse and balanced workforce, organisations need their people to return engaged and motivated to progress their career.

Written in partnership by two established coaching and mentoring professionals, *Mentoring New Parents at Work* makes the case for dedicated mentoring programmes in the workplace as a sustainable way of supporting new parents and improving talent retention for employers. The authors offer timely, practical guidance for each stage of the mentoring journey, from building the business case through to ideas for mentoring workshops. This book is grounded in theory and practice, providing tools, techniques and real-life case studies from a range of countries and organisations to illustrate good practice.

Mentoring New Parents at Work will be invaluable to all HR practitioners and line managers who want to retain and support new parents, helping to pave the way for gender diversity at all levels of their organisations. Its themes and insights will also be of interest to students and researchers of HRM, diversity management, and coaching and mentoring.

Nicki Seignot is an established coach, mentor and facilitator as well as the creator of 'MumtoMum', an innovative maternity mentoring programme introduced to the Asda Walmart Home Offices in 2011. She has recently supported the development of internal Career and Family Coaching at Ernst and Young, is working on behalf of CoachMentoring ltd with the NHS on their return to work mentoring programme and leads Parental Mentoring and Supervision with the Royal Society of Chemistry.

David Clutterbuck is co-founder of the European Mentoring and Coaching Council; Visiting Professor at Sheffield Hallam, York St John and Oxford Brookes Universities in the UK; and practice lead for the global community of Coaching and Mentoring International.

This is an excellent resource for an organisation wishing to support maternity returners; it should be on the shelves of any HR director – and acted on... The book is helpfully organised to give an overview of the subject, practical exercises, case studies and information on evaluation.

—*Esther Cavett, Executive Coach and Director of the*
Cityparents Mentoring Scheme, UK

This book is invaluable to any employer considering the implications of maternity on the careers of their professional women employees... It is a superb resource for how to implement maternity/parental mentoring and for those who want to learn more about best practice in this specialised field of mentoring. A most comprehensive and robust book, which I wholeheartedly endorse as a resource for both organisations and individuals wanting to develop their knowledge in this area.

—*Lis Merrick, Managing Director, Coach Mentoring Ltd, UK*

Mentoring New Parents at Work

A practical guide for employees and businesses

**Nicki Seignot and
David Clutterbuck**

Routledge
Taylor & Francis Group

LONDON AND NEW YORK

First published 2017
by Routledge
2 Park Square, Milton Park, Abingdon, Oxon OX14 4RN

and by Routledge
711 Third Avenue, New York, NY 10017

Routledge is an imprint of the Taylor & Francis Group, an informa business

British Library Cataloguing in Publication Data
A catalogue record for this book is available from the British Library

Library of Congress Cataloging in Publication Data
Names: Seignot, Nicki, author. | Clutterbuck, David.
Title: Mentoring new parents at work: a practical guide for employees and
businesses / Nicki Seignot and David Clutterbuck.
Description: Abingdon, Oxon; New York, NY: Routledge, 2017. |
Includes bibliographical references and index.
Identifiers: LCCN 2016003541 | ISBN 9781138188709 (hardback) |
ISBN 9781138188716 (pbk.) | ISBN 9781315642154 (ebook)
Subjects: LCSH: Work and family. | Parental leave. | Dual-career families. |
Employees—Coaching of. | Personnel management.
Classification: LCC HD4904.25 .S45 2017 | DDC 658.3/124085—dc23
LC record available at http://lccn.loc.gov/2016003541

ISBN: 978-1-138-18870-9 (hbk)
ISBN: 978-1-138-18871-6 (pbk)
ISBN: 978-1-315-64215-4 (ebk)

Typeset in Bembo
by codeMantra
Printed and bound in Great Britain by
Ashford Colour Press Ltd, Gosport, Hampshire

For all working parents-to-be who think nothing has to change.

For those who support them who know nothing will ever be the same again.

For the businesses who recognise the part they can play in ensuring talented people return engaged and energised for continuing their careers.

'This book reflects our understanding (which should not be relied on) of English law at the date of publication.'

Contents

List of figures

List of tables

Foreword from David Clutterbuck

I first encountered maternity mentoring in the early 1990s, when Prudential Insurance launched its programme in London. It was an immediate success and it seemed obvious that there would be a flood of other employers following suit, but it didn't happen. Having shared the idea with thousands of companies, at last, in 2011, retailers Asda (part of the Walmart group) grasped it with enthusiasm. Nicki Seignot took on the role of designing and managing the programme, with support as needed from my veteran gender-based mentoring colleague, Lis Merrick.

In the intervening years, we have seen the rise of maternity coaching, which uses externally resourced coaches to help returning mothers think about the transition back into the workplace. While these coaches (at least those with appropriate training) can provide a valuable resource for some of the practical and emotional preparation that returners need, they usually lack some of the other key ingredients that make maternity mentoring so powerful and effective. Maternity mentors bring both coaching skills and a current understanding of the realities of transitioning back into the specific organisation – with all its politics, cultural assumptions and quirky ways of working.

One of the most underestimated challenges facing the returning mother is the creation of her new workplace identity. Especially if the child is her first, she will not be the same person as the one who left all those months ago. Just as she has changed, so has the organisation; there are subtle and not so subtle differences everywhere and expectations of her and her role will have changed. It's almost impossible for an outsider to help with this process of adjustment, other than at a broad or generic level. But a mentor, who is in the system and attuned to it, can offer frequent, often small insights that give the returning mother what she needs: contextual awareness, self-confidence, and a sense of how to re-align what she has to offer with what the organisation now needs.

Professor David Clutterbuck

Foreword from Rachel Ellison

Many of us are familiar with the 'parents-at-work' shorthand for feeling on the edge of coping – or not quite coping; the juggling, the tiredness, relentless sleepless nights and the challenge of managing work commitments when the baby or the childminder are sick. Unless you have helpful, local family support or can afford a live-in nanny and head of laundry, parenting is a seven day a week job. There are no weekends or holidays. This new job usually comes on top of another job – the job you used to think made you tired!

Some parents gladly come to work 'for a break'; an escape from tripping over toys and wiping bottoms and worktops. It's a chance to have a cup of coffee, while it's actually still hot. For other parents, the thought of balancing working and home life, can feel utterly overwhelming. Coming back from paternity or maternity leave brings up career concerns, issues of self-identity, and worries about family finances.

In my case, I had my first baby at 38 years old and then another when I was 40. If I'd been a PAYE employee, I would never have had the freedom to self-schedule work in the way I do, as someone running their own business. I had more control and freedom than I expected, but I didn't have a caring manager to encourage me, nor the automatic salary switch, to flick back on. I feared my clients would forget me. I really feared forgetting my skills. I worried about forgetting how to pitch for work – the knack of confidently articulating what I do at point of sale. It was a call from a client – coincidentally an Asda client – to book me for some paid work, which gave me self-belief. She genuinely walked the talk of her company's support-iveness to new mums. That made the psychological as well as financial difference, between sitting at home worrying (as the childcare meter clocked up costs), versus feeling positively 'back in business'.

Return to work coaching and mentoring, can be transformative at an individual level. I've seen employees come back feeling self-conscious and under confident, not quite able to squeeze back into their best work trousers. I've seen whole careers saved, because the HR Director had the foresight to send in an Executive Coach before the employee left on maternity leave and again, before she returned to work.

I believe that investing in support for new parents is vital for families and imper-ative for organisations too. It's part of a long-term approach to developing and retaining talent. I would also argue it's part of a societal mindset around parenthood.

Today's parents are raising tomorrow's leaders and tax payers. They're also role modelling how successful parenting can combine with having a successful career.

Not every organisation is concerned with the long term. Many are struggling with immediate concerns in order to survive at all. But the potential for lost business and the costs associated with re-recruiting, would seem far more expensive and wasteful of resources, than looking after the talented people you already have.

There may be temporary compromises for individuals, their managers and organisations. Or could supporting parents of young children appropriately, actually be seen as sound business investing? It may be true that on return from maternity/ paternity leave, parents don't want to stay late in the office and many don't want to travel, but I see evidence of the benefits of these apparently less flexible, more boundaried employees. Parents of young children claim to be – at once – more distracted and more focused than before they had offspring. The working parent offers concise value and intensive output. They are incisive. They challenge the length of meetings and the circularity of discussions to reach a decision. Some claim to see different solutions, faster. They are less likely to lose the thread, if someone interrupts the flow in a board meeting. The post-partum parent is used to distraction and noise. They don't want to waste a moment in the office. Supposed part-time employees, belt through work that might take others a whole week. They are highly motivated.

Working parents might wince at the thought of after work networking drinks. They'd rather be home in time to read stories to their children. In my personal experience, this radical shift in presence from spreadsheets to bathsheets, from reading exec. summaries to turning the pages of *Handa's Surprise* or *Paddington Bear*, deeply refreshes thinking. Time off work tasks, generates more ideas when you swing back into the office. Incidentally, if you know those two children's stories, then you'll see that the after-hours exec at home, is in fact thinking through unanticipated events and global logistics. They're engaged in diversity and difference, nutrition and self care; they're thinking about community and collaborative action.

All this must be tempered with the cultural expectations companies may put on, or appear to put on employees, to respond to the flash of a Blackberry, or compulsively check their email late at night. Everybody's behaviours need to reflect any official policy to support parents of young children and parents returning to work after paternity/maternity leave. By creating a systemic, supportive approach, companies are likely to keep their best workers, and have them working at their best.

The week before I was asked to write this foreword, every client I coached happened to be in a same sex marriage. All of them are in the process of having babies in a multitude of ways – from adoption, to IVF, from surrogacy to woman-to-woman egg transfer. I'm glad Seignot and Clutterbuck offer case studies relating to families in different formats.

Whether it's with a colleague, a People Director, childminder or teacher, I hear myself repeatedly saying:

> Just as I feel I'm getting the hang of this parenting thing, something new crops up. Once again, I feel I'm new in the job…

This unsettling feeling, may indeed allow us to argue, that parents of young children are constantly challenged to refine their resourcefulness, increase their resilience and to keep on learning. That's what this book is asking organisations and the people running them, to do too.

Rachel Ellison MBE[1]

---

[1]   Rachel Ellison was a BBC news correspondent and international project manager working in the UK, Europe and Central Asia. She was awarded an MBE for 'the promotion of human rights and the self empowerment of women in Afghanistan'. Her team won BBC Team of the Year, in recognition of her coaching style of leadership.

Rachel trained as an internal coach at the BBC, before launching her own business. She works with clients in the commercial, public and NGO sectors. Rachel is a trustee for TAG international, a development aid charity and volunteer parent visitor at the Whittington Hospital neonatal intensive care ward. She is married with two children aged 4 and 6 years old.

Acknowledgments

First we must thank the women and men who have shared their personal stories and experiences with us. These case studies and anecdotes add a depth and authenticity to the narrative. For reasons of confidentiality many of these contributions are anonymous; however, you know who you are and thank you so much for sharing.

Many thanks to those individuals and organisations who contributed case studies and tools: Helen Bryce (mentor and founder of Lifebulb www.lifebulb.net), Esther Cavett (executive coach and director of the Cityparents Mentoring Scheme www.cityparents.co.uk), Jessica Chivers (coaching psychologist at Talent Keeper Specialists www.talentkeepers.co.uk), Kathy Denton (executive coach and chartered psychologist), Nicki Hickson (director of coaching UK and Ireland, Ernst and Young), Sue Hughes (training and OD manager, Royal Society of Chemistry), Charmaine Kwame (national programme lead for coaching and mentoring, NHS Leadership Academy), Nicky Lowe (executive coach www.luminate-coaching. co.uk), Jacki Mason (operations manager and consultant, www.coachmentoring. co.uk), Su Nandy (senior HR manager, Imperial College London), Kate Pinder (coach and supervisor, www.piaffirm.co.uk), Sophie Stephenson (Time to Think® coach, facilitator and consultant www.thinking-time.co.uk), and Hayley Tatum (senior vice president people Asda Walmart).

Thanks also to the eagle-eyed reviewers who made time to support the review process and offer feedback and suggestions; Helen Bryce, Esther Cavett, Dorothy Matthew, Vincent Traynor and Vicky Warren.

Finally, this would not have been made possible without the considerable support and input of friends and family who have offered encouragement and essential space for creative thinking. Simon, realising your ambition to sail across the Atlantic came just at the right time!

This project has been 18 months in gestation – you have all helped make it happen. Thank you.

Preface

We all have an aversion to generalities, thinking that they violate what is unique about ourselves. Yet the older we grow, the more we become aware of the commonality of our lives, as well as our essential aloneness as navigators through the human journey.

Gradually the fragments of lives of people I had previously written about and those I was busy interviewing began to come together as parts of a coherent composition. Generalization scared me less and less. I reread an observation by Willa Cather with a mixture of amusement and startled recognition;

> There are only two or three human stories, and they go on repeating themselves as fiercely as if they had never happened before

Gail Sheehy
Passages (1977, p. 28)

Introduction

As an internal mentor and working parent, I started out by supporting a number of colleagues through maternity leave and return to work. With my own experience as a frame of reference and from listening to the stories of these women and working parents in other businesses and professions, I began to notice a series of recurrent themes, which seemed to be determined by the specific timing of where they were on their journey to working parenthood. Pre-maternity there was a resolute optimism and focus on work and career, with limited or no sense of the scale of change that was to come. This was followed by an unexpected disconnection during maternity leave and then, as they began to think about returning to work, there came a new sense of vulnerability and diminished confidence, with unanticipated tensions between career and personal commitments.

Generous policies might have been in place for maternity, yet the extent to which returning mothers had positive or difficult returns was rarely linked to any policy provision. For many it was a matter of 'luck', having a supportive line manager and achieving a return to work solution that met their needs. The personal transition occurred – repeatedly – at an individual level with the collective impact unseen and unmeasured. People were absorbed back into the workplace with virtually no support or discussion around the momentous personal change that had just taken place. Intuitively I believed there had to be consequences, in terms of people's levels of engagement, productivity, and future career choices, and that better preparation of line managers and timely mentoring conversations with peers and working parents from inside the organisation could make a substantive difference.

The experiences of supporting these new parents, introducing maternity mentoring to the Home Offices of Asda Walmart in Leeds, and working alongside skilled professionals Lis Merrick and David Clutterbuck in other organisations as an independent consultant and supervisor, have collectively shaped my thinking and inspired this publication. The aim is to cascade these ideas and learning to a broad cross-section of employers, offering examples of good practice, informed insights grounded in research, knowledge and experience, positioned in a way that makes this knowledge accessible and practical for the end user.

Why do we position this as a book about mentoring and not coaching? The quest to draw a distinction between coaching and mentoring has been underway for a number of years within the professional coaching community.[1] Without seeking to engage in the debate, we propose a definition of maternity mentoring (p. 6), acknowledging that there are many organisations with internal coaching capability that have robust coaching programmes already in place for returning parents. The intention of this publication is to place a new lens on this very specific and pivotal point, exploring the nature of the transition and, having done so, to propose a framework of support that incorporates coaching skills but that fundamentally draws on the contextual experience and knowledge of the mentor as a working parent and/or employee from within the organisation itself.

Maternity mentoring may be regarded by some as a light-touch activity, something that simply brings working parents together for shared conversation and support. Mentoring done well is this and so much more. Careful programme design, planning and preparation of mentors and mentees are all essential, as is having an understanding of the uniqueness of the landscape in which you are working. As one contributor put it, '*With my professional coach hat on, I am wrestling with the skills required to coach/mentor someone in normal circumstances, never mind hormone-induced potentially fragile women.*' The physical process of pregnancy and giving birth is of course specific to women. Having a baby and becoming a mother typically recalibrates a woman's relationship with career and a life outside of work with potential consequences for her employer. Our intention is to offer a progressive exploration of this aspect of a woman's journey: the specific moment in time where her career path converges with the path that is maternity leave and parenthood. We explore how this 'moment' has an impact on her relationship with work and career and the potential for mentoring to support the transition.

With a longer term ambition of supporting steps towards a more gender balanced organisation, we make the assumption that the vast majority of mentees will be mothers taking maternity leave, though many of the approaches and concepts can be applied equally to adoptive parents and fathers taking extended or shared parental leave. (We devote a complete chapter to just this point.) Consequently, the words maternity or parental mentoring appear throughout in an effort to acknowledge the wider social and political ambitions for inclusion and value of shared parenting.

We note our terminology is suggestive of a level of resource and HR structure typically associated with medium to large sized organisations, i.e. working on the assumption that there are additional people to draw on for support and separate functions for Human Resources and Learning and Development. A programme owner may be required to wear multiple hats if setting up internal parental mentoring in a smaller organisation.

This book has as its intended audience:

- **HRDs** – to frame the commercial imperative and recognise the potential contribution of maternity and parental mentoring to a more balanced talent pipeline.
- **Learning and Development Managers/HR Managers** – a 'how to guide' of practical tools and frameworks to get started with your own maternity or parental mentoring programme.

- **Internal Mentors and Coaches** – to offer some timely tools and approaches to support conversations and build understanding of the specific nature of supporting a fellow employee through this transition point and beyond.
- **External coaches and mentors** – who may be working with a client/returner within an organisation and looking for additional insights and frameworks.
- **Postgraduate students** – e.g. HRM, OD and associated academic programmes where consideration of this topic may be relevant in the context of talent management and leadership development.

The individual case studies and anecdotes contained in this book are accounts of maternity and parental leave from across a number of different countries and organisations. They are not offered as empirical representations of a particular country or industry. Rather, they offer a diverse range of perspectives, generating a collective chorus of accounts and insights associated with supporting returners, becoming a parent and overlaying this with work and career. In sharing these, we hope they provide an opportunity to build understanding and appreciate both the differences and similarities associated with maternity and parental leave across differing provisions and cultures.

As David and I were writing this book, we had a number of requests to incorporate a self-help chapter for maternity returners themselves. In practice, there are already a number of useful publications (e.g. *Mothers Work!* by Jessica Chivers, *Baby Proof your Career* by Caroline Flanagan, *Work. Pump. Repeat.* by Jessica Shortall) and online communities and websites (e.g. www.netmums.com, www.workingmother.com, www.mumsnet.com, www.nct.org.uk, www.workingfamilies.org.uk), all of which offer advice and guidance to the individual returner. That's not to say someone might not buy this book (either for themselves, for a partner or friend), take it into work and offer the challenge: *'We need to be doing more of this – please use me as a pioneer/test pilot!'*

Our challenge to you as employers is to view parental mentoring as an essential mechanism within effective talent management and diversity and inclusion strategies. We encourage organisations to make the strategic shift from being passive hosts (reliant on a self-help approach) to active supporters (engaged in positive action through mentoring or coaching), recognising the value of the investment at this pivotal time for the individual, their mentor and ultimately for the business.

We hope this book and the stories within it will give you the inspiration and motivation to get started. Employees will continue to take maternity/parental leave and the patterns will continue to repeat. There is a sense of urgency to spread the word and share learning in order to build momentum for the value of internal support and make a difference to future generations of employees and working parents.

Note

1 A panel-led debate at this year's Annual International EMCC Conference in Istanbul secured collective agreement for a tentative definition which is seeking final approval by the EMCC Council prior to anticipated publication on the EMCC website (www. EMCC.com) in 2016.

1 One maternity leave – two perspectives

When a woman takes time off to have a baby, her rights are generally (and in most developed countries) protected by law. In the UK, for example, these statutory rights are concerned with eligibility for Maternity Leave, Maternity Pay, paid time off for antenatal care and eligibility for Shared Parental Leave and Pay. Her employment rights are also protected while on Statutory Maternity Leave, which includes the right to pay rises, to accrue holiday entitlement and return to work (https://www.gov.uk/maternity-pay-leave/overview).

In the majority of medium to large businesses, procedures for maternity and parental leave and explanation of rights and entitlements are usually to be found in policy documents and handbooks and briefed out with the support of an HR professional. This aside, maternity leave and the practical application of the processes and procedures that surround it can be tricky to navigate and confusing for both the individual employee and line manager, particularly because these are not the everyday types of conversations and both parties are aware they are on emotionally sensitive and legally protected ground.

A line manager's perspective

Ask a line manager how they manage someone through maternity and they might say; *'It's a minefield. I'm not confident about what I can ask and what I can't, for fear of saying the wrong thing. As a company we make provision and on a personal note of course I'm delighted for her. It's an exciting time. Having said that, in terms of the team and what we've got on, it's disruptive. My best manager will be away for at least 12 months, and the new project – which we've been planning for months – won't have landed before she leaves. Any other time would be better than this.'*

Unsurprisingly, maternity can be unpredictable when it comes to forward planning and work schedules. Agreeing dates for the commencement and end of a maternity leave is a challenge, in no small part because while the last working day can be agreed in principle, it may be subject to sudden change, being brought forward in the event of ill-health or even, in some instances, the onset of labour itself if the leave date is close to the date the baby is due. The end of maternity leave and her intentions for return to work may also be subject to change and employees vary in their willingness to keep in touch with their employers.

The absence of a key team member of course requires planning in terms of functional workload and leadership where they have line accountability. It may represent an opportunity for another colleague to step in, or up, and take on an extended role for a period of time. Of course, it's not always possible to secure cover for a maternity leave. This can be down to budgetary constraints (an opportunity to save money), lack of applicants or sometimes specialist skills being difficult to replace. In all these events, there is some sorting out to do by the line manager, who is under pressure to keep the wheels in motion.

If the lead up to maternity is frenetic in terms of handing over and finishing off, the pace of work continues unabated after they have left and quite simply the business carries on. In larger organisations, there is usually a procedure for communicating with employees on leave, but sometimes there can be reluctance on the part of line managers to contact an employee lest this be interpreted as interrupting private time, pressurising them into making a decision or return to work earlier than planned. Clearly contact should be based on individual preferences; however, it is appropriate to make a reasonable amount of contact during leave with the aim of facilitating her return to work. Over time and without contact, an employee can quietly drop off the radar unless lines of communication are kept open.

And then at some point, the email lands in the inbox to confirm the employee is returning on a given date. Over the intervening period, teams will have changed, the work itself may have changed, and perhaps even the original line manager has moved on. Taken at base level, the need is to get the returning employee back in and up to speed as soon as possible. The business focus is typically functional; '*Great, you're back – so let's get started!*'

An individual perspective

Ask any working mother about her experience of returning to work post maternity and the likelihood is she will tell you it was much tougher than she expected. Tough in many respects because before she left for maternity leave, the focus was all about work: handing over and closing down well, with any considerations of the birth and a life outside of work somewhere on the distant horizon. Beyond that, there was an assumption that the rest of life would somehow fit into place, and work and career could continue as planned.

Prior to the start of maternity leave, she hadn't looked for any help because she didn't feel she'd need it. Maternity leave was just a temporary situation, besides which, there was always email and her phone would be on: she'd be accessible and keeping in touch throughout the whole time anyway. Her return would be different to everyone else's – she'd made that commitment to the business and to herself.

Then came the life-changing reality of maternity leave and an altogether different agenda. A complete and unexpected disconnection from work and total immersion into uncharted territory. A life 24 hours a day, 7 days a week, where there could be no immediate prospect of a day off or holiday. A world away from what was known, planned, organised, rewarded (i.e. work). A new world with assumptions of innate knowledge, uncompromising demands for resilience, new measures of success, new skills, new allies, new friendships, new learning every day and at the heart, the excitement and joy of a new baby.

At some point on maternity leave, the prospect of returning to work appeared on the horizon with a whole different set of questions: *'What's changed at work? Can I return to my job role? What skills have I got that are still relevant? What do I need to know and do, to be up to speed and ready to go back? Do I want to continue to work full time or do I ask for part time work? What's the impact of this on my career? What's possible? What's realistic? Do I even want to go back? How am I feeling in all of this? What do I want from work and a career now? What are my priorities? How have I changed? Who do I trust and who can I have these conversations with?'*

These are complex and important questions reflective of the fact the person who returns is not the same person who left. Being out of the business for 2 weeks' holiday can be a challenge, but returning after several months on maternity leave represents a seismic shift.

The mentoring opportunity

The experience of becoming a working parent is highly individual and, of course, not all women find it tough to return to work. Indeed, there are many women who find themselves more than ready to start back and glad to embrace the routine and intellectual stimulation of the working environment. Whatever their experience, each returner will go through a period of adjustment and our experience as practitioners, researchers and working parents tells us this is a critical time for offering extra support as they navigate the transition and re-engage with work as a new parent. Besides which, in the interest of building a diverse and balanced workplace, businesses need talented people to return motivated to stay for the longer term and progress their career.

The benefit of mentoring is its ability to flex and adapt to the needs of the individual returner. With appropriate preparation and development, the best people to offer mentoring support may well be your own employees; leaders, managers, mentors, coaches, working mothers and fathers who have a passion to support, currency of experience and learning to share from within the organisation. We define mentoring in this context as:

> Off line help by one person (who may or may not be a parent themselves) to another in making the transition to working parenthood with self awareness, confidence, and clarity of purpose both professionally and personally.
>
> The role of the mentor is one of emotional and professional support to the mentee. The mentor will bring his or her experience and knowledge of the context to the relationship. The mentor will listen, challenge and offer advice and guidance when appropriate.
>
> In recognition of the uniqueness of the journey to working parenthood, the mentoring focuses on the mentee's agenda, and the challenges that emerge and are important to her. The mentee is responsible for her own learning and

development, acknowledging the mentor may – on occasions – be required to be proactive by prompting time for mentoring in a spirit of moving forward.

In addition to a supportive line manager, mentoring conversations offer a separate, confidential space for exploration of individual questions and concerns, and also somewhere to test out the reconnection with her work self with a view to a smoother and more confident return.

2   An international perspective

While the decision of how long to take for maternity leave is in principle an individual consideration, in practice any maternity leave is heavily influenced by the cultural norms and provisions where the mother-to-be lives and works. With assumptions of an international audience, this chapter offers a brief view of the differing provisions for maternity leave across the world and builds on the individual perspective in Chapter 1 with personal accounts of maternity and working parenthood from three separate countries.

The ILO (International Labor Organization) convention and current European Union (EU) Directive state that mothers should have access to at least 14 weeks of maternity leave. As at April 2014, the average duration within OECD (Organization for Economic Cooperation and Development) countries was 17 weeks with average maternity benefits replacing approximately 78 percent of average gross earnings (www.oecd.org/els/soc/PF2_1_Parental_leave_systems.pdf).

In practice, the range of provisions for paid maternity leave is extensive. The World Policy Analysis Center (worldpolicycenter.org) gathers international data in a spirit of transparency and raising awareness in order to promote equal rights and opportunities. It offers a series of interactive maps related to this topic, including maps for the provision of paid leave for mothers, fathers and both parents. Figure 2.1 illustrates the range of paid leave for mothers of infants.

Referencing data from the OECD Social Policy Division (family database), Table 2.1 provides a detailed comparative summary of maternity and parental leave across a number of OECD and EU countries, ranging from Finland at 161 weeks, through to the United States where there is no national policy for paid maternity leave. (In the United States, having a baby or adopting a child is covered by the Family and Medical Leave Act [1993], which allows qualified employees to take 12 weeks of unpaid, job-protected leave for specific family and medical reasons.)

As indicated, the range is considerable and of course many employers and organisations offer enhanced maternity/paternity pay and conditions over and above any statutory provision. Some would argue the longer the maternity leave, the more challenging it is to return to work both for the mother who will have been out of

Is paid leave available to mothers of infants?

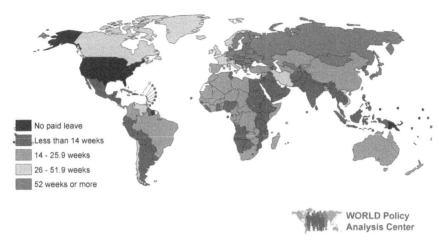

No paid leave
Less than 14 weeks
14 - 25.9 weeks
26 - 51.9 weeks
52 weeks or more

WORLD Policy
Analysis Center

Figure 2.1 Paid leave for mothers across the world.

Source: *World Policy Analysis Center, Adult Labor Database, 2014.* www. worldpolicycenter.org/policies/ is-paid-leave-available-to-mothers-and-fathers-of-infants. Reproduced with permission.

contact with the workplace, her colleagues, stakeholders and customers, and for her child, who necessarily has to be separated from her and cared for by someone else. There are practical considerations for the organisation too, which will have had to secure appropriate cover for the extended absence and will have undergone considerable change in the intervening period.

That is not to say a short maternity leave offers a more straightforward solution. From an employer's perspective a maternity leave of 3 months' duration, for example, in theory may be less disruptive (acknowledging it still requires a degree of planning and redistribution of essential tasks and workload), but for the returning mother still in a hormonal haze at 2 or 3 months post-childbirth, there may be concerns with continuation of breastfeeding, physiological matters of healing and the psychological change coming to terms with a new identity she has yet to grow into before overlaying the demands of workplace agendas and priorities.

At the heart of every maternity (irrespective of geography and timescales) there is a personal narrative concerned with pausing work for the first time, becoming a parent and subsequently re-engaging with work and career. The challenge for any employer is to recognise the significance of this transition and having done so, to plan for additional support which is timely and appropriate to the context in order to secure a positive return and retention of much needed talent.

We now offer a number of case studies, which share insights of maternity from three different countries. Our first is an individual account of maternity in Qatar,

Table 2.1 A comparison of paid parental leave

Country	A^a	B^b	C^c	D^d
	Total weeks paid leave for mothers (B+C)	Total number of weeks paid maternity leave	Paid parental and home care leave available to mothers	Paid weeks leave reserved for fathers
Finland	161	17.5	143.5	9
Czech Republic	110	28	82	0
Norway	87	17	70	14
Sweden	60	8.6	51.4	10
Austria	60	16	44	8.7
Germany	58	14	44	8.7
Japan	58	14	44	52
Canada	52	17	35	0
Denmark	50	18	32	2
Italy	47.7	21.7	26	0.2
Greece	43	17	26	0.4
France	42	16	26	28
Netherlands	42	16	26	26.4
United Kingdom	39	39	0	2
Portugal	30.1	6.4	23.7	21.3
Poland	26	26	0	2
Turkey	16	16	0	0
Spain	16	16	0	2.1
Switzerland	14	14	0	0
United States	0	0	0	0

Sources: Data taken from OECD (2015), Family database www.oecd.org/social/family/database.htm, © OECD Paris (December 2015).

Notes

a Column A refers to total paid leave as of April 2014 (expressed as a total of Columns B and C)

b Column B refers to paid maternity leave

c Column C refers to parental leave and subsequent periods of paid home care leave to care for young children (sometimes under a different name, e.g. 'childcare leave' or the Complément de Libre Choix d'Activité in France)

d Column D refers to entitlements to paternity leave or periods of parental leave that can only be used by the father

where maternity leave is just 50 days' duration. Our second is an account from Finland, which as indicated, offers the longest provision for maternity and parental leave. Finally, our third case study is a reflective account from an executive coach in Portugal who has worked with many senior women returning to work after maternity leave. What becomes apparent is that while the locations and timescales may be different, the stories have a resonance with each other, for example, the importance of provision for pay and leave, the value of connections outside and inside work, concerns about going back, crucial questions of childcare, the need for compromise and impact of working on the family and ultimately the desire to be parents and continue their careers.

Case study

Maternity leave in Qatar

My experience of becoming a first-time mother has ultimately been a positive experience, albeit challenging because of the unfamiliar ways of doing things here. Eighty percent of the population where I live and work are expatriates and there are many groups that seem to form when people are away from their usual countries. Consequently, I found it easy to connect with other mums and also work colleagues, which has been invaluable.

The minimum entitlement for maternity leave in Qatar is 45 days and my employer offers a 60-day entitlement. We do get a lot of annual leave, and I was lucky that I found out about my pregnancy just before my leave entitlement refreshed, so I was able to plan and save that too. I am also allowed a small amount of unpaid leave (2 weeks) so in total am having 3.5 months maternity leave on full pay.

There is no such thing as paternity leave here. In fact, when my husband asked about it, the question was asked '*What is paternity leave? Why do you need leave when it's your wife who is the one having a baby?*' (So typically men take annual leave to be with their new baby.) If we were at home in New Zealand, I'm pretty sure we would use the whole year available to us and my husband and I would share 6 months leave each, which is very common in New Zealand now, especially if the mother is advanced in her career and has a well-paid job.

I found the transition to being a parent at home very easy, but I suspect that is because I know my time as a full-time parent is short, so I'm making the most of every moment. Admittedly I am still connected to work. I check my work emails most days but I don't answer usually unless specifically requested (my out of notification is on) and I have coffee and a 1-1 with my line manager once a fortnight. I work for a Qatari male manager. He is very family oriented, so is extremely supportive of me, baby Leo and making things work. I am quite lucky in that sense.

I am 3 weeks away from returning to work. I am pretty anxious about it, mainly because I won't be at home with Leo looking after him and other people will be brought into our lovely team to help us. My anxiety is alleviated however because we have 2 months of family care (in-laws and my mum) before having to think about nursery or a nanny. It is very common here to have a live-in Philippine nanny, however I think we prefer the nursery route. Childcare is not as expensive as in New Zealand and seems to be very good.

I'm not really sure how I'll go with the transition back to work. I will really have to be organised because I have just been promoted. I have done well in my career to date because I've put my heart and soul into work working whatever hours were required. Now, however, I'll be working

(*Continued*)

7.30am–2.30pm. (For the first year I am able to take a 'Breastfeeding Hour,' which means I can leave an hour earlier than usual.) I'm going to try to express milk during the day, so I guess I will feel "mum" at work because I'll still be expressing. I know I'll be looking forward to seeing Leo every day but I know I have to go back to work. It's part of why we are here in Qatar. For the next 12 months, working is the better option for our 'team.' Then when we move home we may be in a better position and I'll have more time at home when Leo (and maybe baby 2) are older.

I believe there is a very strong case for organisations to improve how they retain key female talent including flexible working hours, child support, ensuring an understanding line manager and team. These are all things organisations can invest in to ensure women remain able to progress their career – if they want to. As someone specialising in talent management and succession planning, I'm a huge advocate for programmes that enable women to have families and remain in their career, adding value to the organisation. Unfortunately this type of investment is not common here in the Middle East (yet) and there are still very traditional notions around the roles of women at work – even if they are expatriates.

Senior Manager
Oil and Gas Industry
Qatar

Case study

Parenthood in Finland

In Finnish society, cultural norms and expectations emphasise equality between men and women. It is conventional for mothers and fathers to bring up and take care of their children together and I think the father's role in parenting has grown in importance over the last few years.

Both of my children were born premature, so consequently the transition from work to being a parent happened very fast. I found I had little time to prepare myself and struggled with the newborn baby. The Finnish maternity and childcare systems, however, have a crucial role in improving the health of mothers-to-be and babies. Maternity clinics take care of mothers and their children, but also offer psychosocial support to the families. This (public) service system had a significant impact on our lives. I felt grateful that we got all the support we needed with a premature baby.

Altogether I spent 3 years at home on maternity, parental and childcare leave. In Finland, mothers have 4 months of maternity leave and fathers have

54 days. After the maternity and paternity leave there is parental leave (around 158 days), which can be taken by the mother or the father, or they can even share the days. I went back to my job when my youngest was 1 year old and my husband stayed at home for 2 months to look after the children while I returned. After that we had a babysitter at home, but quite soon both children started at kindergarten. My daughter was about 1.5 and son was 3 when they both started at kindergarten.

The transition back to work happened quite smoothly and all the practical arrangements between my employer and myself were (in theory) easy to organise. In Finland, parents have a statutory right to work part time (80 percent) until the youngest child goes to second class at grammar school. Unfortunately, the reality of combining work and parenthood was a little different. At the time I was working as a specialist in the Finnish Red Cross and my job required quite a lot of travelling and staying away from home. I became extremely tired with travelling and found it difficult to motivate myself. My husband was also travelling quite a lot with his job and it became increasingly difficult to combine these two careers in our family. So I decided to change my job.

While I was on parental leave I had started post-graduate studies and graduated as a work counsellor soon after returning to work. I now work as an entrepreneur in my own company with two other partners. For me and for my family, this is the optimal way to combine career and parenthood (when the children are still young and need me a lot). It took a long time to gather all the courage to start as an entrepreneur, but now I am really happy about my decision. This situation offers me flexibility and I also have the opportunity to work from home.

Being a mother isn't an easy job, but in Finland we really are fortunate to have a lot of time off and to enjoy being a mother. I believe the Finnish maternity and childcare system, and the strong Finnish support system, make the combination of work and parenthood/motherhood easier in Finland.

Entrepreneur and Business Owner
Finland

Case study

Women's experiences of maternity and working parenthood in Portugal

While maternity mentoring as a practice has yet to arrive in Portugal, I have no doubt that mentoring at this point in someone's career is unequivocally the optimal means for employers to support talented women through the transition to working parenthood. Moreover, I strongly believe that mentoring

(Continued)

has a significant contribution to make in getting more women into the top decision-making echelons of companies, especially in countries like Portugal, where resources for leadership development are still scarce. Mentoring is a two-way learning activity and can be the seed for changing mind-sets, impacting a business systemically because it enables powerful inter-group exchanges (inter-generational, cross-gender, cross-hierarchical and cross-department) and gains empathy for different contextual realities and perspectives. With mentoring, I believe relationships are strengthened, and communities of learning and sharing are built.

In this case study, my contribution is anecdotal, based on my professional experience from the last 10 years as an executive coach and executive development consultant. It is also specific to a special group of Portuguese working women – well-educated executives who operate mostly in competitive and demanding settings (some of them within a male-dominated culture), who are passionate about their jobs and advancing their careers, in order to develop and thrive.

In a country where despite the fact that more than half the workforce is female, women continue to be under-represented at senior levels. The predominant culture is patriarchal and the transition of an executive woman into working parenthood is a considerable challenge, though it is not recognised as such. Maternity can materially affect women's development and careers, but in my view, this is a taboo.

From my experience, the challenge of this transition is mostly lived in solitude and even, in some instances, repressed. With this as a backdrop, mentoring can have a significant impact in terms of the support it provides to address the emotional, cultural and business issues facing women as they change identity to become working parents. Becoming a working mother is a change in identity (both personally and professionally) and this can be daunting. Added to which, in Portugal there is a need for many families to have a double income source, and flexible working practices (such as home-working, reduced hours, compressed hours and job sharing) are few and far between and not typically seen as an option for economic and cultural reasons. Furthermore, there still exists a working culture of presenteeism and long working hours in Portugal.

Although every Portuguese executive woman's situation is different, there are commonalities and transversal issues, which connect them as a group. The following themes emerge consistently across the women I have worked with in a coaching and/or leadership development setting:

- Unequivocally, these women still undertake the greater share of family related responsibilities. Even if they have a support system (either family or one they afford and invest in), they are responsible for planning and coordinating that help, which represents a significant 'plus' in a busy workload. Typically they tend to not to question this, rather assuming it is their role and try to incorporate this at their expense – both emotionally and physically. They take it all! Amazingly, in many situations, this supplemental burden could be softened if they took the initiative to acknowledge the practical constraints it causes. Examples of this include the conversations and expectations of out-of-hours working by line managers that often conflict with family routines and responsibilities, such as nursery pick-up or children's bed times. Calling this out is a challenge, requiring the individual to clarify expectations and boundaries and negotiate some adjustments in order to meet their family commitments.

- It seems simple and obvious that when one has a baby one needs to rethink and adjust daily routines and that this might impact the work schedule, but this causes a great deal of tension, especially inner tensions for a new mother. Typically, they feel embarrassed to even raise the issue and have a genuine fear of being criticised or having their commitment to work brought into question. It is helpful to bounce ideas off someone independent of the immediate situation, who has been there themselves or who can be sensitive to what they are experiencing. A mentor can support by putting things in a wider perspective to find solutions that sometimes question the status quo, but may also offer new working solutions. For a mentee, realising that she is part of the system and therefore also jointly responsible for what she gets from it and that she can influence it (namely on the family front, especially with her partner and on the work front, with her line manager and direct reports), is liberating and enables things to be changed for better and attain win-win solutions. Empathy and sensitivity to women's family caring responsibilities can't be expected to be practiced by others (especially line managers and male executives), unless they have had the chance to be brought in a context where they have learned it by themselves. If this is not the case, women need to acknowledge it not from a victim standpoint, but from a creative and responsible one, as well as focusing on output achieved. The opener for this conversation might sound as follows: 'Here's how you're going to get the very best from me at work as a working parent.' Mentors are precious in this respect.
- There is, surprisingly to me, a naivety about how these women address this phase in their lives. They come to maternity as educated autonomous individuals, yet struggle with the all-consuming reality of what is about to happen. Any change in life has the potential to cause negative stress, especially this one for its consequences and impact. For instance, they do not necessarily think about and prepare in advance for their maternity leave and if they do, their plan in many cases is emergent and with a lot of assumptions that are not checked, namely with their partner and line manager/company. I notice that women worry about a lot, but they do

(Continued)

not necessarily take thoughtful actions. Having a structured mentoring programme along with this period of becoming a working mother (pre-pregnancy, pregnancy, maternity leave and returning to work) opens the door to address this life event in a systemic perspective, bringing more awareness to the impact at the different levels personally, in their family, in their team, in their company, as well as enabling them to have a more conscious, strategic and longer-term view of career development and life purpose and lifestyle. Also, from a very pragmatic view, it enables getting support and advice on how to deal with specific concerns and common questions at each stage of the maternity process.

- Becoming a parent, especially for the first time, is a major life change. It is underestimated how this change affects not only the more evident parts of life, like the daily routine and coping with sleep deprivation, but also issues more profound, such as the ones related with one's identity and perception of identity. For instance, it is common that maternity leave affects the sense of self-confidence. In parallel, parenthood enables the development of leadership skills, such as time management, decision making, creativity, problem solving, planning and organisation, assertiveness, flexibility, multi-tasking, and so on. Providing support and advice through mentoring is definitely a way to benefit from a wider view and putting things in perspective. The intensity of the juggling of the early years does not last forever.

- It is common for these women to strive to live up to a stereotype or an ideal of parenting. There is also sometimes huge social and family pressure to adopt a position that just does not fit the needs and views of the new mother. Curiously, the pressure and the tensions experienced might come from someone very close e.g. the mother of the new mother and might be very stressful. Coping with these pressures and tensions takes courage and is emotionally draining, especially when it comes to the guilt these women often feel for not being the idealised mother they aspire to be or others expect them to be. Being able to voice any concerns and doubts freely with a 'sympathetic ear,' someone who has been in the same situation is comforting and confidence is boosted to find their own way, as well as to find the emotional resilience that it is needed. Mentoring conversations are not only collaborative; they are generative.

I am an advocate and passionate exponent of mentoring. There are clearly immense benefits of having a mentor supporting someone through this life transition. It is not just a nice thing to do; it is an essential practice if companies aspire to have on board the other half of talent.

Ana Oliveria Pinto
Executive Development Consultant and Coach
Portugal

Further information

The lack of provision for paid (and unpaid) maternity leave in the United States continues to generate heated debate. (The United States is the only developed country in the world with no national paid leave.) In an enlightening and impassioned TED Talk, Jessica Shorthall (TEDx. *The American Case for Paid Maternity Leave.* November 2015) shares disquieting data and disturbing anecdotes from working mothers, setting out the *'staggering economic, financial, physical and emotional costs'* associated with this policy.

For a more global perspective, there are a number of useful websites that offer insights and interactive maps indicating the range of provision for leave of absence (by mothers, fathers and both parents) in countries across the world:
(http://worldpolicycenter.org/policies/is-paid-leave-available-to-mothers-and-fathers-of-infants).

Parental employment benefits around the world:
http://www.citation.co.uk/news/parental-employment-benefits-around-the-world

Maternity and Paternity at Work, International Labor Organisation (PDF report 2014):
http://www.ilo.org/global/topics/equality-and-discrimination/maternity-protection/publications/maternity-paternity-at-work-2014/lang--en/index.htm

3 The business case for mentoring maternity

The commercial and business benefits associated with diversity of talent in organisations are well documented. For a number of years, McKinsey has been conducting global research into the value of diversity in the workplace. Its first report 'Women Matter' (2007) identified *'a positive relationship between corporate performance and elevated presence of women in the workplace in several Western European countries, including the UK, France, and Germany'* (p. 1).

The McKinsey 'Women Matter' report 2012 benchmarked the diversity programmes of 235 European companies indicating the best performing companies had a *'critical mass of initiatives'* in place and that these initiatives were contained within a *'supporting ecosystem'*. Sixty-three percent of companies had at least 20 different initiatives in place as part of their gender diversity programmes. Within this list of initiatives were in fact a number of enablers including programmes *'to smooth transition before, during and after maternity leave'* (p. 23).

Most recently, the 2015 'Diversity Matters' report (analysing 366 public companies across a range of industries in the United Kingdom, Canada, the United States, and Latin America) found *'a statistically significant relationship between a more diverse leadership team and better financial performance. The companies in the top quartile of gender diversity were 15 percent more likely to have financial returns that were above their national industry median'* (p. 1).

The makeup of the senior leadership team is a critical and symbolic point, but it is also just the tip of the iceberg. As essential is the pipeline of talent that precedes it and *'without successive waves of talented ambitious women, the whole edifice of female advancement crumbles'* (Clutterbuck, 2011). The ambition has to be to maintain and grow the supply of talent at every level of leadership, recognising and acting upon those factors which continue to have an impact, i.e. for the purposes of this publication, the transition to parenting and potential impact on the gender balance of a talent pipeline.

Why mentoring

Business enthusiasm for maternity mentoring tends to be influenced by two primary factors: familiarity with the specific concept and how seriously they take the issue of gender diversity. Cost is rarely a significant factor (it's an inexpensive intervention) although the budget generally has to be allocated from somewhere.

It's not surprising that the concept of maternity mentoring is novel to many business leaders and HR professionals – after all, it is relatively recent and has not been accompanied with great publicity. Moreover, gender equality pressure groups have been slow to recognise maternity mentoring as a significant part of their cause. This is, in our view, a serious mistake, because the time when women feel most marginalised is on return to work after maternity leave. It would be unfair to suggest that archetypal childless career women discount women who have chosen to be parents, but comments made suggest that this is a factor that should not be overlooked in terms of organisational readiness and essential internal support for maternity mentoring. Certainly, it has been disappointing that women's networks within organisations have not always pressed the case for maternity mentoring more energetically and that HR directors are sometimes less empathetic with the issues facing working mothers than might have been expected.

The advent of social media, however, means individuals are better connected than ever before and there is a culture of openness and readiness to share experiences of life as an employee and working parent using online forums, blogs, and specialist websites such as www.fairygodboss.com and www.pregnantthenscrewed.com all of which can substantively impact marketplace perceptions and the reputation of a business as an employer of choice. Fairygodboss, for example, is a website that posts employer reviews by women for women on their company's pay and benefits, working hours, culture and maternity provision. In December 2015, company reviews included Apple, Deloitte, General Electric, Google, Hewlett-Packard, McKinsey, Microsoft, Sony, Thomson Reuters and Vistaprint. These types of forums are visible shop windows for good and poor practice.

Getting clarity on the metrics

Our experience is that many organisations still approach gender equality from a reactive rather than a proactive perspective. In other words, they respond to political pressure from both inside and outside the organisation. However, they also respond to sound economic arguments, where there is a clear and direct correlation between investment and return. Unfortunately, employers don't always recognise the cost of poor return to work practices – for example, the cost of women not returning, the cost of longer than necessary readjustment once back in the workplace, and the cost of delayed loss of talent when returning mothers feel unsupported and vote with their feet a few months later.

Convincing a sceptical board of the need for investment therefore requires a compelling case and evidence of the status quo. We invite HRDs to seek answers to the following questions for their organisation:

- What is the gender balance of your talent pool/pipeline across all levels/grades?
- What is evident when percentages of male and female employees at all levels/ grades are plotted using separate lines on a graph?

- At what job levels or grades do the volume of maternity/parental leave typically occur?
- What is the gender balance at the levels above and below the point at which maternity typically occurs?
- How many employees take maternity/parental leave typically each year? (i.e. What is the scale of the opportunity?)
- Over the last 5 years, is the trend increasing/decreasing/more or less static?
- How many women do not return to work after maternity leave?
- What is known (and acted on) in terms of reasons for leaving?
- Is there a difference by department or job role?
- What are the attrition rates for employees who leave after having returned to work?
- Is there evidence of a later tipping point, e.g. 9–12 months post return?
- What costs are being incurred for replacing lost talent and essential skills (i.e. external search and recruitment costs, loss of productivity, training and development of new hires)?
- To what extent are people's career trajectories being maintained through maternity?
- What is evident when comparing promotions and talent matrix positions for employees pre- and postparental/maternity leave?
- What is the business doing to support women at this key point in their careers?
- Who and where are the role models?

When this data can be gathered and considered, then a proactive response becomes more probable.

The impact on the bottom line

Mentoring can be seen (sometimes by both HR and line managers) as a nice-to-have rather than a significant contributor to achieving business objectives. Yet we know from research and experience that the impact of mentoring on retention of talent is higher than for any other people management intervention.

At a *macro* level in an organisation are the HR business metrics (of engagement scores, performance measures, labour turnover figures, sickness and absence rates, promotion statistics, recruitment costs) and generally a robust set of supporting policies and procedures for maternity, shared leave and adoption (confirming legal rights and entitlements, any enhanced provision for maternity pay and time off, procedures for flexible working, requests for job sharing, etc.). At a *micro* level, the individual experience is the reality of those policies played out in practice.

The issue with many behavioural development interventions is that it can be difficult to demonstrate positive and financial return on investment. Being clear on the opening picture of key HR metrics and revisiting these same factors post intervention, the financial returns and benefits associated with mentoring this specific transition point are much more easily evidenced.

In our view, an effective maternity and parental mentoring programme should deliver:

- Increasing numbers of women returning to work post maternity.
- Reduction of costs associated with replacing lost talent.
- Positive comparison of returners versus new hires. (Some studies suggest new hires fail to live up to expectations 60 percent of the time!)
- Improved retention rates in the 6–12 months immediately post return to work.
- Improvements in the relative speed of getting back to an expected level of performance.
- Measurable improvements in levels of performance (as evidenced through appraisal ratings).
- Measurable improvements with key relationships at work (e.g. line managers, stakeholders).
- Increased levels of engagement (as evidenced in employee surveys, focus groups, for example).
- Changes to the gender balance of the talent pipeline longer term.
- Increase in reputation as an employer of choice (winning talent being an ongoing management challenge).

Fuelling the talent pipeline

Mentoring maternity is one part of a constellation of good practice towards building a more diverse organisation. By taking a proactive position supporting individual journeys, mentoring becomes an enabler, building collective momentum for a long-term investment in the future talent of the business, improving retention, supporting a faster re-engagement and return to productivity. It can also provide timely insights and raise awareness of broader issues, which can lead to improvements in culture, policies and processes.

For the returner who has, in all likelihood, given so much to the business in the past, this support is symbolic of the value the organisation in turn now places on them as someone with more to give and potential to contribute:

> When I first came to mentoring, I thought my issue was that I didn't want to leave my son and it turned out, at the end of that journey, I learned so much more about myself; my confidence, my skill set, what I bring to the workplace and for an employer to invest that much time in you is just phenomenal.
> (Mentee, Royal Society of Chemistry)

> Having additional support helped me to recognise those things which give me energy (or not) and helped me to redefine my values and what I stood for. It allowed me to be true to myself, highlighting successes and giving me self-motivation. It was somewhere I needed for self-reflection, and testing out; to try new things out

with my manager and challenge my balance of working and living. I was thankful
for the support, felt more motivated and committed to the company. I felt able to
express my needs to achieve personal goals and also the goals of the business.

(Senior Manager, PayPal France)

We close this chapter with two illustrative case studies; the first from Asda Walmart,
makes the business case for supporting the individual returner and the commercial
value of improved diversity at the top table; secondly, we share a detailed case study
of Career and Family Coaching at Ernst and Young (EY) which evidences compelling results and hard data to substantiate their continued investment in supporting
EY employees during this time.

Case study

The business case for parental mentoring
at Asda Walmart

– crucial for returning talent and our target customer base.

MumtoMum mentoring was first introduced to the Asda Home Offices in
April 2011. The programme began with a small pilot group of just 12 mentoring pairs; working mothers and one father, who came together to begin a
groundbreaking project, to improve support for colleagues returning to work
post maternity. Four years on, momentum continues to build and in a spirit
of inclusion and valuing difference, the mentoring now incorporates new
fathers, adoptive parents, and same sex couples.

The inspiration for the programme came from Nicki Seignot, a working
parent and member of the People Team. Nicki was a passionate exponent
with a clear sense of purpose and an unfaltering belief in the value of what
she was doing. Its inception demanded tenacity and an ability to influence across senior leaders and different functional teams. In the 4 short
years since its introduction, nearly 150 new parents have been supported
through the transition, all of whom have more than given back to the
business, both in their re-engagement and delivery in role and many have
since become mentors themselves. The willingness to give back makes programmes like this sustainable for the long term and future generations of
working parents.

MumtoMum has added value that we never dreamed of at the time, with
benefits at individual and business level.

For the individual employee pre-children, it's possible to be relatively self-
ish and to be flexible in terms of what you choose to do and when. However,
once children are factored into the equation, suddenly those commitments
can't wait, won't wait and you have to find a new way of being. For someone

who has always been in control, it is about working out how to function differently and make peace with that. That's where the mentoring comes in; to empathise with the emotion of returning to work as a new parent, to help someone connect with previous relationships or forge new ones and offer essential space to think through issues such as balancing time, dealing with conflicting priorities and maintaining career momentum.

Being a parent is a business issue too. From an attraction point of view, people want to know why they should choose to come and work for a company. Programmes like this offer a cultural sign to future employees, whether they are planning to be parents at some point or not, and are an amazing part of the employment proposition.

As a business it is also critical to have a blended set of experiences around the board table. We make better decisions when we reflect the communities we serve and represent people from different walks and different stages of life. That blend of people for decision making and debate is critical throughout the organisation when you think of Asda's target audience. Our prime customer is a mother with children under the age of 12, so if we don't support and retain those people who also work in our business, we lose the customer voice in and amongst us. So there is an ambition of retaining talent, which we can't afford to lose and also a strategic recognition that working parents give validity to a life experience and appropriately put this voice at the centre of our decision making.

MumtoMum whilst established by Nicki's determination and belief, is now self-sustaining. This makes it ever more powerful. It's in Asda for a purpose and our purpose. Colleagues own it, handing the baton over to new parents all of the time. It is no longer an HR initiative or an Asda programme – it's much more dynamic and important than that. I believe this provides a competitive advantage retaining talent we might otherwise leak. I'm amazed more businesses haven't noticed this hole they are letting talent fall through.

Hayley Tatum
Senior Vice President People Asda Walmart

Case study

Ernst and Young career and family coaching

EY is a global leader in assurance, tax, transaction and advisory services. The insights and quality services they deliver help build trust and confidence in the capital markets and in economies the world over. The UK and Ireland

(Continued)

region of EY employs over 13,000 people, at 5 levels: Level 1 to Level 5. Level 1 are our school leaver and graduate recruits, plus a large proportion of our business support employees. Level 3 is a significant promotion point, following qualifications and experience, to manager. Levels 4 and 5 are our senior managers, directors and, ultimately, partners. Fifty-four percent of our total UK&I workforce are female. Twenty percent of our partners are female.

Our 2010 analysis showed that women were more likely to leave the firm than men (22 versus 19 percent) and that women were under-represented at all levels. Between 2007 and 2010, 20 percent of women taking maternity leave did not return to work following their leave and a further 20 percent left within 24 months.

EY deploys a flexible working culture whereby our people are expressly and actively encouraged to 'exercise greater choice over when, where and how they work.' This flexible culture is supported by 6 key behaviours that were activated during a 2-year culture change programme across the business, and are now measured annually in our Flexible Working Survey and bi-annually in our Global People Survey. This means that our people operate informal working arrangements that work for them, their teams and their clients and are agreed locally, such as flexing hours, working from home, working from other sites closer to home and taking time out to attend personal commitments (e.g. family, sporting, charity). In addition, formal flexible working policies enable fixed working patterns to be put in place, such as part time, annualised hours, term time working. Nine percent of our workforce has such a contractual arrangement.

Our 2011 Global People Survey told us that talented EY women were choosing to leave before starting families or to step off the career fast track after their maternity leave; there was significant opportunity to improve the quality of conversation between line managers and our women; and there was an absence of support enabling women to meet their personal and professional goals. Our view was that coaching could enable high touch, personalised conversations to drive the culture change required to overcome many of these issues.

Career and family coaching was implemented in 2011 and is now available for all employees taking maternity, adoption, surrogacy or shared parental leave. Initially known as 'maternity coaching,' it comprises an offer of 4 coaching sessions (prior to leave, during leave and two on return to work) to support women with their thinking, planning and actions to enable an effective transition out of the workplace and a smooth return to work following their leave. The coaching is delivered one-to-one for senior managers, directors and partners, and in small groups for managers and below.

The coaching is likely to include discussions around managing a positive handover, ensuring the support of the team, preparing for the journey ahead, dealing with anxieties and communication on leave; then to preparing for a confident return, looking at changes in identity in relation to becoming a parent, alternative work patterns, managing expectations, re-engaging with clients and, later, finding balance, defining career aspirations, managing dual careers, handling sickness and leave and career momentum. The delivery is flexible; coaching can be face-to-face, by telephone or webinar, meaning that it is inclusive for those working on client sites.

At the same time, the line managers (known in EY as counsellors) are required to attend two coaching webinars, one prior to the leave and one prior to the return to work. These interactive webinars position the shared accountability for a successful transition with the counsellor. They look at their prior experience of maternity leavers and how this might influence their expectations and behaviours this time; unconscious bias; good communication practise; sources of support and help; planning for leave; supporting the return to work and helping to manage their career.

The coaching was provided by an external provider from 2011 to 2013, but once the coaching infrastructure was in place, the decision was taken to bring it in house in a phased manner throughout 2014 and 2015. This has enabled the firm to benefit from harnessing the skills of trained internal coaches, who understand the cultural context from within and who offer a currency of thinking and business knowledge. This more cost effective solution ensures the sustainability of the offering in the long term.

To date, over 1500 women have taken up the coaching and over 1100 line managers. In terms of direct impact, career and family coaching has:

- Contributed to reducing the percentage of women leaving the firm. Since 2012, women are now less likely to leave than men across all levels.
- Improved retention after maternity leave to 94 percent, significantly reducing attrition costs and also ensuring EY retains skilled and experienced women.
- A survey of those who received coaching said it made them feel valued at EY, increased their engagement with the firm, helped to maintain their relationships with key stakeholders, and increased the likelihood of them staying with the firm.
- The feedback scores for the coaching average 4.5 out of 5.

The coaching focuses on accountability and good management at each stage of the maternity transition, and gives both the line manager and the individual space and time to address the changes peculiar to the maternity/paternity/adoption transition. Importantly, too, it improves the confidence of both parties to do so.

(*Continued*)

The programme has delivered organisational learning to EY about the experiences of working parents, enabling us to develop further support programmes (e.g. new fathers programme, EY parents network mentoring scheme), to understand and help overcome the barriers to flexibility, and inform our innovative shared parental leave approach.

Nicki Hickson
Director of Coaching UK and Ireland
Ernst and Young

4 Maternity coaching and mentoring – internal or external support?

Having established the value of providing additional support for new parents, what is the best solution for your organisation? When it comes to maternity and parenting, there are many bespoke businesses and coaches offering specialist external coaching support. However, at a time of tightening learning and development budgets, more and more organisations are looking at investing in their internal resources as a source of localised and more sustainable development solutions (Ridler Report, 2013, 2016).

We invite you to make a comparison of options using the information in Table 4.1 and consider the questions that follow, thinking about which approach might be best suited to your business' needs and available resources. For example, a small to medium enterprise, with limited numbers of employees taking maternity, or a single member of the senior leadership team going on maternity leave, may be best served by working with an external provider. Alternatively, a low cost business with large numbers of employees taking maternity leave across many levels may view internal mentoring as more a cost-effective and sustainable solution, by up-skilling the internal resource that is their own group of working parents and mentors.

Table 4.1 A summary of external and internal support

External Maternity Coaching or Mentoring	Internal Maternity Coaching or Mentoring
Who is offering the support?	

External coaches or mentors.
  Professionally qualified (often, though not always, parents themselves).
  Usually specialists in this subject area. Examples of providers include Talking Talent (www.talkingtalent.com), My Family Care (www.myfamilycare.com), and Talent Keepers (www.talentkeepers.co.uk).
	Internal mentors or coaches, some of whom may be professionally qualified or accredited. In practice, mentors and coaches are up-skilled for parental mentoring and many are working parents and/or development mentors already.
	  Good practice is for the mentor to be a peer at the same level (though for reasons of maintaining confidentiality not the same business function) as their mentee. Peer mentoring offers the mentee someone at their level who understands the grade-specific challenges of managing this personal transition in a professional context.

(Continued)

External Maternity Coaching or Mentoring	Internal Maternity Coaching or Mentoring
What does support consist of?	

One-to-one coaching at senior levels, planned sessions before maternity and during the return-to-work transition.
 	
  Group workshops designed to support more junior employees (before, during and after maternity leave).
 	
  Workshops for line managers supporting maternity.
 	
  On-line forums and resources.
	One-to-one support from within the organisation, before and during maternity leave and on return to work.
	
	  Internal mentoring programmes also benefit from wider constellations of supporting activities, such as line manager workshops, HR led briefings for employees taking maternity leave, informal parenting networks and online intranet forums.

What about costs?	

External coaching can be expensive. Services are typically costed by each individual or group assignment.
 	
  The cost of maternity coaching for an individual over a maternity leave will vary according to the provider and volume of participants will typically give scope for some negotiation on price.
 	
  Additional costs are incurred for extra services – e.g. web hosting, access to online resources, etc.
	Internally resourced coaching and mentoring programmes are less expensive. (Though of course there is an intrinsic cost to the business insofar as both parties are focused away from day-to-day tasks while engaged in mentoring.)
	
	  Is there a coaching culture, with coaching and mentoring programmes already in place? Depending on the existing culture, levels of skills and experience, there will be setup costs associated with building a parental mentoring programme and investing in up-skilling and mentor development.

Who is the target audience?	
Depending on budgets and finance available, external maternity coaching may be limited to senior women for 1-1 support, and possibly group coaching for more junior women.	Has the potential to be open and inclusive to all, subject to size of the pool and availability of internal coaches/mentors.
What do they do?	
External providers frequently offer a combination of face-to-face coaching, some group workshops, webinars and access to online platforms and apps. Generally there is a schedule of planned support. Many are set up to manage a programme end-to-end for the client from marketing through to matching and evaluation, sharing updates, themes and recommendations.	Most mentoring takes place on a one-to-one basis: Face-to-face conversations while the mentee is in work, moving to telephone or e-mentoring support while on maternity leave and then face-to-face on return to work. The design of the programme will determine the approach taken. Some organisations will have a set framework for support, e.g. one mentoring conversation before finishing work, online support during maternity with a one-to-one session prereturn and then a final session three to 4 months post return. In others, internal mentoring takes a more fluid approach with individual mentoring pairs determining the plan for support and responding to different needs at different times.

External Maternity Coaching or Mentoring	*Internal Maternity Coaching or Mentoring*
Some pros and cons associated with each approach	
Pros • Professional coaches, experts in their field • Independent view – free from business culture and politics • Able to share best practices and insights from having worked with a volume of clients across a range of businesses and industries • Offer a broad approach informed by their experiences as coaches and parents Cons • Both coach and client are 'outside' of the organisation • The external coach will not necessarily have currency of knowledge nor an understanding of the culture and politics of the organisation • The expense associated with external coaching means in practice, it is more likely to be reserved for senior employees and may not be available as one-to-one support where the volume of maternity occurs • There are new costs associated with each assignment, i.e. further maternity leaves/groups require further investment. Plus costs for external management support of the programme	Pros • Internal mentors and coaches familiar with the specific organisational culture, its particular challenges and context • Mentors offer relevant and 'current' experience • Ease of access to mentors within the organisation • Support from 'inside' the business – particularly where mentees feel marginalised and on the 'outside' during maternity/parental leave • Internal mentoring retains a sense of 'connectedness' to the organisation both while on leave and after return • Builds capability of individual mentors and coaches • Costs – the costs associated with an internal programme tend to be up-front and associated with setting up; thereafter, the costs are a matter of internal resource • Returning mentees may become mentors post return. In this way a maternity/parental mentoring programme has the potential to become sustainable and scalable, building for future generations of working parents. Cons • Mentors are not (usually) professionally qualified • Depending on the culture of the organisation, there can be risks associated with confidentiality or internal politics (which should be addressed as part of the mentor's development) • Mentoring takes place in addition to the day job, which can add complexity to a busy diary
Safety in practice	

Accredited external coaches should have regular supervision in place as part of their ongoing professional development.
     The AC and EMCC Global Code of Ethics (www.emccouncil.org/webimages/ EMCC/Global_Code_of_Ethics.pdf) requires that all members have regular supervision.
	Regular group supervision should be in place for all mentors. This is a complex and sensitive transition for the mentee and therefore it is important internal mentors are supported, and continue to develop their mentoring skills and practice in an ethical manner.
	     There may also be collective themes the business needs to be aware of.

(Continued)

External Maternity Coaching or Mentoring	*Internal Maternity Coaching or Mentoring*
Return On Investment (ROI)	

ROI measures are equally applicable across both approaches. As noted earlier in Chapter 3, the impact may be measured through:

- Improved rates of return
- Improved rates of retention post return
- Comparison study of new hires versus returners
- Improved engagement scores of returning employees
- Performance grades of returning employees
- The relative speed of getting back to an expected level of performance
- Longer-term impact on gender diversity at senior levels and through the talent pipeline

Making an informed choice

Good practice! To facilitate your decision, we recommend consideration of the following questions:

- What is the scale of maternity and shared parental leave across the different levels in the organisation?
- If costing support on an individual and or group basis, what might be the anticipated costs in order to do this using (a) internal resources and (b) external support?
- What are the pros and cons of each given your particular business circumstances?
- How established is the organisation culture in terms of support for coaching and mentoring?
- What might be some of the blockers?
- What additional help might be needed?
- Who are the internal champions who have the passion and influence to lead this project successfully?
- What resources are there available in terms of people and budget?
- What is the appetite for this as an ongoing commitment?
- How sustainable is your solution for the long term?

We now offer three case studies as examples of current practice and different solutions for supporting returning parents. The first is an internal mentoring programme at Imperial College London led by Su Nandy, secondly Esther Cavett shares insights from Cityparents, a mentoring programme that operates across a range of professional organisations in London and finally Jessica Chivers shares insights from her work as an external coach supporting returning parents at PayPal.

Case study

Maternity mentoring at Imperial College London

Background

Following her own experience of return from maternity leave, Su Nandy, Senior HR Manager at Imperial College (IC), recognised the college did very little to support the transition back to work for new mothers. With this experience and the recognition that there was an opportunity to improve representation of women at senior levels and address the high attrition rate amongst women (particularly at early postdoctoral level, which tended to coincide with early child rearing), Su worked with a research consultant to create a robust survey to understand more of others' experiences of returning to work following maternity/adoption leave at IC.

The survey covered maternity returners who had taken maternity/ adoption leave between July 2008 and July 2012. One hundred ninety two staff responded, which represented an astonishing 85 percent return rate. The outputs from the survey were shared in full with the Board and there were a number of recommendations made, one of which was the introduction of a Maternity Mentoring Scheme to support returners and raise the visibility of female role models at IC.

The mentoring was designed to assist and support women on maternity leave to make a smooth transition back to work and also to give more focus to the continuation of their career. Mentoring was made available to all staff who were pregnant, on leave or had returned from maternity leave. The mentors were all mothers, the rationale for this being that staff would hopefully feel able to raise concerns and doubts openly with someone who had been in the same situation. They were all trained ahead of time in terms of mentoring skills.

The programme

The mentoring programme operates on a self-select basis and is accessed by means of a web page within the Organisational and Staff Development section of the main IC website. The site hosts details of the programme and individual mentor profiles. The profiles are a personal introduction to prospective mentees, outlining

- Each mentor's department and/or academic discipline
- Professional experience and job role
- Family background

(Continued)

- Top tips for working parents
- Key issues and subject areas the mentors feel able to give advice/offer support with

Academics and researchers in particular are identified as a group in most need of support. (The challenges include urgency around continued academic publication and the male dominated competitive nature of the environment.) The insight offered here is that the mentor profiles highlight those topics that are of most relevance to their specific context and discipline, examples of which include:

- Career progression with children, especially those in medicine/clinical posts
- Managing maternity leave as an academic
- Keeping research going through maternity leave
- Information about all that the college has to offer to help female academics particularly those with caring responsibilities
- Coping with the triumvirate of demands from your kids, your patients and the need to publish – each one a full-time job, but there is only one of you!

With contact details directly on the site, the emphasis is on staff self selecting and getting in touch with the mentor whose background and experience feels most suited to their needs.

The scheme is further supported by an informal buddy system that connects staff pre- and post maternity leave and also has input from an external coaching provider who leads workshops pre- and post maternity for new and expectant parents. With a 95 percent recommendation, the view is that the balance of internal and external support is working well.

Next steps

- The IC programme is about to relaunch as Parent Mentoring from the end of 2015 with up-skilling sessions planned for additional mentors, seven of whom are fathers from different disciplines across the college. The principle is one of inclusion for all parents and also to raise expectations and validate caring responsibilities of both male and female staff.
- The intention is to resurvey returners in 2016, by which time the hope is that the mentoring and wider activities (instigated as a result of the initial survey) will have begun to have an impact, e.g. a lowering of attrition rates – particularly with senior academics

Su Nandy
Senior HR Manager for the Faculty of Engineering
Imperial College London

Case study

Cross-business mentoring as offered by Cityparents

Citymothers and Cityfathers (now Cityparents) is a networking organization open to parents and people supportive of parents working in London. It was started in 2012 by Louisa Symington-Mills, who had just returned from her first maternity leave, and felt she needed more support than was available from her employer and more generally in the City. From that start, as one woman and a web page advertising high-quality talks and seminars on topics of interest to mothers in the City, including networking opportunities for members, the organisation now has more than 7000 members, including fathers, and Louisa and the organization itself have succeeded in achieving a number of diversity awards. Esther Cavett structured and now runs the mentoring scheme (the 'CMS'), which was open initially just to Citymothers but is now open to all members. Key to progression of women in London is provision of support to fathers in the City too, so that being a parent is something that is openly acknowledged and 'normalised' for both genders.

The purpose of the mentoring relationship is for the mentor to offer the mentee a supportive and confidential environment in which to discuss and think through issues regarding work and parenting from the perspective of managing her career progression and work-life balance.

Mentoring at its best provides a reflective place where mentor and mentee can focus on issues of concern raised by the mentee. Both pool their experiences and both learn from doing so. In the case of this mentoring programme, the mentor may have greater seniority in a mutual area of work, such as law or banking, and thus can offer advice and some direction, but the core skill required is that of open questioning, nonjudgmental feedback and willingness to focus closely on another with empathy. As a consequence, the mentor gains valuable insights into other perspectives, challenges and lifestyles, as well as the satisfaction of helping someone progress perhaps more easily and effectively than they did.

Too often in a business context, employees work in a strict hierarchical structure. Sometimes it is possible to plateau and work to a particular level without aspiration for further progression, and that may suit certain mentees whose immediate wish is for good work/life balance; in other careers, such as those within big City law firms, systemically and often explicitly, the direction is up or out, so discussion might centre around looking at options for the future, and when is the optimum time to make a move.

The mentoring relationship provides a safe place in which to practice challenging the 'paternalistic' hierarchy which 'gives opportunities,' 'offers a pay rise,' 'allows exposure to another type of work' where the mentee can perhaps role-play a difficult conversation, visualize what success looks like and ask for it, and generally develop a greater sense of control over a future career.

Esther Cavett
Executive Coach and Director of the Cityparents Mentoring Scheme

Case study

Support from an external provider at PayPal (UK, France, Germany)

PayPal is a great example of where there's been a significant shift toward women actively seeking out coaching when returning to work. We started with a small pilot in the UK in 2013 and the programme has now grown to include women in France and Germany. Women are talking to one another about feeling more energised in their day-to-day role and how maternity comeback coaching has helped them think about longer-term career possibilities and plan related activities. These peer conversations and endorsements mean women are now aware of support being available, how it can be useful and are seeking it out, rather than it having to be 'sold' to them by HR.

At the other end of the spectrum I'm often approached by individuals wanting coaching at the point of returning to work and intending to pay out of their own pocket. This is usually for one or two of a only a handful of reasons:

- She thinks it would be cheeky to ask for her employer to pay for coaching when they've been 'really good to me' ('good to me' is often code for flexible working requests being granted).
- There isn't a coaching culture where she works and/or coaching is seen as being a resource for people who are underperforming or not coping.
- She doesn't feel comfortable asking for this kind of investment because there's no precedent.
- She feels her employer has invested in her enough and says she would feel guilty asking for more.
- She is anticipating having another child in quick succession or leaving her employer and says she would feel guilty having this investment made in her at this time.

After we've discussed the purpose and benefits of coaching and their reasons for not wanting to approach their employers, about half of the women go on to have conversations with their line manager or HR team.

Jessica Chivers
Coaching psychologist and author of *Mothers Work!* (Hay House, 2011)
Founder of The Talent Keeper Specialists (www.talentkeepers.co.uk)

5   Phases of a maternity mentoring relationship

The dynamics of every mentoring relationship will be different, with each partnership bringing its own unique set of circumstances and challenges. And yet, research (Kram 1983, Megginson et al. 2006) indicates that there is often a predictable pattern to mentoring relationships.

For example, work-based programmes for development mentoring appear to go through five broad phases:

- Rapport building (introductions and getting to know each other)
- Setting direction (developing a sense of purpose – where do I want the mentoring to take me?)
- Making progress (peak learning and progression for both mentee and mentor)
- Winding down (reflecting on the journey and celebrating success)
- Moving on (to new sources of learning and development)

These five phases are illustrated in Figure 5.1, which reveals the dynamic nature of the relationship, with levels of learning increasing in intensity before reaching a natural tailing off point, and closing down of the relationship.

The trajectory of a maternity mentoring relationship

Within the context of maternity mentoring, the trajectory of this relationship is radically different. Maternity mentoring relationships are much more fluid, ebbing and flowing with periods of intense support, preceded and followed by limited or no contact, the most apparent feature of the maternity mentoring trajectory being the steep inclines into and out of maternity leave.

This is illustrated in Figure 5.2.

In the context of maternity mentoring, the agenda and relationship are driven by sheer practical matters of geography and the introduction of an all-consuming agenda (i.e. the whole business of becoming a parent for the first time and caring for a new baby for 24 hours a day). The orientation moves swiftly from work to

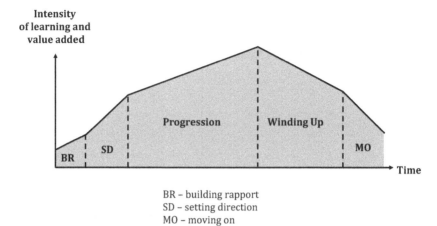

Figure 5.1 The mentoring framework.

Source: Reproduced with permission from Megginson, D. et al. 2006. *Mentoring in action: a practical guide.* 2nd ed. Kogan-Page, London).

Figure 5.2 The mentoring trajectory for maternity.

domestic concerns and then a heady – often conflicting – combination of the two, with consequential impacts on the mentoring relationship:

- **Building rapport** – Initial mentoring conversations are tentative and about getting to know each other and exploring early agendas. There is some progress as rapport is established; however, until the date for leaving starts to feel close for the mentee, many women often don't feel the need to be mentored.

Their main concerns are around work priorities and closing down, rather than focusing on what may be beyond the birth. That is not to say that initial objectives may not be agreed for the mentoring, but at this stage, she doesn't know what she doesn't know and it's helpful to acknowledge that goals and agendas are likely to emerge and be defined once the future context is more 'known' and understood. The key to building rapport is for the mentor to begin to build trust and confidence, knowing that the time spent up front will pay dividends later. Mentors may have to be proactive to ensure these early meetings actually happen against the backdrop of a busy mentee's diary.

- **Maternity leave** – In contrast with development mentoring (Figure 5.2), where learning continues to build as the relationship progresses, the start of maternity leave means the initial rapport building is followed by an immediate drop in dynamics. The need for work-based mentoring is temporarily 'switched off' since she is physically out of the working environment and embarking on a new life as a parent. This will occupy all her energy and resources possibly for a 3–6 month period (subject to the provision for maternity leave). For the mentor, the challenge is how and when to interrupt the radio silence of maternity leave.
- **Setting new direction** – The reconnection of mentee and mentor is often made through e-contact (e.g. email, text or social media). This may be a timely note from the mentor, to 'check in,' or a specific question now on the mentee's mind. While there is no set 'point' where this occurs, typically it is in the later stages of a maternity leave that questions relating to work begin to surface, and there are likely to be some visits to the workplace, perhaps 'keep in touch' days or even team meetings, all of which may open a window for a mentoring conversation. With this in mind, the mentoring trajectory evidences peaks of input and a desire to begin to set direction, which effectively re-engage the mentoring relationship.
- **Progression** – The period of most learning and support typically tends to be in the phase immediately prior to return and the actual return itself as she negotiates dates, details around job role, practicalities of working arrangements and begins to consider how to make the return physically and psychologically as a working parent. For many women, this can be an emotional time; returning to work (with all that has changed since she finished) and returning to the working self, only this time with additional (often conflicting) priorities that were just not there before. The mentor plays a significant role in learning and exploration at this point.
- **Winding up and moving on** – With the navigation of her return to work completed, there is a point perhaps 6–9 months post return where the mentoring relationship becomes less 'essential' to the mentee. She begins to discover her independence and achieves a new equilibrium as a working parent. Mentors may continue to offer an experienced 'sounding board' and a relationship may be left 'open' with the offer of a catch up, should she need it. The key here is to acknowledge the end of this stage of the journey and take time to reflect what the relationship has delivered, what they may want to agree in terms of an ongoing 'informal' relationship and the future mentoring needs the mentee may have that may be best met by other people from this point.

The relevance of this trajectory to your maternity mentoring programme

The purpose of the model is not to typecast all experiences of maternity mentoring, but to note that there is a rhythm and a dynamic to this type of mentoring which has some common themes. The relevance of this is in the programme design and preparation of your mentors.

It is important to recognise the potential impact of a mentees' disconnect (during initial maternity leave) on her mentor. From my own dissertation research into the maternity mentoring programme in Asda, the mentors (all working parents themselves) had experienced the same disconnection from work. However, what I hadn't anticipated was the mentors' interpretation of the extended time gap as a negative reflection on their performance as mentors. Over the course of their mentee's maternity leave, the mentors had themselves become disconnected from the programme, consumed by their own busy work agendas and with their mentee effectively 'off the radar.' In conversation with her mentee, one mentor describes this as follows:

> I didn't even realise you'd had your baby until I saw you visiting work. That made me pick myself up – we'd swapped numbers, but I'd got so self absorbed, I felt I'd let you down. I didn't even know you'd had the baby.
>
> (Mentor, Asda)

What is striking in this quote is the impact of this discovery on the mentor, though critically, this concern was not echoed by her mentee. In contrast, another mentee offers a reflective – pragmatic – view of life absorbed and away from work:

> My mentor contacted me a few times and I put it off, just because my life was so busy. It was more about finding the time and it not being a priority. As soon as work became a priority for me, that's when I started engaging.
>
> (Mentee, Asda)

The challenge of a maternity mentoring trajectory is twofold:

- To encourage mentors to reflect and be able to reconnect with their own experience of maternity leave and return – either as a working parent or from observation of other working parents – acknowledging that at a given point, 'staying out of touch' could be really helpful for their mentee
- For programme owners to find an effective way to keep mentors connected with the mentoring programme throughout the duration of a mentoring relationship

The key message is to manage expectations. In order to minimise the problems and maximise the benefits of maternity mentoring, both the mentor and the mentee need to be prepared for how the relationship may evolve, with all its peaks and troughs. We return to this in Chapter 13 where we share a number of tools and ideas for preparing your mentees and mentors.

Case study

Individual accounts of mentoring at Cityparents

What do you feel you've gained from your mentoring relationship so far?

Mentees

- A regular scheduled slot dedicated to talking about me, meaning that I really have to focus on what issues I need to address and how I feel about them, rather than them dropping off the radar amongst all the other things I am juggling.
- Someone on the same wavelength as me to share ideas with in a safe environment.
- An honest and impartial sounding board for issues that have arisen in the past year connected with promotion and upcoming maternity leave.
- A sense of perspective, that one's career goals are long-term strategies and then sometimes what feels counterintuitive can be the most sensible course of action.
- Time out and space to reflect on what it is I am really looking for in my career and what options there are to get me there and also a sounding board to help facilitate those thoughts.
- A fresh pair of eyes on some issues that have been on my mind for a long time. Having a fresh perspective on them has helped to put them in context. My mentor and I would often talk about how to address these issues, which has encouraged me to be more proactive.
- I've found it helpful that my mentor works in the same field as me and so has been able to give me an external perspective on things.

Mentors

- I have had two very different mentees, though they are from the same profession and trained at the same place. What has surprised me has been how savvy they appear to be, though they are stuck in many of the same dilemmas as those we faced 20 years ago, purely stemming from being a mother in both cases.
- I have gained a more feminist approach to 'strengthen' my mentee's resolve and unfortunately, whilst encouraging them to be true to themselves and their femininity, sometimes I have suggested they would be better off acting like a man – one hypothetical example being not being so honest when slipping off early for the nativity play! Having through the years mentored some women in different areas of work I have not previously felt the need to adopt this approach.
- I have gained new insight into some employers' expectations of professional women, including perhaps their double standards.

(Continued)

- On a personal level I have felt I have gained in confidence in my mentoring/coaching abilities. I now believe my parents were right when they said that there are often many things to be learnt from those younger than you but when you have grown a little you have something more to give!

Feedback provided to
Esther Cavett by
Members of the Cityparents Mentoring Scheme

6 The journey framework and mentoring support

If the mentoring support was a metaphor it would be a lifeline.
That might be a bit dramatic, but the way I was feeling was dramatic.
It was a massive shift.

(Mentee, Asda)

When we are frightened, we don't want to see too much.
At such times mentors can appear lantern in hand,
helping us to see the way ahead,
perhaps strengthening us in our downward journey,
promising in some way to help us fill the void left by the loss
of our former certainty.
At such times we need to think of them as part divine,
and it comforts us to believe that they have been here before,
that they can see the way through.

Daloz (1999)

Underpinning the ebbs and flows of a maternity mentoring relationship is the unique journey of the mentee herself. The journey is unique because every set of circumstances will be different. However, through research and our own experience as working parents, we have identified a number of distinct stages in the journey to working parenthood which are concerned with:

- Early pregnancy
- Ending work
- Maternity leave – early days
- Maternity leave – countdown to return
- Return to work
- Moving forward

We explore each of these stages in turn, looking from the mentee's perspective, what's generally happening at this point and with that in mind, offer some timely mentoring approaches and ideas designed to support each particular stage in the journey.

(Some of the mentoring approaches in this chapter are shared in more depth in Chapter 18. These are referenced alongside the relevant points.)

Stage 1 – Early pregnancy

What's happening for the mentee

The very early days of pregnancy are characterised by a spirit of simple pragmatism: 'keep calm and carry on.' Morning sickness aside, in the work arena at least, life continues pretty much as before. The prospect of actually giving birth is in the distant future and a pressing task list and work agenda continue to occupy her immediate attention and time. At this stage, she's not anticipating major change: the baby will come, she will make provision and working life can carry on.

That being said, there is a seed change in her relationship with work. Perhaps for the first time, she is not able to be completely open with her line manager. She has momentous news, which – for now – she is not disclosing. It is estimated that approximately 20 per cent of all pregnancies miscarry, with the majority (up to 85 per cent) doing so in the first trimester (weeks 1 to 12).[1] Most likely, she will save her news until after the 12-week point when she can be more certain.

She may also begin to feel less in control, sensing an impending clash of priorities. Perhaps the schedule or timing is out – the baby is due a month before a major project lands or a new contract comes to fruition. There is some nervousness about how her news will be received and an automatic desire to reassure work colleagues that nothing is going to change beyond taking some time out. It's important to note that at this point, she truly believes this. Work is what she knows. Technology makes her available and she can keep 'in touch' remotely if she has to. Work has defined her to date and she has yet to experience what becoming a parent might mean for her relationship with work and career.

At home, there is a wonderful sense of elation at the discovery of being pregnant. Having the space to talk openly and celebrate with her partner and family is very important at this time. Away from work, typically, she moves into research mode, through online forums, books, and websites, following her baby's progress and acknowledging milestones of growth with an emerging excitement.

The impact of this and connection to work is as yet unrealised.

What does maternity mentoring look like in this context?

In practice, a first time mother is highly unlikely to be seeking support at this early stage. The focus remains on work and career. However, the point where she notifies her employer of her pregnancy does provide an opportunity for a conversation about what support is available when – and if – she feels it might be helpful.

Good Practice! It is useful to have information relating to your mentoring programme readily available: either a link to an intranet site, or a leaflet giving further details of the programme and key people (e.g. mentors) she can to speak to in confidence. While she may not feel the need for support now, the likelihood is she will refer back to this at a later stage.

Stage 2 – Ending work

What's happening for the mentee?

> Everyone was busy making plans around me, but no longer with me. I suddenly felt invisible and yet I was enormous. I was the elephant in the room.
>
> (Senior Manager, Asda)

At the later stages of pregnancy, there is a point where the personal agenda inevitably collides with the work agenda. She is now visibly pregnant in the workplace and there is a dawning realisation that there can be no going back. This baby is going to arrive. On her calendar, she notes her expected delivery date, but frustratingly (for someone used to being in control) this biological package comes with no guaranteed delivery date.

The prospect of departure comes close. Plans are being made, deadlines set, future meetings arranged that for the first time won't include her. It indicates the start of separation and a reminder that work is going to continue even when she's not there.

> I didn't want to go! Things were really exciting at work and I was worried I was going to miss out on some great opportunities.
>
> (Director, EDF Energy)

She feels the tension of close down; so much to do, to finish, to complete. Her diary is jammed and there is an urgent mission to leave with everything in a great place. No one will say she left without doing a great job.

> I remember thinking I need to make lots of plans and be clear how my area of the business is going to be looked after when I'm not here. So there was a great deal of planning with my managers to ensure we had someone in post while I was off and I wanted to be part of the process of finding that person. I did comprehensive – ginormous – handover notes. I'm sure I bored him with all the little things he needed to know before I went off.
>
> (Senior Leader, Public Sector Organisation)

The big question; how to make the break when giving up work is inconceivable?

> The question on my mind was … 'How the hell am I going to cope with not working?' I wasn't even thinking about the birth, thinking about what I was going to do when the baby arrived, because I just thought; it will be what it will be. The birth? I never read that chapter … it was all about giving up work.
>
> (Senior Manager, Asda)

What does maternity mentoring look like in this context?

The maternity mentor – someone who's been there ahead of her, experienced the challenges of closing down and made it back – comes into their own from this point. In the context of the mentoring relationship, the mentee is able to bring her pregnancy to a conversation in the work environment. Critically in the transition to working parenthood, the mentor may begin to explore changing identities and these conversations can trigger early foundations for a new identity as a working mother.

> The sessions prior to my maternity leave were really useful in getting my priorities right and making sure I optimised my maternity as maternity leave. Talking through my motivations and particularly the assumptions I was making (i.e. that the team wouldn't cope, I needed to be in touch and having a watching brief, I would be able to keep in touch with work throughout and enjoy looking after my baby) was a really useful exercise. I explored why I felt I was indispensable and my concerns that everything would fall apart in my absence – which didn't happen of course. My team were wonderful. We also looked at the sort of parent I wanted to be.
>
> (Director, EDF Energy)

What maternity mentors should be doing at this stage:

- **Contracting the mentoring** – Agreeing upon the ground rules for the mentoring relationship is the essential starting point, and being clear as to the nature of the support being offered. (Maternity mentoring is concerned with supporting a return to work as opposed to antenatal advice and guidance, for example.) Our experience shows that maternity mentoring is quite distinct from sponsorship and development mentoring. In practice, maternity mentors are typically called on to offer professional friendship, to be a confidential sounding board and offer practical and emotional support through the transition to working parenthood. Thoughts of career and sponsorship are not usually a priority for this form of mentoring. That represents a future mentoring opportunity post return and in all likelihood with a different mentor.

  See Figure 6.1 for a suggested outline for a mentoring contracting conversation in this context.
- **Considering the line manager relationship** – Without preparation or guidance from the HR team, many line managers can be uncertain and nervous because they don't know what they can ask for or expect from their colleague. Discussion relating to her pregnancy can simply be put off, ignored or in the worst cases, discounted. Note a mentor's role is not to act as an intermediary between a mentee and her line manager. Instead, the mentoring can be a useful forum to prompt the mentee to consider what she can do to help her manager and how she intends to manage his or her expectations (for example, thinking about ways of working, flexible working in later stages of pregnancy, involvement in recruitment for maternity cover, preferences for keeping in touch during maternity leave, etc.) with the aim of creating an approach that works for both parties.

Agreeing ground rules for the mentoring relationship

- How long do we expect our mentoring relationship to last? (Typically mentoring relationships span a couple of months prior to the start of leave and between 6–9 months following return.)
- How often do we want to meet and for how long each time? (Aim for a minimum of two meetings prior to start of maternity leave.)
- Where would be good places to meet? (Consider different locations with the mentee being away from the workplace for an extended period of time.)
- What happens if one of us needs to cancel / rearrange a meeting?
- How do we want to keep in touch during the course of maternity leave? (Consider alternative media such as email, phone, texts, Skype or Face Time.)
- Who is the onus on to get in touch?
- How confidential will our relationship be?
- What about note taking?
- What is the nature of this mentoring? (Discuss mentee's expectations of the mentor.)
- What do we hope to achieve?
- What are the boundaries to our relationship?
- How will we know when issues are outside our agreed boundaries?
- What sits outside this mentoring? (e.g. Mentor discussions with line managers on behalf of a mentee.)
- How will we give each other feedback and measure progress?
- What if we simply don't get on..? (see 'no fault divorce clause' p. 96)
- Are we both in agreement with this?

Figure 6.1 Outline for a contracting conversation.

- **Supporting safe close down** – The pressure of close down and immediacy of change on the horizon can all conspire to make this a stressful time for the pregnant mother-to-be. Rather like vents on a volcano, the mentor can offer a space to:

  - Let off steam and share how she is feeling about closing down and leaving work.
  - Test out ideas and prioritise what needs doing by them personally, acknowledging that some tasks might require additional help, or alternatively could be delegated, 'handed over' or simply may just not get done (see 'Either Side of the Line' p. 158).
  - Create a robust handover plan with clear timelines and accountabilities.
  - Plan for contingency (for health reasons some maternity leaves commence without notice).
  - Prompt thoughts and ideas of a future life as a working parent (see 'Coming Back with Confidence, p. 162).

- **Giving permission to bring considerations of health and baby into the work arena** – *"It's nice to be in the room and just be pregnant."* *(Manager, Asda)* In a busy work environment and particularly for a first time mother-to-be, there is a guilty tendency to put her pregnancy to one side and to go above and beyond, working harder and longer hours in order to prove the rule that nothing has changed and pregnancy is not an illness. The mentor can explore this with her, encouraging her to reflect on how she is working and explore good practice in a way that enables her to be health aware and still get the job done. (See 'Massively Difficult Questions,' p. 153 and 'Vision for a New World,' p. 156.)
- **Networking in work and at home** – As maternity leave draws near, one of the things to consider is an individual's network. A mentor can help by exploring options and narrowing down to key individuals to connect with before she finishes work. But this is only half the story. In the absence of work and the ever-present support of peers and colleagues, the mentor can encourage her to begin to think about the benefit of a different network at home, in the community, which can be a vital source of support during maternity leave and early parenting. (See 'Powering the Network,' p. 159.)

Stage 3 – Maternity leave

What's happening for the mentee?

> My baby was 9 days late and I remember sitting there thinking; this is ridiculous. Needless to say I was run off my feet when she arrived!
>
> (Senior Leader, Public Sector Organisation)

As she comes to terms with a new life as a mother and a new 'job' that occupies every waking moment and more, early maternity leave has zero space and carries no requirement for a work-based mentor. Many mentees simply 'drop off the radar' for a few weeks or even months, as they are immersed in a whole new world and for many, maternity leave is a lovely experience. As one mentee describes it: *'I had a blast on maternity leave – it was just the best time ever'* (Mentee, Royal Society of Chemistry).

What does maternity mentoring look like in this context?

Good Practice! Unlike most work-based mentoring relationships, where the onus is typically on the mentee to be proactive and get in touch with her mentor, things are different for a maternity leave. The mentee is out of work mode and – for now – appropriately less focused on business timelines and agendas. So a date in the diary 3 to 4 months from when the baby has arrived helps to prompt the mentor into getting back in touch if there has been no contact by that point. During this time, the most helpful thing a mentor can do is simply to keep in regular contact via email, text or social network, depending on what has been agreed between them.

The benefit of keeping in touch via email is that conversations can continue at a pace that suits the individual mentee. She isn't obliged to take a phone call when her baby is crying or is in the middle of trying to feed. An email can be read later and responded to when she's ready. (See Chapter 8 for an exploration of mentoring using alternative media.)

Stage 4 – Countdown to return

What's happening for the mentee?

There will come a point on maternity leave where considerations of work enter her consciousness. This may be triggered by a financial need, a friend making her own return, the approaching end date for maternity leave, or perhaps a desire to be 'using her brain' and be back in wider adult company. The likelihood is that in the latter stages of maternity, she will need to go into work to meet her line manager to agree plans for her return. This in itself can be a significant undertaking. She may not have worn business clothes for several weeks or months. Physically, she may not be where she wants to be – yet. She may be concerned about what to wear, whether to take her baby in with her and what might be asked of her at that meeting.

In any event, there is another change of direction ahead, bringing with it a new vulnerability, a sense of uncertainty and a whole new bunch of questions to be thought through:

- What job am I able to go back to?
- What do I know/not know?
- What do I need to find out as a priority?
- What has changed? (e.g. work agendas and priorities, the team, colleagues, line manager, personal values and priorities, career goals)
- How do I negotiate?
- Where is my currency and sponsorship?
- How do I feel about all of this?
- What do I actually *want*?

And for some returning mothers, the question uppermost in their mind now is; 'How do I return to work when leaving my baby is inconceivable?'

> I just remember how absolutely wretched I felt at leaving her. Then I'm frightened, I'm frightened about coming back.
>
> (Manager, Asda)

> My biggest fears? Juggling work and home, feeling guilty for leaving my beautiful new baby and wondering would I still enjoy work as much and be as ambitious as before?
>
> (Director, EDF Energy)

What does maternity mentoring look like in this context?

The mentor takes on the role of the professional friend at this stage. For many women, the return to work is charged with emotion, loss of confidence in the professional 'self' and a new sense of vulnerability. The mentor can offer a space to test out/share early thoughts of return, air questions and work through some of the practical and emotional dilemmas facing their mentee. While a mentor will not provide 'the answers,' shared conversation with someone who can draw on their personal knowledge and experience from within the context of the organisation is immensely helpful to prompt thinking and aid preparation, as well as perhaps gaining some much needed reassurance around emotions.

A mentor can offer:

- **A different conversation space** – Some mentees find it extremely helpful to meet their mentor away from the workplace prior to their actual return to work. It is a kind of staged reconnection with work, yet free from the trappings of the workplace itself and, importantly, on neutral ground. Subject to the availability of the mentor and their diary commitments, meetings at this point could take place off site, at a quiet café or even outdoors. Walking in fresh air and green open space can have a positive psychological impact on a mentee wrestling with questions around her return. It allows both mentee and mentor to engage with each other and the environment around them, perhaps gaining inspiration and fresh ideas. There is an added bonus that a walk offers plenty of metaphoric possibilities to add to the discussion – e.g. new pathways, unexplored avenues, new route maps, bridges to cross, rich landscapes, variety and colour, the need for preparation (destination, appropriate kit/clothes, contingency), the value of refuelling (support, conversation over a cup of tea and cake) and even rubbish bins (what could you let go of …?) can all be woven into the discussion.

   Good practice! Agree with the mentee where to meet and explore possibilities associated with different locations.

- **Working through the big questions. What do you want?** The mentor can help their mentee to work through the questions on her mind, weighing up pros and cons in order to reframe a situation and move forward with a renewed understanding and sense of purpose. The aim is to encourage a mentee to stay in the driving seat and help her to be as clear as possible about what it is she wants. If she doesn't know what that is, the likelihood is someone else will decide for her with a risk to confidence, where she doesn't feel in control.

   A useful approach here is Rene Descartes' Cartesian questions, the key to which is asking the questions in the specific sequence with sufficient pause to capture different thoughts each time. Here we illustrate how the questions might flow in support of whether to return to work, for example:

1   *What would happen if you did* return to work?
2   *What would happen if you didn't* return to work?

3   *What wouldn't happen if you did* return to work?
4   *What wouldn't happen if you didn't* return to work?

At first glance, these questions appear to be asking the same thing. Yet, following the questions in sequence helps the mentee to look at the issue from several perspectives. It is useful as it expands the boundaries of the original problem, helping to bring clarity to the issue and discover new ideas and solutions. The opportunity is in the reflection of the notes/words which pop up following each question and discussion around what they might want to take away from the conversation.

- **Preparing for the line manager meeting** – Coming in for a first conversation with her line manager is an important milestone for the returning parent. The mentor can help the mentee to be ready for the discussion by:

  ◦ Prioritising the questions on their mind for discussion at the meeting
  ◦ Clarifying what they want to discuss/ask for and why
  ◦ Exploring return to work preferences (See 'Learn Exploit Coast model,' p. 170)
  ◦ Giving consideration to the possible impact of a specific request (e.g. change in role, reduced or compressed hours, flexible working patterns, request to job share, changes in availability for long distance travel)
  ◦ Understanding which elements of their return are non-negotiable
  ◦ Gaining clarity as to where they may be able to offer some flexibility (e.g. staying away on business might be possible at a later date) and encouraging them to be open to considering alternative ideas and options if appropriate
  ◦ Rehearsing the conversation ahead of time

The ability to see things from the point of view of someone else is a key communication skill. For example, the mentor can help by inviting the mentee to physically sit in different positions and experience the return to work conversation from different perspectives:

  ◦ Firstly, from the perspective of herself (What are you saying? What are you not saying? What do you see/hear? How are you feeling?).
  ◦ Secondly, from the perspective of her line manager. (You are now 'X' the line manager. What do you notice? What do you see, hear? How are you feeling about this conversation?)
  ◦ Lastly, from the perspective of an outsider looking in. (What do you notice in this conversation between these two people?)

The skill is in the mentor's facilitation of this, encouraging the mentee not to try and mind read, i.e. '*I think they would say …*'. Instead the mentor encourages her to speak as the individual '*What I (as X the line manager) notice is … The way I am feeling is …*' This can be a helpful and insightful way to prepare for a difficult line manager conversation.

  o Offering tips and guidance (for example, revisiting the pre-maternity performance review to reinforce a positive perspective and summary of her performance before she left to take maternity leave. Encouraging the mentee to talk about what she can do, as opposed to what she can't do.)

  o Thinking about practicalities such as

    – Timing for a meeting (is there a day of the week to avoid, e.g. Mondays because people are typically caught up in 'start the week' activities?)

    – Personal preparation/presentation in order to feel at her best

    – The pros and cons of bringing the baby in for the meeting

- **Working through their ideal return to work plan** – A planned approach to reintegration can make all the difference to someone's experience of return. Some organisations may have comprehensive induction programmes for returners already in place in which case, it is helpful for a mentee to have sight of this ahead of time in order to have visibility of the timetable for her specific return and be able to build in relevant activities, meetings, etc.

  Good practice! In the absence of a plan, it is useful to help the mentee create her own return to work plan, which could then be shared with her manager. Some suggestions include:

  o Dates and activities for connecting with work prereturn. (In the UK, a parent has entitlement to a number of paid Keep In Touch (KIT) days during parental leave. Ideas could include team meetings, away days, corporate briefings, events and conferences)

  o Networking opportunities. (Who could they meet for coffee or lunch on a KIT day?)

  o Housekeeping basics. (Confirmation to HR for payroll set up, a reminder to nominate a team member to reconnect email, mobile phone, set up the desk ensuring pc and printer are connected. These things can make a big difference.)

  o Agreeing a plan for return to normal working hours (e.g. phased return, flexible start and finish times for the first few weeks)

  o Key people to meet with in the first 4 weeks

  o Business updates (e.g. current documents, strategy papers, latest project plans, performance summaries)

  o Anticipated handover of projects/work tasks/team activities

  o Dates for skills training and updates (as appropriate)

  o People and team update (e.g. performance reviews, appraisals, current issues and challenges)

  o Key priorities, diary dates and commitments coming up

  o Planned time for one-to-ones with their line manager over the first month

  o What if? (agreed contingency in the event of emergencies)

  o Communications announcement to the team/wider stakeholder relating to the return to work, role and working arrangements

Suggestions for a countdown to return

> Definitely the preparation, the absolute practicality and logistics of how you
> come back to work. Should I feed her before she goes to nursery or give her
> toast in the car? You find you've got this massively unknown factor and I just
> couldn't get my head round it. It was literally down to that – those practicalities
> were absolutely the most important thing for me before coming back to work.
>
> (Manager, Asda)

The days counting down to return can be helped by:

* Offering practical suggestions – e.g. encouraging the mentee to do a
  'practice run' of her morning drop off and travel to work. Inviting her to
  consider what her routine might need to look like in order to get to work
  on time and ready, and also what support she has available to help.
* Planning contingency (frequently a first week back coincides with a baby
  being ill – what are the plans for if this happens?).
* Exploring how to be 'at my best,' e.g. emotionally and in presentation of
  self. What might she want to wear to help her feel confident and in work
  mode? (Not a question a line manager could ask, but absolutely fine for a
  mentor to check in on!)

Stage 5 – The return to work

What's happening for the mentee?

The word 'return' has an inherent suggestion of going back to something, yet in the
context of maternity leave, where she has been absent from work for an extended
period of time, with perhaps little or no contact, the world that 'was' pre-maternity
is no longer there. Projects, activity and work are going to have moved on; there
may be changes in the team, with perhaps even a new line manager. Fundamentally
she has changed too.

> A massive amount had happened with me but also there had been huge
> changes in the team. Everything was just closed down. We'd got a full team,
> which we didn't have when I left. I came back and everyone was in their place.
> It was all buttoned down and everyone was doing their job. I felt like I was
> trying to edge in. I'm back – find me something to do.
>
> (Manager, Asda)

Early days back are typically concerned with juggling competing priorities and
identities with a new routine and structure of life as a working parent yet to emerge:

> I was torn between desperately wanting to stay at home with my son and feeling a
> huge sense of loss at not being at work every day. I think in those early days you're
> in transition from one identity to another. You just want some sort of familiarity.
>
> (Manager, Royal Society of Chemistry)

> My challenges were sleep deprivation, feeling tired, out of date, fat and a little unable to cope at times. I also missed my little son. And on top of that, requesting slight changes to my hours from an unsympathetic boss to support childcare arrangements.
>
> (Director, Russell Group University)

Some returners find themselves in a dilemma and confused about what they want, despite being so clear (pre-baby) about their intentions for resuming work and career. Often there is an overwhelming emotional desire to be with her baby when at work and a concern she should to be at work or working when she gets home. In addition to this, the choice of childcare can often feel like a compromise and she worries about how her baby is being cared for in her absence.

> My mentor gave me permission to separate work and being a parent. The job was important, but was no longer the be all and end all of life. I found I had new priorities. Before having my daughter, even though I had a big family life, my job was everything. I would spend more time at work than at home, more time thinking about work than anything else. Then you have a baby and 99% of your time is spent thinking about the baby and where they are. Even now (18 months in), I'm checking to see have nursery called, is she okay, is she wearing the right clothes? There is a whole secondary dialogue which never stops running, about what might be going on for your child, even when you are at work.
>
> (Senior Leader, Public Sector Organisation)

In addition to these concerns, for some returners there are fundamental concerns with self-confidence and their perceived ability at work. As one mentor describes her mentee:

> There was a real concern about her being able to do her job. She really worried that she had complete baby brain and was no longer able to function – and that when she went back they would find out, or somebody would say you're clearly not able to do this anymore.
>
> (Mentor, Asda)

What does maternity mentoring look like in this context?

Typically the mentor is called upon to offer practical guidance and emotional support to the returning mentee in the early weeks postreturn. Things a mentor might do include:

- Proactively scheduling in a coffee and informal catch up on the first week back
- Planning in a first mentoring session post return to work
- Encouraging the mentee to set small goals, recognise new skills developed on maternity leave, and celebrate success (see 'Stars in a Night Sky,' p. 163, and 'The First 30 Days,' p. 165)

- Building confidence by mapping internal and external resources (see 'Systemic Approach,' p. 176)
- Exploring boundaries for work and home, which make this new life possible and manage expectations of others in the workplace (see 'Massively Difficult Questions,' p. 153)
- For a mentee struggling to feel 'back', the Kubler Ross Change Curve can be a helpful tool to reflect on the nature of journey thus far, acknowledging highs and lows as part of the natural process of dealing and coming to terms with change and also offering hope for future progress (see 'Change Curve,' p. 167)

Stage 6 – Moving forward

What's happening for the mentee?

> I have to constantly juggle being a writer with being a wife and a mother. It's a matter of putting two different things first simultaneously.
>
> Madeline L'Engle

As the above quote suggests, being a working parent demands ongoing adaptation and balancing of priorities. There is no 'magic solution' to getting it right and as most working parents will tell you, some weeks things go well, while others are a challenge. In her book *Mothers Work!* Jessica Chivers offers a timely reminder that working parenthood '*is a journey, not a destination*' and that '*getting back to work and coping with the first week or month is just the beginning of things*'. In practice, the returner begins to manage the balancing act, recognising the need for give and take and perhaps re-evaluating what constitutes success. Over time, new routines and patterns begin to establish themselves. There may also be an emerging reconnection with their professional identity and increasing self-confidence as they restore currency of knowledge and skills and are now delivering in role. Appraisal meetings or one-to-ones may be opportunities to set out intentions for a next move or longer-term career choices. There will come a point where the mentee begins to step away from the mentoring, with original objectives and needs having now been met.

What does mentoring look like in this context?

The mentoring support may well begin to slow down and change gear at this point. The key is for the mentor to be sensitive to the personal progression of their mentee, noticing changes in agendas, their preparation, perhaps the language they are using and the nature of what gets 'brought' to mentoring conversations. Equally, noticing where a mentee may seem 'stuck' or becoming dependent on the mentoring support.

Things a mentor could be doing at this point include:

- Reflecting on the journey and personal learning (see 'Massively Difficult Questions,' p. 153).
- Recognising and celebrating the things that have gone well.

- Exploring longer term career options in the context of who they are now as a working parent.
- Revisiting personal and professional networks in support of moving forward and maintaining career momentum (see 'Powering the Network,' p. 159).
- Exploring next steps for coaching or mentoring support. This is a critical point for women as Joy Bussell (2008) notes: *'The transition from working woman to working mother is complex and longer lasting than current assumptions acknowledge. This transition does not start with pregnancy and end with a return to work, rather is a process that continues and evolves with the needs of children.'* Key to this stage in the journey, Bussell's research identified a *'very critical period 9–12 months following return to work'* in which women questioned and reflected asking, *'What am I doing?'* The maternity mentoring may be drawing to a close, but there may be new challenges ahead for which additional support might make a difference to retention and/or continued career progression.
- Moving toward the end of the relationship (see Chapter 15).

We close this chapter with two case studies, which set out different approaches and structures for support from Cityparents and Talent Keepers.

Case study

Cityparents mentoring

In the Cityparents Mentoring Scheme (the 'CMS'), which matches people from different organisations, we say that the mentee is in charge of the relationship, setting the parameters of the discussion, reflecting after it and acting on things arising from it, based on her own judgment of what is going to be most effective, and taking charge of practical matters such as arranging the dates and times of sessions.

The essential features of the CMS are set out in a Mentoring Code to which all participants are asked to agree, and are summarised as follows:

- A requirement to undertake an induction
- Commitment by participants to meet (in person/virtually) approximately every 6 weeks for a maximum of a year
- The mentee is responsible for her own development and steps taken, and drives the mentoring relationship
- Ongoing input from scheme director is available if requested
- Mentors and mentees provide occasional feedback to Cityparents
- Personal information is held subject to the Data Protection Act
- The mentoring relationship is on a voluntary only basis (after the mentee pays an initial, modest joining fee)

- Participants agree to the CMS Code and confirm that they understand that the role of Cityparents is to introduce mentors and mentees and set reasonable expectations for the continuation of that relationship, in line with current best practice, but it does not manage the relationship on an ongoing basis.

The CMS Code also emphasises:

- Confidentiality (subject to exceptions required by law), respect and honesty.
- Mentors and mentees are asked to honour boundaries and establish a clear framework for relationship in the initial meeting and, subsequently, through clear 'contracting.'
- Appropriate reflection following meeting is encouraged.
- The mentee is asked to actively consider next steps.
- Both mentor and mentee are asked to consider appropriate conflict management.
- The mentor is asked to work within their own competences and skills.
- Members agree to a no-fault clause to end partnership.

These aspects of the Code are taken from various sources including the ethical codes of The Association for Coaching and the European Mentoring and Coaching Council. We also considered our responsibilities under the Data Protection Act as regards the holding of personal information and we reviewed the British Psychological Society guidelines for research involving individuals and would adhere to those guidelines in any evaluation of the scheme.

Overall, we have tried to devise a scheme that encourages transparency, trust, reflection and respect between mentors and mentees and between participants and the organisers of the scheme.

Esther Cavett
Executive Coach and Director of the Cityparents Mentoring Scheme

Case study

External coaching insights from Talent Keepers

To kick-start our maternity comeback coaching relationships, we invite coachees to complete a reflective exercise before their first coaching session. It's a series of questions to get minds whirring about what's going well at the moment, what a good 'comeback' might look like, anticipated challenges and

(*Continued*)

3–5 objectives for the coaching relationship. Along with this we invite coachees to complete the Realise2 strengths tool. Taken together these resources help coachees build their sense of self-efficacy and begin to work out what they want in the transition phase between maternity leave ending and returning to work, and beyond.

Recurrent maternity comeback coaching themes centre around time management, others' expectations and self belief, with coachees wanting to tackle questions such as:

- How can I show I'm still committed when I can't do as many hours as I did before?
- How can I continue to get the job done when I won't be able to get in early/stay late on a regular basis?
- How can I get on the right people's radars and still have time for career development when I need to (and want to) get home?
- How can I cope at work when I am still sleep deprived?
- What can I do to make it easier separating from my child(ren)?
- What if my maternity cover did a better job than me?
- How can I feel generally more confident about the job I'm doing? (A question that comes up constantly when coaching women whether or not it's at maternity time)

I find that women having the time to ask and think about these questions goes such a long way to feeling prepared for their return to work. Coaching time can be hugely valuable at many points in our careers and especially in times of transition when we can feel so very uncertain, unsure and anxious about what lies ahead.

Jessica Chivers
Coaching psychologist and author of *Mothers Work!* (Hay House, 2011)
Founder of The Talent Keeper Specialists (www.talentkeepers.co.uk).

Note

1 National Institute for Health and Care Excellence, *Ectopic pregnancy and miscarriage*, clinical guideline CG154, London NICE, 2012. Available at: http://guidance.nice.org.uk/CG154.

7 Mentoring roles in this context

Mentoring in the context of maternity leave and return to work is concerned with development. It has at its heart helping mentees to do something for themselves. It is concerned with co-learning (since both mentor and mentee will learn and change through this relationship) and helping the mentee through a period of significant transition. So what does this mean for the role of the mentor?

There are **two dimensions of 'helping to learn' in mentoring**.

In principle, mentoring as a learning relationship operates across a spectrum, with two dimensions:

- The first relates to **who is taking the lead**? Where a mentor takes charge of managing the relationship, setting up meetings, driving the agenda and general direction, the relationship is directive. In contrast, where a mentee is encouraged to set her own agenda, to be proactive and encouraged to come to her own conclusions, the mentoring is relatively nondirective.
- The second dimension relates to the individual's **primary need** for the mentoring. Is it about learning – being stretched and challenged – or about nurturing – being supported and encouraged?

The skilled mentor is consciously able to move along these different dimensions, in any direction in response to what the mentee needs at a given point. Again, it's worth reiterating that the early stages of mentoring (where the mentee is perhaps struggling to decide if she even wants help, not to mention what might be on her agenda to discuss), may well require a mentor to be slightly more directive at that point in time.

Styles of 'helping to learn'

We identified four primary 'helping to learn' styles based on the above dimensions (see Figure 7.1):

- Traditional coaching – which is relatively directive since the goals may be set by the coach or a third party

- Counselling – in the context of learning and support (as opposed to therapy), translates to a sounding-board, helping someone explore career influencing decisions and simply listening in order to help the mentee take responsibility for her development
- Networking – effective mentors help their mentees develop self resourcefulness, focusing on information networks (what do I need to know?) and influencing networks (who do I need to influence to get something done?)
- Guiding – being a role model and on occasion offering advice (but only where they are sure that the mentee can't work something out for herself. The core question being: 'Is this going to help my mentee work out the right solution for her?')

Maternity mentoring draws on all four of the 'helping to learn styles'. The roles a mentor adopts are influenced by the nature of the mentoring programme (how it's set up in terms of declared aims and objectives), the cultural context of the organisation and the background of the mentor and mentees themselves. Plus, of course, each mentoring pair brings their own set of expectations (both of content and behaviour) and hopes for the mentoring.

Supporting their mentee as she navigates her way out of the workplace and returns with a new identity as a working parent calls for a degree of flexibility on the part of the mentor and an ability to diagnose what might be appropriate at different times along the journey and according to the need. In the beginning, the mentor will need to develop a safe environment, taking on the role of a friend and guide, but as the mentee develops more confidence and becomes more independent, the mentor may need to become more challenging and a critical friend.

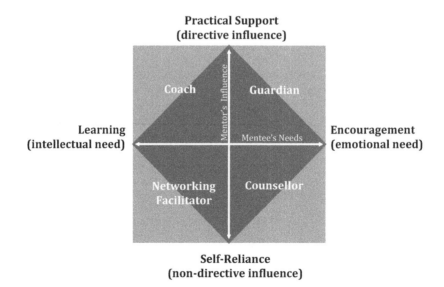

Figure 7.1 Dimensions of mentoring.

I needed some real practical guidance' and a 'friend' who could help me answer this question:'I am choosing to be here, so how do I find myself back as a professional?
(Manager, Royal Society of Chemistry)

Figure 7.2 outlines different roles and behaviours a mentor may adopt in developmental and sponsorshop mentoring. From our research and experience of mentoring maternity, the kinds of roles that emerge typically include:

- **Role model** – For mentors that are parents, a key role they assume is that of a role model. This role is dual-layered, in that they offer a combined professional/work identity with the private/personal identity of being a parent. A sense of shared experience, someone who's done it before and has experienced similar challenges of combining these two identities is highly relevant for a maternity mentee. The mentor becomes a role model for what might be, with the mentor's journey somehow giving hope for their own transition.
- **Emotional supporter** – The need to feel confident at work is a recurrent theme for returning mothers. The mentor offers confirmation and validity to what the mentee is feeling as well as sharing tips and perhaps offering suggestions or advice from their own experience and knowledge. The role of mentor as someone who offers reassurance, ongoing support and acceptance of the emotional dilemmas the mentee is working through is essential.

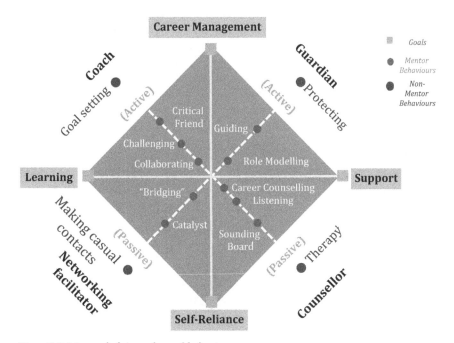

Figure 7.2 Mentor helping roles and behaviours.

I needed reassurance that it's quite normal to feel this way – reassurance that the walls weren't going to fall down when I wasn't there.

(Manager, Asda)

- **Trusted counsellor** – Trust is at the heart of a mentoring relationship. In this context, trust is the foundation stone of a confidential forum – a safe space for airing the raw tensions associated with working and early parenting. The mentor as trusted counsellor also offers a place to discuss the difficult questions and test out thoughts and ideas: *'I knew I could vent and raise fears and concerns in a really safe environment.' (Manager, Asda)*
- **Friend/Critical friend** – The level of disclosure in this context, exchanging of personal information and confidences, can sometimes generate a level of mutuality where both parties find they are benefitting from the relationship. The net result can be a personal friendship between mentor and mentee. This is particularly important for the returning mother who may not feel able to bring her 'whole self' to her working relationship with her line manager. Rather the mentoring offers a legitimate place for doing just that and bringing personal stories of family to the work context. As the mentee grows in confidence, the mentor may adopt the role of critical friend – someone trusted to offer an alternative view in a safe space without fear of reprisal.

At a more practical level, the mentors can also find themselves taking the role of:

- **Network reconnector** – Immersed in a new role with new objectives and new demands on time, frequently the one activity that gets put on the back burner is networking. The mentor can play a useful role in prompting thoughts around refreshing connections and helping the mentee work out with whom they need to build and rebuild working relationships.
- **Contextualiser** – What's new? What's current? What and who's changed? What do I need to know? These are all questions to be explored in the early days of return to work and while a line manager takes responsibility for bringing their returning team member up to speed with functional/local changes, the mentor is a valuable offline source of information and key to helping their mentee understand relevant changes in the broader business landscape, particularly in relation to wider strategy, people changes and company politics.

What this means for your maternity mentoring programme

In setting out examples of the roles mentors may take on, the learning points are again for the mentors. Much of the success of a mentoring programme rests with the up-front preparation and readiness of your participants. With this in mind, a key aspect of your mentor training (see Chapter 13) is to raise awareness of the nature of the mentoring and what the roles they may be called upon to take on at different times as the relationship develops.

8   E-mentoring as an alternative means of support

Emails don't feel as intrusive – you can sit on them if you want. There were times when both of us didn't reply for a day or two – and that was okay. Not like telephone – I wouldn't have felt comfortable with the immediacy of the interruption.

(Manager, Asda)

The need for e-mentoring

Most work-based mentoring relationships can be conducted in person, on a one-to-one basis, either in the office or a café close by and usually during work time. In a maternity context, of course, this all changes. The advent of maternity leave will result in the mentee's physical absence from work for a period of time, and her separation from the standard working day, so for the mentoring to continue and keep on track it's an opportunity to be a bit more creative and agree the most appropriate ways for the following:

- How to keep in touch informally (with simple text exchanges – "It's a girl/ boy!" Informal updates/check ins)
- When it's okay to be out of touch (e.g. the first three to 4 months of maternity leave)
- How they will reconnect (who's going to make contact and latest by …)
- How they might want to table early agendas (using email, for example)
- How and when they might want to meet face to face again, to continue the formal mentoring conversations
- What times of day are likely to work best for each party

This book is written at a time when there are more means of connecting people than ever before, with the range extending from email and telephone mentoring, through to Face Time, Skype and video conferencing. So there are plenty of alternative options open to support mentoring when the mentee is out of the work arena.

Maternity mentoring therefore requires its mentors to be flexible with their communication methods and media. No one approach is better than another – each may be helpful for different conversations at different times. The key thing is to be aware of the pros and cons of each method; see Table 8.1.

Table 8.1 Some pros and cons of e-mentoring mechanisms

Mentoring via email	
Pros	Cons
• The 'conversation' can take place at a time that suits both parties, and they can each respond when they are ready. Unlike a telephone conversation, email doesn't have to be synchronous. For example, when the baby goes down for a nap, the mentee may have time to make a coffee and respond to an email. • Offers reflective space and time to think. • Good/better/best – an email can be drafted and revisited before sending. • Provides an ongoing record of conversations and learning. • Mentoring can happen when it's needed rather than waiting for an actual meeting to take place. • Questions or concerns can be tabled ahead of time, before a meeting, for example, to enable preparation and thinking.	• There can be a loss of spontaneity. • Sometimes text can be misread or misinterpreted, since the intonation of the actual spoken word is missing. • Because the communication is written, there is no opportunity to observe body language which in face-to-face conversation gives more clues as to what is being said or not said, how someone might be feeling, their emotions and the extent to which what they are saying is in tune (or not) with what their body language is indicating. • Words in CAPITALS may be interpreted as aggressive or negative. • Email correspondence may not always be fully confidential. • A busy mentor's in-box may result in a delayed response to the frustration of a mentee looking for an immediate response.

Telephone mentoring	
Pros	Cons
• Great 'just in time' mentoring method, where there is more of an immediate need for a conversation or question to be asked. • Benefit of reassurance to hear a friendly voice for a mentee in crisis pre-return to work. • A mentor can gain much information from the 'auditory clues' in the conversation, e.g. how urgently the mentee is talking, when they hesitate, etc.	• Despite best planning, the timing for a phone call may just be a disaster – perhaps the baby is feeding, needs their nappy changing, has just been ill, or is crying. Where a mentee is distracted, the conversation is likely to struggle. • As with email, phone conversations can lack the 'visual clues' we get from talking face-to-face with a mentee. • Silence while someone reflects on a point or question is a key part of a mentoring conversation. Silence in a phone conversation is potentially difficult – it can be hard to know they are still there.

Skype or FaceTime

Pros	Cons
• An opportunity to 'meet' face-to-face – it's the next best thing! • No requirement to travel to meet up. • If you have the system set up and broadband connection, there is usually no cost to using these applications. • Some mentees use it as an opportunity to introduce their new baby.	• As with the phone call above, despite your best planning, there may be a crisis which gets in the way of the conversation taking place. • Depending on the company systems and firewalls, there may not be scope to conduct virtual mentoring through the company network, which may require a conversation outside working hours and from home. • Broadband connections can sometimes result in conversations 'dropping out' or 'freezing' which can be frustrating if midway through a conversation. • Finding a time to suit the mentor and mentee diaries can be a challenge.

Good practice suggestions for e-mentoring

Email

• Agree some rules up-front for how emails need to look and sound, e.g. how long should they be? How much detail is helpful without drowning in content? Is there a maximum size for attachments into your in-box? What about use of CAPITALS?

• Agree to a maximum frequency for emails and a window for ideal response time.

• If in doubt about a word or phrase – check understanding/interpretation before assuming you have understood the message.

• Check in at the beginning and review at the end of an email exchange.

• Be clear as to next steps and actions.

Telephone and Skype/Facetime

• The environment is key. Is it a space where you can talk without distractions or interruptions?

• Have a clear agenda.

• Set the time boundaries for the conversation.

• Make a personal exchange at the start part of the agenda too.

• Check in and check out at the beginning and end of the conversation.

Finally, some thoughts regarding use of online social media. Sites such as Facebook, Instagram and Twitter are very much public spaces. The benefit of for this form of media is the instant visibility and access to personal information that they offer. Social media is, as the name suggests, a way of connecting friends socially, though 'soundbites' of text, external links, photographs and images and there is perhaps a risk of blurring boundaries here. While mentee and mentor may ultimately become professional 'friends,' there is no guarantee of this from the outset, and there is something about maintaining a helpful distance in order not to over immerse themselves and lose sight of the professional objectives of the mentoring.

There is of course no substitute for mentoring face to face. Meeting in person at the outset of a mentoring relationship is critical to establishing rapport and building early trust. From the start of maternity leave, the mentoring methods used for ongoing help and support need to be chosen carefully and agreed, knowing there are pros and cons associated with each. Mentoring conversations using e-communication methods are most helpful where participants are able to engage in a depth of 'conversation' (be that an email exchange, phone call or Skype) with confidence and at a level of detail.

9 Being an effective maternity mentee

Having a maternity mentor is a privilege and a responsibility for the individual mentee. It is a privilege because it represents a uniquely personal opportunity for one-to-one learning and growth. It also brings with it a level of responsibility because the mentee will be expected to invest time and energy at a point where she may feel she has little or no spare capacity.

For the mentoring to work well, it is helpful for all participants to have an understanding of what they are signing up for and their part to play in its success. Mentoring is a shared learning relationship, not something which is 'done to' someone. As we have seen earlier, the challenge with mentoring in this context is often that in the early stages of pregnancy, the mentee is not anticipating any need for support. This contrasts dramatically with conversations post maternity, where horizons have changed and the need becomes much more tangible and immediate. So it's worth the programme owner outlining expectations from the outset in order to help set your mentoring relationships up for success.

For example a mentee should be expected to:

- **Respect time** – Mentors typically offer their mentoring support in addition to the day job. Therefore, good use of time in a busy mentor's diary expects that a mentee:

  - Is proactive and sets up mentoring meetings
  - Commits to time (and doesn't cancel last minute)
  - Arrives on time
  - Comes prepared, having given some thought to what they want to discuss
  - Is conscious of what is achievable to explore in the time allocated

  In addition, particularly while the mentee is on maternity leave, agreeing times for when and how to communicate is critical. For example, early evenings may be perfect for a mentee when her baby has just gone down for the night, but the worst time for her mentor, just back in from work and juggling children's bath time/homework with evening meals and personal time with their partner.

- **Be honest** – Maternity mentoring should be a safe space to share insights and explore hopes and concerns. It will only work well where participants are ready to be open and honest with themselves and each other. Both mentor and mentee should also remain open as to how the relationship is working and be prepared to give and receive feedback.

- **Maintain confidentiality** – Mentoring conversations in this context frequently involve a high degree of disclosure from both mentee and mentor, since conversations frequently reference both a work and home context. Contracting a commitment to confidentiality up front and practising this builds trust and enables the relationship to grow.
- **Prepare ahead** – Appropriately, a mentor will expect their mentee to have done some preparation for a mentoring meeting and the quality of this thinking will have an impact on the conversation. For example, here are four simple questions which might be helpful to prompt thinking and preparation:

  o What's happened/progressed since my last meeting?
  o What's on my mind as priority to explore/discuss today?
  o How can I help my mentor to best understand the issue (e.g. bringing an outline summary, documents, post-it notes, images) and in doing so, give greater clarity to myself?
  o What type of help am I looking for in this conversation (i.e. listening, challenging, sounding board, personal insights/experience)?

- **Be open to challenge** – A mentee, struggling to think about topics for discussion in the early stages of mentoring, may be challenged by her mentor. This is particularly so where the mentee is perhaps making assumptions or has set expectations about what will 'be.' Questions, which asked sensitively and at the right time, can prompt thinking, and open horizons to new possibilities; *'She asked me powerful and challenging questions, getting me to spend time thinking things through. Thought-provoking questions to help prepare for the journey and what I might want, respecting my opinion and thoughts' (Senior Manager, Asda)*
- **Make time for reflection** – In the vortex of 'close down' pre-maternity leave, finding reflective space can be a big task. However, it is important for the mentee to take time to reflect on the conversation, their learning and what they want to take away as commitments and actions. Reflection does not have to be an onerous activity. A few minutes immediately following the conversation, where the mentee makes simple summary notes of learning points and actions can suffice. The risk is that they dive straight back into work and those important insights are lost.
- **Follow through on commitments** – The mentee that does not follow through on actions will ultimately frustrate themselves and their mentor. If there are difficulties or resistance, this in itself can be explored through the mentoring. What additional help might be needed?

    And what of our expectations of the mentor?

10 Being an effective maternity mentor

Taking on the role of maternity mentor carries with it a dual responsibility; responsibility to the mentee, as the mentor will be supporting them through a significant period of transition, and responsibility to themselves in terms of bringing their own experience, learning, insights and sometimes personal vulnerability to the table. In short, as a working parent and mentor, they bring their whole self (work and home) to the mentoring.

An effective maternity mentor is someone who:

- **Protects time** for mentoring. A mentor should be willing to invest sufficient time for the relationship to be effective. Time for their own preparation (e.g. letting go of their agenda to be 'in the room' in support of the mentee) and reflection (What am I taking away? What did I notice about my mentee/myself in that conversation?)
- **Is willing to challenge** and be prepared to be **proactive**. For example, while the mentor should not be scheduling mentoring meetings, they may need to nudge a busy mentee if they have missed a session or not set a meeting up. In addition, a mentor may – where appropriate – challenge the mentee to address difficult questions or think more broadly.
- **Is honest.** We reiterate maternity mentoring should be a safe space to share insights and explore hopes and concerns. It will only work well where participants are ready to be open and honest with themselves and each other. Both mentor and mentee should also remain open as to how the relationship is working and be prepared to give and receive feedback.
- **Balances listening with sharing insights.** A mentor may use their own experience to provide guidance, but will be conscious that what 'worked' for them may well be different for their mentee. There is no one best way to return post maternity. Each return presents a unique set of circumstances and a maelstrom of emotions, choices, priorities and compromises. The effective mentor comes prepared to listen to – and value – their mentee's ideas, being aware that there will be points where a well-phrased question may be most useful to a mentee wrestling with an issue. They hold the space for exploration and working things through.
- **Keeps confidences** and themselves 'safe.' The conversations between mentor and mentee should remain confidential except in very special circumstances, which should be outlined and planned for by the programme owner. A mentor

who has concerns their mentee may be a danger to themselves or others, or has concerns that someone may be suffering from postnatal depression, for example, should know the procedure to offer a referral for specialist support – in confidence – via the programme owner or HR team.

- **Works within the limits of their own competence.** '*Competence is defined in human resource terms as meeting the standard requirement to properly perform a particular job.*' (Cox, Bachkirova and Clutterbuck 2010) Competence in this context is concerned with knowledge (of the particular sensitivity and context of maternity and new parenting, different approaches, frameworks), skills (in applying that knowledge, understanding and practice) and behaviour (how they work and grow as a parent mentor). It's about remaining open to continued learning, developing skills and practice and, critically, noticing where something may be beyond their level of expertise. Recognising when they themselves need help or a fresh perspective is key for the effective mentor.
- **Is conscious of their learning through the process**. It is good practice for mentors to keep a record of their mentoring conversations, to maintain continuity between sessions, log questions or concerns, reflect on personal learning and capture points they might want to take to supervision. This feels like a relatively simple activity, but requires commitment and the discipline to complete as close as possible to each session while the conversation is still fresh. Notes should be recorded using a standard template to ensure consistency of approach. Examples of points to incorporate include:

  ○ Date and timing of the mentoring session, mentee name
  ○ Mentoring format (one-to-one, telephone, Skype/FaceTime, email)
  ○ Key themes and questions
  ○ Observations from the conversation
  ○ Questions, patterns, points to follow up next time
  ○ How the relationship is progressing (feedback given or received)
  ○ Reflections on own practice
    – What might I do more of/less of/build on next time?
    – How am I growing as a mentor in terms of my practice?
    – Questions/concerns for supervision review or referral

- For the purposes of mentee confidentiality, security and privacy, the maintenance, storage and disposal of any records (including e-files) relating to mentoring are typically protected by law. In the UK, for example, these would be termed 'client records' under The Data Protection Act 1998 (www.gov.uk/data-protection/the-data-protection-act) and protected accordingly. Programme owners should seek formal guidance to ensure the processes and procedures relating to notes and records comply with relevant legislation.
- We now share a number of short case study insights from parent mentors reflecting on their mentoring relationships and learning. Finally, we have a reflective account of a mentee supported by an external mentor and how his support made the difference to her return to work.

Case study

Insights from maternity mentors

There is so much in this for the mentor. Having that experience of supporting someone, developing your own skills, fine-tuning and realising you still have blind spots to work on. It's that tension of feeling uncomfortable, challenged and recognising I'm in a learning space and an '*I don't know where this is going*' place. I believe I'm a better person when I'm coaching and mentoring because I'm more conscious about what I'm doing and hopefully the impact I'm having.

Sue Hughes
Training and OD Manager
Royal Society of Chemistry

Each mentoring relationship is entirely bespoke and that's what makes it so exciting. My best mentoring relationships have moved and flowed according to what the needs of the mentee were. For example, one mentee was very concerned about line manager continuity before finishing and nervous about the whole process. I expected to hear from her frequently in the run up to her return but actually it never turned out to be a problem and she had a really positive experience. At the other end of the spectrum, I had a mentee who was relatively relaxed about returning to work, but had her flexible working request turned down. We had a number of conversations about what next that went far deeper than I had expected. She was actually comfortable with the decision but wanted to focus on how to make things work going back full time. We talked about everything from how to keep clear boundaries during the first few months back through to what this meant for her career long term. I learnt so much from her about resilience and focus. She went back and had honest conversations with her manager about how to make it work. He was hugely supportive as a result.

Helen Bryce
Lifebulb

Case study

Insights from a father mentoring maternity

I joined the maternity mentoring programme as a single dad with residency care of my kids, in the hope that some of the traditional issues seen with balancing work and parenting by mothers could benefit from a male perspective.

(Continued)

The process was really interesting as I was paired with a pregnant colleague who was facing up to life as a single parent; therefore we had lots in common. The key areas where I hope I offered some perspective were around the guilt felt by a lot of women as they try to be the best mother and the best career person. My innate competitiveness plus the pressure I put on myself to be a mother and a dad to my kids, whilst holding down a senior role in my organisation, meant the first year I spent working and sole parenting was very stressful. However, by sharing and discussing my learning around the importance of communication, managing expectations, the value of routine and structure, I hope I helped my mentee to develop a successful balance.

I believe traditional gender strengths of men in the workplace (such as being more confident in asking for what they need – a point often cited in pay gap discussions and analysis) absolutely worked for me in the parenting/career balance sphere. I was very clear with my boss that I had flexible support outside work and with notice I could achieve whatever was required for the business, however there were some 'non-negotiables' that I would not change without very good reason as this was protected time devoted to my kids.

Through the mentoring I shared my experience of the importance of clear communication with all stakeholders (at home; the kids, childcare support, my network of friends, family and school, and at work; my boss and the team) which alleviated any guilt. When everyone knew what they could expect of me and had agreed the parameters of engagement, it was easier to focus on the immediate task without being distracted by thoughts of what I "should" be doing in the other half of my life. I think this was the key element of mentoring that we shared.

In summary as a mentor, I feel it's about the people involved rather than the gender of the mentor per se. Another mentor may have supported my mentee more around the process of return to work and the emotional isolation associated with maternity leave, however my sole parenting experience and male perspective gave a different slant to some of the challenges she faced as a single mother.

Buying Manager and Parent Mentor
Asda Walmart

Case study

Insights from a mentee supported by an external male mentor

My mentor is outside the organisation, which is valuable to me because he offers a perspective without being deeply involved in the business. He is someone I have worked with for nearly 7 years now and he has supported my transition from administrator through to my current role as a senior leader. With that depth of relationship and trust, he assisted my return to work in a number of ways and I sought out his help in particular in the lead up to my return and in early days back.

In my absence, there had been major issues with change across the department, which hadn't been supported by my maternity cover. Over a couple of 'Keep In Touch' days prior to my return, I had one-on-ones with all my team, in which every single staff member either cried, ranted or had a 'moment.' They were so angry about the change and didn't feel supported or listened to. Mainly they were angry because they thought I had masterminded the change from home – which frankly I hadn't. I explored with my mentor how to step into this and not get completely overwhelmed by the mountain of pain that seemed to be there. He worked closely to help me identify work streams and activity so I went back in with a plan and instead of reacting to emotion by being emotional, I responded with empathy without getting caught up in it. My mentor was the one I could be emotional with outside of the team! He assisted me by taking myself out of the context, looking back at the situation, and going in prepared. He asked the tough questions and called me to account for activities, working through ideas so they went from being half-baked to being proper plans.

Early on in the mentoring, he worked with me on a personal SWOT (Strengths, Weaknesses, Opportunities, Threats). A potential threat which became apparent was my need to be liked by the people who worked for me. My management style came from a place of wanting people to like me. That was more important than them respecting my decisions. On maternity leave, I found I had a baby who loved me unconditionally. I didn't need the team to like me – it was about respect. That time out brought with it the realisation although I could be friendly, I was their boss, their supervisor as opposed to their friend.

I recognised my previous management style was akin to being a parent with the team somehow in role as children; I fixed their problems, found solutions, I was there to listen to grumbles and mop up the mess (even though the majority of the team are older than me). I saw then that was the relationship I had fostered as their manager. Mentoring gave me space to reflect and I knew the relationship I wanted moving forward was something much more adult. I had changed and was coming back as an adult. I didn't want children – I had that at home. Away from work I had had time to make that transition. The challenge was to communicate that to the team.

Senior Leader
Public Sector Organisation

11 Building your business case for maternity and parental mentoring

Most mentoring programmes begin with enthusiasm and a good deal of excitement both for the participants and the business at setup. Unfortunately, almost one in three programmes don't make it beyond their second year, finding themselves floundering with questions of ownership, sponsorship and competing priorities. Success for any new mentoring programme therefore starts with firm foundations: being clear about why the mentoring is needed, what it is intended to achieve and crucially having endorsement and sponsorship from the senior leadership team.

As the programme owner the challenge is:

> To build a programme that
> meets its objectives for the participants, is sustainable and responsive to
> the needs and expectations of the business

So if you are considering introducing parental mentoring to your business, start by building a compelling proposal to secure the investment. Your business case will need an outline framework and informed answers to the questions in Figure 11.1.

What's the starting point?

Good practice for a business case begins with doing a chunk of research into the current experience of maternity/paternity/adoption leave in your business and knowing your start point. Data should be accessible via your management information or talent management systems. (We touched on this earlier in terms of gathering essential data up front. See p. 19 for some suggested research questions.)

You could also conduct a survey of maternity/paternity/adoption leave from across the business and across job levels/grades, to understand more about

- The influencing factors for length of time taken for maternity/parental leave
- Experiences of closing down, reintegration and return

- **What's the starting position?** Research statistics and trends for your organisation. What are the recurrent themes, stories and anecdotes? Inclusion of these will add a level of insight and depth to your proposal and create the burning platform that makes this investment a 'must do.'
- **Why now?** Be ready to suggest the potential risks if you don't make the investment.
- **How will mentoring address this?** Who will the mentoring support? (Increasingly programmes are about supporting both new mothers and new fathers). What will it do? Why internal mentoring and not external coaching?
- **What are the objectives of the mentoring?** Be clear what the scheme intends to achieve and how it dovetails with other practices and provision for working parents.
- **How will you evaluate success?** How will the business know the investment has been worthwhile? What are the measures of success? What will people see/hear that is different?
- **What's needed to set up and run this programme?** Your anticipated budget for resources in terms of costs, people (both internal and perhaps external) and time.
- **Who are the stakeholders and sponsors endorsing this idea?** Starting at the most senior level, identify sponsors and how they support the scheme and be clear who are the stakeholders critical to its success.

Figure 11.1 Outline framework for a business case.

- Typical concerns associated with returning to work as a new parent in the organisation
- The factors that support/detract from the experience of return to work
- The time it takes for someone to fully adjust back into working life
- Some of the working practices for parents within the organisation, i.e. how they make it work
- The impact of parental leave on perceptions and experiences of progression and choices relating to longer-term career development

Results from your research and survey should be summarised in a formal report, outlining the background, key themes arising, narrative and commentary, along with clear and recommended courses of action.

What else might be needed?

Maternity/parental mentoring may be just one recommendation of many from the research. For example, in addition to introducing maternity mentoring, the recommendations of the maternity survey conducted at Imperial College London in 2012 also included:

- To prepare line managers to manage maternity more effectively
- To implement career coaching specifically for maternity returners
- To connect working parents across the college, with a dedicated parents' webpage and forum

Capture stories and anecdotes

What are people saying? What are the recurring themes? Who are the people regarded as role models? Personal stories and anecdotes can be hugely powerful in engaging others in the journey and illustrating the opportunity for mentoring support. Ensure you seek permission to use direct quotes and make it clear whether these will be attributable. Generally, people are more likely to be open where their comments remain non-attributable.

Review the current provision

What support is in place right now? How is it working and how might it be improved? What's missing? How does this compare with other employers?

Why now?

What have you discovered from your research? Use the business' statistics and anecdotal insights to indicate the potential risks if the mentoring is not introduced. These may include

- Short term risks (e.g. stress levels in the workplace, absence levels, engagement scores, talent retention, costs associated with loss of skills, recruitment)
- Longer-term risks (e.g. the balance of the talent pipeline, external perception of the organisation)

How will mentoring address the issues?

Explain how a mentoring approach will help meet the needs identified. Set out details of your target audience and who the mentoring will support. In practice, the volume of support is likely to be with women taking maternity leave, but the principles and approaches in mentoring are equally applicable to a father taking paternity leave or an adoptive parent. A programme that sets out to be inclusive from the outset is much more appealing to stakeholders in that it speaks to a more diverse agenda. You might also want to make a comparison of internal mentoring versus external coaching in terms of sustainability and cost implications.

What are the objectives of the mentoring?

This is your opportunity to 'rewrite the script' and set out the objectives and ambitions for your mentoring programme. Note it is worth positioning objectives from the perspective both of the individuals involved and more broadly for the business. Each set of objectives is equally relevant, but both contribute to the overall business case.

Some examples of objectives for a parental mentoring programme are illustrated in Table 11.1. Note this is not an exhaustive list. Based on your research, there will be localised objectives you will want to add, which will be relevant and appropriate for your business' needs.

How will you evaluate success?

How will the participants and the business know the investment has been worthwhile? What are the measures of success? What will people see and hear that is different? It's worth setting out the plans for evaluation, but also remember that parental leave (maternity/paternity/adoption leave) can mean a significant time lapse between someone going on maternity and being back in the workplace. In the UK for example, there could be a gap of just over 12 months, given the current provision for leave. (See Chapter 17 for detailed information and suggestions for programme evaluation.)

Table 11.1 Example objectives for a parental mentoring programme

For the individual	For the business
• Provide one-on-one support for the individual in transition to working parenthood • Keep in touch and connected while on maternity/paternity/adoption leave • Demonstrate they are valued by the business • Support individual preparation and a smoother return to work • Keep talented employees on track for continuing their career with the organisation	• Retain 'sight' of talent on maternity/paternity/adoption leave • Improve re-engagement and pace of delivery post return • Increase retention of talent and skills • Positive impact on diversity of talent pipeline and at senior levels • Provide a simple, cost-effective development solution, using the skills and expertise of people within the organisation • Self-sustaining – mentees may become future mentors • Develop coaching and mentoring skills of managers as mentors • Contribute to corporate social responsibility • Contribute to building a reputation as an employer of choice

What's needed to set up and run this programme?

External costs can generally be kept to a minimum for an internal mentoring programme. Remember of course that an internal programme means using your own employees, so there is an intrinsic cost where these resources are diverted from doing something else – though of course it is still an investment in the business! You may decide there is value in seeking external expertise up front to help with design, get the programme off the ground and support with initial supervision of mentors (see Chapter 16). Thereafter, it is a matter of deciding where ownership for different aspects of the programme resides, which can then be formalised into part of an individual's performance contract or job role. What is clear is that a maternity/parental mentoring programme needs a programme manager with this as a contracted part of their job role and someone with a real passion for their subject.

An effective mentoring programme also requires a sound administrator and you will benefit from having a 'go-to' individual with the skills to set up a mentoring 'hub' with records of mentoring partnerships; someone who can be available to email out biographies/profiles and act as the point for day to day queries. In a larger organisation, this task may be best performed by a member of the central HR team, who manages the administration of maternity, paternity and adoption leave. In this way, the information remains within one team.

At a time where finances are tight, it's worth pointing out that mentoring activities may represent just one aspect of an individual's job role, be that the programme manager, the administrator or a mentor. There should be no automatic requirement to bid for any additional headcount. Table 11.2 offers a brief summary of your two key roles to get started.

In addition to these core roles, it helps to find yourself some **champions** for your programme. Ideally, these should be from a diverse range of people, including:

- Managers from the senior leadership team
- Influential middle managers (both male and female)
- Managers from a range of different functions

Table 11.2 Two key roles

Programme Manager	Administrator
• Overall project owner • Scopes the programme • Creates the plan for implementation • Conducts research • Builds the business case • Manages key stakeholders • Is an ambassador for the programme • Communicates • Trains the mentors and mentees • Coordinates mentoring matches • Prepares ongoing summaries and evaluation reports	• Sets up the mentoring database • Keeps accurate records of mentoring partnerships • Supports the matching process • Circulates mentor biographies • Handles day-to-day queries • Supports the evaluation process, e.g. issues evaluation forms postmentoring, prepares summary reports

The champions to 'sign up' are those who have a personal interest in making it happen and want to get involved. They may be line managers (with someone on parental leave) or they may be working parents themselves. Your champions can be helpful activists to open doors, raise energy levels generally about parental mentoring and encourage participation. You may decide to create a steering group (p. 84) and ask your champions to sign up for specific actions. They could also become mentors for your programme.

Who are the stakeholders and sponsors endorsing this idea?

Separate from the champion role, you will set yourself up for success by having sponsorship at the highest level for your programme. A programme sponsor plays a key part in securing airtime for your ideas and gaining support across the senior leadership table. The best sponsors are those who offer influence (at a strategic and fiscal level) and interest (are a passionate exponent of the power of mentoring and the importance of parent mentoring in particular). It goes without saying your HR director should be a key advocate for the mentoring programme; however, with them on board, good practice is to secure sponsorship from a director of an alternative function (for example, a director of operations, finance, production or marketing), which indicates support and ownership beyond HR and the importance of this to the wider organisation.

Do your homework. When you have an outline plan for your programme, and have some compelling research and insights to share, ask for time with some of your most senior working mothers and fathers. Invite their comments and builds and go back again with revised plans. Ask for permission to include these insights as appropriate in your business proposal.

Identify your senior sponsor and make a personal request for their specific involvement. Think about what you want your sponsor to do for the programme and contract this with them. This should be more than acting as a figurehead. The type of things you might want to ask of your sponsor could include:

- **Reviewing the business case** – Your sponsor is a great sounding board for the draft business proposal and for giving critical feedback and suggesting input.
- **Gaining business agreement for the investment** – Your sponsor may be needed to make the case and lead your request for investment at board level.
- **Launching the scheme** – Your sponsor should be present at the launch, and come prepared to share his or her own experiences of being mentored. What did he or she gain from previous mentoring support? What difference has mentoring made to his or her career and life as a working parent? What are his or her hopes for this particular programme? What obstacles does he or she anticipate and how will he or she support?
- **Steering groups/business updates** – Ask your sponsor to update the wider business on progress/themes from the mentoring as it progresses.
- **Focus groups** – You could ask them to set aside diary time on a quarterly basis to meet with groups of mentors and returning mentees to gain feedback and insights.

Case study

Senior sponsorship at the Royal Society of Chemistry

I am the sponsor for the maternity mentoring scheme at the Royal Society of Chemistry and I understand the importance of having mentoring support at such a crucial time in somebody's career. I've had two lots of maternity leave, 10 years ago and 14 years ago, and I recognise the opportunities that maternity leave brings in terms of offering a period of reflection and also an opportunity to review future career paths.

The business' impact of having a maternity mentoring scheme means that not only do we offer the individual support in that crucial stage as they plan to go on maternity leave (and that helps with productivity and ensuring we have continuity), but it also helps to bring them up to speed for returning and integration back into the workplace. This can often be a challenging part of the return to work having been on maternity leave, whatever length of time that might be. Supporting an individual at that stage is important to them, and is also really important to us and we've seen the benefit of that support.

Senior sponsorship is crucial to this kind of activity not only because you set role models, you are also working with the experience of those who may have already been through maternity leave and returned. It shows support for our staff and I think it also sets the tone for cultural expectations and good practice. We have an empowerment culture at the Royal Society of Chemistry, which is very much about providing direction, autonomy and support to our staff. Senior sponsorship ensures that this is felt throughout the organisation in supporting the individual but also supporting the team around that individual as well.

Helen Pain
Deputy Chief Executive
Royal Society of Chemistry

In addition to the sponsor, there will be significant others in the organisation that you'll want to have 'on side' as you prepare to launch your programme. Draw up a list of your key **stakeholders** and decide who to engage with as a priority. Good practice is to have a mix of supporters and some 'nay sayers' – that way, you get to understand the different perspectives and really test out your thinking.

You may find the following questions helpful to prioritise your stakeholder list:

- How does their role have an impact on the success of the programme?
- What might they be called upon to do in support of the programme?
- How much influence do they have and over whom?
- What information or experience do they have which could be helpful to a maternity/parenting mentoring programme?
- Are they a potential mentor? (Either as part of the pilot or ongoing programme)

- What is the risk to the programme if they are not included/consulted?
- What questions/concerns might they have that you need to have considered?

In summary

We have outlined some of the foundation stones for your business case. There may be more, but the list feels long enough! Experience tells us the more thought that goes into preparation and the more people you engage with the concept, the more likely your programme is to succeed. A mentoring programme of this nature connects with people at a pivotal point in their lives and careers and has the potential for lasting impact on the organisation too. This is legacy building work.

We close this chapter with a case study from the NHS, which outlines the context and factors central to their business case. It also illustrates the value of having a passionate owner to lead a programme of this nature.

Case study

NHS Return to Work Mentoring

The NHS Leadership Academy's new Return to Work Mentoring programme aims to support people transitioning back into the workplace following an extended period of time away.

Within the NHS, there's a major focus on talent management, supporting organisations at national and regional levels with building robust talent and succession planning processes. These aim to deliver a diverse and inclusive pipeline right through to board level. We're getting better at developing a more inclusive leadership workforce than ever before but we can still do better. If we're more supportive of those returning to the workplace, including those returning back after maternity, paternity and adoption leave, we're more likely to retain a diverse range of talent and have those people continue through the pipeline. This investment is fundamentally about inclusion, supporting people across the whole organisation regardless of where they are on their leadership journey. Our staff have families and lives outside work, and we want them to come back feeling supported and ready, with mentors available to help at key transition points. This way, they're more likely to come back, more likely to stay and more likely to progress their career with a whole new range of valuable skills to offer our service users gained from their personal experiences outside of the workplace.

Making the business case

To secure funding, we looked at evidence from current research, business articles and practitioner case studies. Evidence-based decision making is in

(Continued)

the nature of the industry, i.e. to gauge value for money with any request for NHS expenditure and investment.

The questions I needed to answer were these:

- Where's the proof that this makes a difference to the quality and experience of patient care?
- How will this make a positive difference to the performance of our leaders and their unique contribution?
- How will this support the continued development of an inclusive workforce?

We're working to help equip our people with the right leadership skills and behaviours and it can be a challenge to substantiate behavioural investment and return. We talked about stabilising productivity and transition after a person returns to work, i.e. if it typically takes someone 6 months to return to full productivity and we're able to half that time, there's a clear measure and benefit. We also looked at sickness absence in the first year post return and how better-supported transitions into what can be a changeable and complex system can help to reduce the likelihood and/or rates of sickness and occupational health referrals. It's also about seeing how things evolve over time and building a bank of stories which evidence the change at a personal level.

The aim is for people to feel supported, nurtured and included, whatever their chapter in life but especially around the touch points of starting a family, caring for a loved one who is sick, or supporting the community by becoming a foster carer. Like our patients, our leaders are equally diverse and unique and by taking an inclusive approach, we become more reflective of the communities we serve and the workforce we're aspiring to have in the future. I know that this will make a difference. If our returners are supported, it follows that they'll make happier, more supported, resilient leaders. In turn, the quality of care and experience of our patients will be better.

A passionate owner

My passion for return to work mentoring is informed by my own personal experience of becoming a first time, single working mother within the NHS and the difference I believe mentoring would have made to my return. It's this experience and the stories of other working parents that I also brought to the table in support of making the investment.

I took my first maternity leave at a really difficult time in the NHS. There were fundamental changes taking place, including the strategic move away from Strategic Health Authorities (SHAs). For my part, 2 months before taking maternity leave, I had to make members of my team redundant which was a very emotive process. I didn't know what the organisation would look like when I returned post maternity and if I'd have a job. My line manager left, as did other colleagues and members of my own networks, and there was very little line manager support available. I went on maternity leave confused, under stress with my own role formally at risk of redundancy and overwhelmed at the options available to me. Thankfully I developed a good relationship with a member of the HR team who hadn't already left and while on maternity leave, maintained regular contact about the state of play. When a role came up, a band lower, in a different specialty and a different location, I made the choice to return to work earlier after 5.5 months rather than take redundancy. I was thankful I had a job to go back to and hopeful I could make the transition into what was a new NHS architecture. After having a short interview, I got the job but wasn't made aware of the options available to me once I returned. These included phased or part-time return, using annual leave and childcare vouchers. I jumped back on the bandwagon; I think I was just so grateful to have a job to come back to at all.

My transition to being a working parent was hard. At work, I returned to an interim role still within the SHA, but working in an area where I had no experience or influence. I was working in a team where once again, people were concerned about their jobs. My line manager was lovely but because the relationship was new I felt I couldn't open up about the difficulties of returning. My main concern was about being back, making a great impression, finding my next role and maintaining my career trajectory.

On a personal level, I was isolated. No one else in the team had young children. I worked 9:00am – 5:00pm and became 'that person' who was the first to leave work each day, worried that people were judging me. I literally gave myself an hour to get out of London and of course I was always worried about making it back on time for the nursery run. Looking back, I didn't make it easy for myself: I stopped breastfeeding earlier than planned (unaware of any provision for expressing or storage of breast milk), and that special bond with my daughter just stopped. There were jobs that had to be done each evening like sterilising and making up bottles. It was very very difficult and in some respects, I lost out on the pleasure of being a new mother. On top of this, my confidence was rock bottom and I wasn't feeling very resilient or a good leader as I had done previously. I felt ill-equipped to deal with the new NHS and behind in my knowledge of the system. My sphere of professional networks was almost gone; most colleagues had moved on into new jobs.

When you go back to work you're functioning on autopilot. I had friends in the community, but I didn't feel I had anybody I could connect with in my organisation to make this adjustment easier for myself and benefit my team and the organisation. I needed someone to help me think through my own career trajectory: what could I negotiate? What did I want? What type

(Continued)

of leader did I want to become? I had a new identity as a mother and loved it, but I wasn't sure what that meant for my career. A return to work mentor could have made all the difference.

I'm really passionate about family and community – it's a beautiful thing and an essential part of being a human being. The NHS is a caring business – it is about looking after our people and communities who in turn, are caring for other people at vulnerable times in their life. Returners need time and attention and I'm passionate about providing this, believing that we'll see more improvements in productivity, efficiency, resilience, motivation and overall leadership than we would without that support. Better leadership offers a better NHS.

Becoming a parent has changed how I see the world. What I recognise is I work very differently now. I'm more compassionate and my experience has given me clarity and understanding of the gifts you bring back to the workplace as a parent. In some cases, becoming a parent or carer has been regarded as a deficit model in the business world, yet in practice people come back to work with a whole new set of skills and experience that could benefit the service we offer to our communities. The question is, why wouldn't we do this?

Charmaine Kwame
National Programme Lead for Coaching and Mentoring
NHS Leadership Academy

12 Getting started

Piloting your programme

The advantage of piloting a programme is the opportunity it offers to test out your ideas and assumptions, to see what works well, what needs improving and how the ideas and practice are received by both the participants and the wider organisation.

The challenge with a maternity/parental leave pilot is that it could be very lengthy if the intention is to see a complete series of mentoring cycles through before launching the programme to the wider business. End-to-end a maternity mentoring relationship (in the UK) may span up to 18 months or more; i.e. a mentee may begin her mentoring support 2 months before finishing for maternity leave, then she may take up to 12 months off work and find that the mentoring comes to a natural close at the end of her first 4 months back at work. With this in mind, it will be important to manage the business and stakeholder expectations that this is a long-term initiative and represents a long-term commitment. And of course, if the ambition is to have a positive impact on the talent pipeline, the return on investment may be 5 to 7 years in the making.

In practice, many organisations choose to start off with a small number of mentoring partnerships, testing out their processes for matching, mentor and mentee preparation, and evaluating learning on an ongoing basis. In other words, there is a range of activities within a programme of this nature which can be piloted, built on and improved as you go. You can plan for this by setting out dates for mentors to get together to share learning and review progress, identify where they might need further help, and their experience of any barriers or challenges, for example.

It's worth noting that with initial maternity mentoring underway, conversations will be had between expectant mothers and parents across informal networks. The stories filter out and having heard that support is there, programme owners can frequently find themselves approached by employees who have heard of the mentoring and want to request a mentor themselves. The message here is to be prepared for plenty of interest!

Steering group

In support of setting up your pilot programme, you may decide to establish a steering group. Chaired by your sponsor – which hopefully encourages attendance and participation – this group should quite literally 'steer' activity for the programme, including:

- Supporting the initial set up of the mentoring programme's purpose, goals and measures of success
- Marketing and communication across the organisation
- Making key decisions, e.g. budgets, wider roll out
- Meeting regularly to review progress and discuss improvements
- Reviewing evaluation data and feedback in order to make improvements
- Being the sounding board for the programme manager

Good practice is to keep membership of your steering group small, between three to six active members. In identifying members of your steering group, consider the extent to which they will:

- Help influence and manage internal politics
- Be in a position to understand the needs and perspectives of the mentors and mentees
- Add credibility to the programme by their association with it
- Act as unofficial mentors for the programme
- Be willing to sign up and do something, thereby sharing the workload

Finding maternity/parental mentors

In Chapter 10, we touched upon what makes an effective maternity mentor. Starting your pilot programme off, you will need to seek out some willing volunteers to be your pioneer mentors. Think creatively how to engage with your prospective mentors; this could be through an existing parent's network within the organisation, an intranet mentoring site or by recommendation. It is also important to consider the criteria you might want to apply to potential mentors, examples of which might include:

- Working parents (mothers, fathers, adoptive, same sex parents) who have returned to work within 3 to 5 years[1]
- Mentors who are not parents themselves, but are interested in supporting someone through this transition point
- Already trained or established internal coaches or mentors
- Qualified or accredited the work internal mentors (this might be a bonus rather than essential criteria)
- Recognised as performing in role (you may decide to apply a minimum appraisal grade)

- Regarded as behavioural role models
- Individuals with a track record of developing themselves and others
- Endorsed and supported by their line manager
- Have the passion and capacity to mentor
- Willing to attend an initial workshop or webinar to up-skill and commit to further development sessions as appropriate
- Offer diversity of job levels to enable matching at same level (if using peer-to-peer mentoring)

Not all mentors have to be parents themselves, indeed some may be step-parents while others may simply have an interest in supporting a colleague during this time. For a first pilot, good practice is to identify your mentors in conjunction with the HR team, your champions and sponsor, who should have visibility of potential mentors – indeed may become mentors themselves. Further into the programme, you may decide to advertise internally for mentors.

The numbers of mentors for your scheme will be largely determined by the volume of maternity/paternity/adoption, which you will have established from your business case research. The key is to have a diverse range of mentors across job levels and different teams (so you minimise the risk of any conflicts of interest), and also to have plenty of mentors at the level where the volume of maternity/parental leave occurs if matching peer-to-peer (i.e. same level matching).

Communicating the pilot

The start of a pilot is a perfect opportunity to 'broadcast' what you are doing internally and externally and to raise awareness about the programme. Think about how best to communicate your message using any existing mechanisms available, bearing in mind where employees typically go to access information.

Ideas for communication could include:

- An announcement on your internal communications website (easy to access information about the mentoring programme, perhaps with short video clips from mentors, key sponsors and relevant documents available to download, e.g. Mentor/Mentee profiles, contact names, FAQs (frequently asked questions) and any planned dates.
- Creating a bespoke site on your intranet with links from pages on your learning and development site.
- Presentation at a senior leaders' briefing (to raise awareness across senior levels of the business, lead by the sponsor and programme owner).
- Hosting an event across lunchtime in the reception/main entrance area (informal and involving champions, mentors, mentees; creating an opportunity for individual exchanges and questions).
- Making the launch part of a broader diversity and inclusion event (which weaves the programme into the broader diversity agenda).

- Launching your mentoring programme as part of the annual International Women's Day celebrations (with potential for external PR). This says something about the business and its willingness to support women at a key transition point in their working life.

Matching mentors and mentees

Matching mentors with mentees to create effective mentoring relationships is at the heart of your programme.

The decisions around your mentoring partnerships start with your criteria for matching. These criteria should relate to the purpose of the mentoring programme, i.e. in this instance, the primary focus is concerned with connecting someone with experience (of the organisation itself either because they have experienced maternity/paternity/adoption leave and return, or simply offer insights as an established mentor and fellow employee) with someone about to embark on the journey to working parenthood. For the returner, a mentor's level of empathy, *'the ability to understand and share the feelings of another'* (Oxford English Dictionary) is key.

In all mentoring relationships, effective matching looks for an appropriate balance between **rapport** (being similar in personality, background, interests and circumstances) and **potential for learning** (which implies difference). The principle is that 'difference' adds value by stretching thinking, looking at problems or challenges from alternative perspectives and 'similarity' helps generate trust and the special chemistry of the mentoring relationship.

In maternity/parental mentoring, the need for similarity may carry more weight in terms of matching (i.e. the shared circumstance of combining parenting with work and career), though the risk is that this could lead to a tendency to invite a mentee to 'do what I did' rather than, 'let's look at how you create your own path.' We revisit this point in the next chapter as we explore how to prepare mentors and mentees.

Typically, most development mentoring programmes have as their start point the matching of more senior mentors to junior mentees. With the emphasis on similarity and building rapport, experience has shown peer mentoring to be the most helpful approach in this context, recognising that the participants are more likely to have a similar/shared understanding of the job challenges at a given level. That is not to say the 'peer matching' rule has to be hard and fast. For example, a prospective mentee may be close to being promoted and in these circumstances, it may be more helpful to match them to a mentor at the next level or job grade.

By and large same gender matches seem to be an important criterion for this type of mentoring too, i.e. someone returning from extended paternity leave may find it helpful to confide in a male mentor and a woman returning post maternity may prefer to work with a female mentor, not least because of the experience of childbirth and physical changes associated with having a baby. But how important is it to have someone of the same race, education, personality, or someone who has a deep faith (irrespective of whether it is the same as your own)? Each journey is unique to the individual and each individual will seek different things from a mentor. The general rule seems to be: *If it's important to the mentee, it's important to the programme*. With this in mind, good practice is to encourage prospective mentees to table the specific criteria that are important to them in their choice of mentor and for your mentors' profiles to be clear on all these points.

It's also worth taking into account learning maturity. People vary widely in their ability to learn from experience (their own and that of other people). The more mature you are as a learner, the more learning styles you will feel comfortable with. So while you might not specifically use learning maturity in deciding whom to match with whom, sharing how mentors and mentees learn (perhaps referencing any current organisational profiling/diagnostic tools, such as the Myers-Briggs Type Indicator [MBTI] or Honey and Mumford Learning Styles, for example) may facilitate the setup and ongoing mentoring relationship.

While the experience of working parenthood is a point of difference at the outset, it becomes a crucial, shared point of *similarity* where both parties meet as indicated in Figure 12.1. In summary then, the criteria for matching in parental mentoring should prioritise the need for similarity by giving consideration to:

- Job level (either peer or next level of seniority)
- Working arrangements (the mentee may aspire to, e.g. full time, flexible or compressed/reduced hours)
- Any specific criteria that are important to the mentee (which may include gender, faith, race, education, or personality, for example)

But the criteria should also consider *difference* as an appropriate criterion for building a learning relationship.

- Cross-functional diversity (usually from a different department/team to help minimise risk of conflicts of interest)
- Geographical location (single or multisite, international)
- Learning style (e.g. MBTI profile)

Good practice! The choice of which mentee to match with which mentor may also be driven by sheer availability of mentors. Maternity mentoring can be an intense process, so there is a need to have a large enough pool of mentors to enable people to come in and out of the mentoring, balancing this with the demands of busy work schedules. In addition, it is helpful to have a range of mentors from across the spectrum of business teams and job levels and in particular, a good number of mentors at the level where the volume of maternity and parental leave occurs to enable peer matching.

Experienced programme coordinators would say that there is also no substitute for a personal connection and having prior knowledge of the participants can be hugely helpful when making decisions around matching mentors to mentees. With this in mind, consider who is best placed to coordinate the matching for your

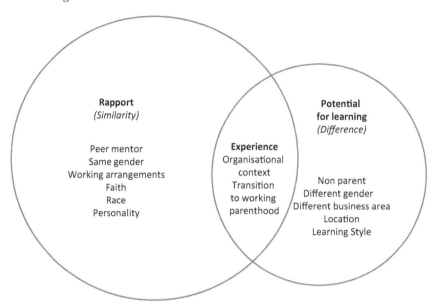

Figure 12.1 Points of difference and similarity.

programme. You may decide that matching is best conducted with support from a central administrator (for coordinating paperwork, connecting emails and following up with information), while the decisions around specific mentoring pairs remain with the programme owner.

Where mentoring programmes operate across different countries, e.g. for pan-European or international businesses, the programme owner is unlikely to have personal knowledge of every participant. In these instances, good practice may be to work with the local knowledge of the HR or learning and development team and work together to complete a match.

We now share three case studies as examples of different approaches and ideas for matching mentors and mentees; firstly from the Royal Society of Chemistry, secondly from an external provider and lastly the matching process in place at Cityparents.

Case study

Matching mentors and mentees – Royal Society of Chemistry (UK)

With over 51,000 members and a knowledge business that spans the globe, the Royal Society of Chemistry (RSC) is the UK's professional body for chemical scientists, supporting and representing members and bringing together chemical scientists from all over the world. Here training and OD manager Sue Hughes shares thoughts on mentor selection and matching from her experience of adding maternity mentoring to the RSC development portfolio in 2014.

Prospective mentors for the broad mentoring pool fill in a mentoring form to help with the matching process. As part of that process we also ask them if they desire to mentor internationally, mentor graduates or mentor in a maternity capacity. Equally when we do the mentor training, we talk about maternity and that's where people actively say 'I'd like to do it because I'm a working parent' for example. So with this kind of mentoring it's about self-selection and people offering to be maternity mentors.

I would choose maternity mentors based on people wanting to do it, but also that they have that empathy and the ability to step in someone else's shoes for a moment. My sense of things is that you need to be a 'mentor-plus' to be a maternity mentor. In this context someone is feeling vulnerable as they go through a major life transition. We want to have a pool of mentors available for just that moment.

In terms of the matching process, there is an extra element of sensitivity you need to apply. This is very much about personalising and knowing the individuals. As the programme moves beyond its initial pilot, I will continue to select the mentor and mentee matches. For the longer term, it may not be me that makes those matching choices. Over time, I will prepare one of my team to do the matching, based on their knowledge of the individuals and the information on the mentoring forms. We would initially work in partnership, i.e. they could work alongside me to understand my thought processes. We might perhaps end up with two mentors and share a discussion and thoughts on making a final choice. In other words, a nice development conversation and perfect learning opportunity for wider team members!'

Sue Hughes
Training and OD Manager
Royal Society of Chemistry

Case study

External matching with CoachMentoring Ltd.

For many years as an external outsourced mentoring coordinator providing programme design and delivery, I have helped with the matching process for large and small organisations and membership associations/professional

(Continued)

bodies. I have found that those relationships that have been matched most successfully are where relevant questions are asked of both mentees and mentors in some form of application questionnaire.

The key to a good match is to ask the mentees what it is they would like from a mentor, and this might include the experience, skills, gender, sector, and even geographical location. I also try not to ask too many questions, otherwise you have far too much data to look at and you also risk not being able to find a mentor who has everything the mentee has requested.

As an external coordinator it is of great benefit to have a meeting with someone from within the organisation who has some knowledge of the mentors and mentees. They can give a final overview and check that no one has been inappropriately matched, i.e. dotted reporting lines/close relationship to the mentor. I use a simple spreadsheet for matching and this can quickly highlight the easy matches where the requirements of the mentee match up to the skills and experiences offered by a mentor. However sometimes, and especially where there have not been enough mentors or a shortage at a particular level, I have made a match based on lesser factors. By making sure you make a brief note of what criteria you have matched on if it's not obvious, you can convincingly advise the mentee and mentor why they are being paired. It is also more difficult to match a mentee where they have given very little information, or are vague about what they want to achieve and you may need to contact them to find out more before trying to match them.

There may be instances where you cannot match everyone, either because you don't have enough mentors, or because the skill sets do not match up. You may need to match creatively, or decide not to match at all. As long as you manage expectations by explaining why you cannot match them at this point, then this may be the best option until you are able to source some additional mentors who may meet their specific needs.

Matching is just a common sense approach to looking at what the mentee requires, and what a mentor can offer, and linking them together. It is very satisfying when you get it right, and even more so where you have been creative in the match!

Jacki Mason
Operations Manager and Consultant
CoachMentoring Ltd

Case study

Matching insights from Cityparents (CMS)

The CMS has two application windows a year and scheme members are assumed to stay in a mentoring relationship for a year. To date, the rolling membership has been up to 300 people per annum, but this does fluctuate.

Applicants for the CMS fill out an electronic application form at www.surveymonkey.com, which has evolved during the life of the scheme. Mentors and mentees provide information to assist matching, including their age, type of job and years of experience in that area of work; ages of children, preferred location for meeting. The mentee forms list a number of skills, such as work/life balance, inter-office relationships; developing business acumen, parenting and so on, and asks applicants to prioritise which of these areas they wish to focus on with their mentor; there are also free text questions such as *'What would you wish to gain from a mentoring relationship?'* and *'What experience in your mentor might be most useful to you?'*

The mentor forms have a parallel sequence of questions, thus mentors rank the skills they feel most able to assist mentees with and answer free text questions including *'What might you bring to a mentoring relationship?'* and *'What might you gain from one?'* The network has such a large membership that it is often possible to match parents with similar issues if they wish, such as single or gay parents or parents with disabled children or miscarriage or infertility problems. Mentors also provide an anonymised biography in their application forms, and the second stage of the matching is to send all mentee applicants a copy of these biographies so they can indicate their 'top picks,' thus involving them in the selection process. We take account of 'top picks' but, where more than one prospective mentee requests a particular mentor, we then look at other factors applicants have identified as important to them.

Esther Cavett
Executive Coach and Director of the Cityparents Mentoring Scheme

Materials to support the matching process

Taking a systematic approach, matching is helped by having some form of structured profiling whereby the mentor can introduce themselves, their personal and work contexts, working arrangements, experience and what they feel they can offer a prospective mentee. Equally, the mentee should also be encouraged to outline their own situation, initial preferences and perhaps early agendas for the mentoring. Mentoring pairs can hopefully be set up based on the needs expressed by the mentees and the practice and experience of the mentors.

With mentoring of this nature, the profiles of both parties are likely to include personal information; therefore, you may feel it is not appropriate to have full profiles available for open viewing. If you post mentor profiles on your intranet mentoring site, you may decide to prepare a précis profile for each mentor, with a link through to the programme coordinator to request further information.

Figures 12.2 and 12.3 are examples of templates which are maternity/parental mentoring specific, while Figures 12.4 and 12.5 are examples of mentor and mentee templates kindly shared by the Royal Society of Chemistry, which allow employees to apply for mentoring more broadly and tailor to maternity/parental mentoring as part of a later/follow up conversation with the programme owner.

Maternity / Paternity Mentor Profile	
Name	
Current role, location, team	
Job level / grade	
My working pattern (Full time, part time, compressed hours, etc.)	
How I make work possible as a parent	
The three biggest challenges I found returning to work	
What helped me most coming back	
What I hope to bring to mentoring	
Any additional information e.g. gender, faith, ethnicity	

Figure 12.2 Example mentor profile.

The matching process

Thought should be given to the actual mechanics of the matching process itself. Questions for consideration include:

- How transparent do you want your matching process to be?
- Will mentees self-select or be offered a choice of mentor? (If so, will this be open selection or guided choice?)
- Will mentees be allocated a mentor centrally (i.e. on the basis of their profile versus that of a mentor)?
- Will a mentee have an opportunity to review the profile of their mentor first?
- Who makes the initial connection? (The programme administrator or mentee?)
- What happens if they are not happy with the suggested match?

Maternity / Paternity Mentee Profile	
Name	
Current role, location, team	
Job level / grade	
The date my baby is due	
My last planned day in work	
My preferences for a mentor (Note, wherever possible we try to match mentees with same level (peer) mentors unless you indicate otherwise. Mentors will always be from a different team / department in order for your mentor to be as independent as possible)	A mentor at my current level / grade or A mentor at the next level / grade or No preference
	A mentor who works full time or A mentor who works part time / reduced / compressed hours or No preference
Other factors important in my request for a mentor, e.g. working parent, gender, faith, ethnicity	
My initial aims and objectives for the mentoring support	
Any additional information	

Figure 12.3 Example mentee profile.

Depending on the availability of mentors and knowledge of the different partici-pants, you may decide the best approach is to match mentors and mentees centrally and give the mentee the opportunity to confirm they are happy with their match before progressing to connection and introductions. Whatever method you choose, good practice is to share the process with participants and the wider business, e.g. on your intranet site, so all are clear how it works.

RSC Mentoring Form

Introductory form for mentors

Thank you for volunteering your time to be a mentor on the RSC mentoring scheme. To help us in the matching process (of mentor and mentee) could you please fill out the following form with information about yourself and send it through to XXXXX. Provide information you feel comfortable sharing and leave any areas blank if you would rather not answer. The information will be treated confidentially; however, we will share it with any mentee matched to you.

We also ask all mentees to fill out a similar form and will provide you with the information on your matched mentee prior to your first session. We do not send mentees this information.

Name:

a. Tell us a bit about yourself:

- *What is important to you in life?*
- *What does success mean to you?*
- *When in life have you been successful and what strengths did you use to help you get there?*
- *How would you describe yourself?*
- *What did you do before you came to the RSC?*
- *Do you have any hobbies/interests?*
- *How long have you been at the RSC?*
- *Anything else you'd like to share about yourself?*

b. What do you hope to get from mentoring?

c. In a nutshell what do you think mentoring is?

d. What are you able to bring to mentoring?

e. Describe yourself in three words.

f. Have you had any previous experience of mentoring or using the skills used in mentoring?

g. Is there anything you would feel very uncomfortable dealing with?

Preferences for mentoring:

Could you indicate below (by marking in any of the boxes) if you are interested in any of the broader mentoring services we aim to provide across the RSC. Additional training/ information would be provided for these:

I would be happy to work with someone from a different location to my own.
I am interested in being a potential maternity/parental mentor.
I would be happy to mentor a graduate as part of our graduate mentoring scheme.

Figure 12.4 RSC mentor profile.

Royal Society of Chemistry Mentoring

Introductory questionnaire new mentees

Welcome to the start of your mentoring experience here at the Royal Society of Chemistry. Please provide us with some information about yourself and what you would like to gain from the mentoring experience by filling in the questions below. The information will be used to match you with a mentor and to give to your mentor prior to your first meeting. Provide information you feel comfortable sharing and leave any areas blank if you would rather not answer. Your mentor will use this information as a basis for discussion at your first meeting and as a way to get to know a little more about you before you start this process. The information will be treated confidentially.

Name: .... **Area/Directorate:** ....

a. Tell us a bit about yourself

- *What is important to you in life?*
- *How would you describe yourself?*
- *What does success mean to you? \What did you do before you came to the Royal Society of Chemistry?*
- *Do you have any interests/hobbies?*
- *Anything else you'd like to share about yourself?*

b. Describe yourself in three words.

c. What do you perceive are your strengths and development areas?

d. What would you like to do in the future?

e. By the end of your mentoring process what do you hope to have gained from the experience?

f. What do you want to work on/explore with your mentor?

g. What do you know about mentoring – have you had any experiences of mentoring before?

h. What are your expectations of your mentor?

i. What can your mentor do to help get the best out of you?

j. Please add below some objectives discussed and agreed with your line manager to share with your mentor:

Figure 12.5 RSC mentee profile.

If things go wrong

Despite best intentions, not all mentoring relationships work out. It may be down to an initial mismatch, or simply that one party (or both) feels they are not able to work with the other.

Good practice therefore is to plan for this at the design stage and have a simple 'no fault divorce' get-out clause (Clutterbuck 2004), which participants understand is there in the event of being needed and which makes it possible for either party to request a change at any point. Consider who is best placed to field these conversations and to make any decisions necessary in terms of offering alternative solutions and next steps.

Note

1 The point referring to time back after maternity/parental leave is an interesting one. In your pool of available mentors, it is helpful to have some mentors who are relatively recent returners. They offer themselves as 'current' role models; colleagues who have experienced the tough times and made it through. That is not to say all working parents believe they have the boxes ticked in terms of balancing work/career and parenting. It is an ongoing dialogue but suggestive of a challenge worth taking on. And it is perhaps the recency of their experience that gives hope to a returning mentee, struggling to rationalise a pre-maternity vision of life with the reality of managing life back in work with a new baby.

13 Preparing mentors and mentees

Investing time in preparing your participants ahead of the start of mentoring will have a significant effect on the success and outcomes of your programme. As we have shown in previous chapters, the nature of mentoring in this context is quite distinct from most work-based development mentoring and with this in mind, the introduction of a maternity or parental mentoring programme calls for bespoke preparation. It's about setting out expectations, what might be expected of the participants, exploring why and how this mentoring landscape differs from other mentoring contexts and building a practical understanding of helpful mentoring approaches and practices in order for this to be a positive learning experience for both mentor and mentee.

There are a number of questions to consider here:

- What format is best for preparation – a briefing, a workshop or webinar?
- What might the content need to look like?
- Who is the target audience – mentors, mentees or both?
- How much time should be allocated to this?

From our experience of mentoring programmes across organisations, we have found a clear correlation between the format, the audience and successful learning outcomes as indicated in Table 13.1.

When starting up a brand new programme, our recommendation is to run development workshops for all participants (mentors and mentees) where it is practical to get people together in one location. Where your potential participants are spread across geographical areas (internationally, for example), the next best solution may be to use online video conferencing or webinars. In this way you still have an opportunity for shared discussion and a level of participation in the session. Webinars used as 'follow up' can also support ongoing messages and have the added benefit that they may be recorded if someone is unable to attend at the time of broadcast.

There are advantages to training mentors and mentees jointly on some aspects of the programme. For example, it has the advantage of enabling them to get to know each other, perhaps help the matching process through meeting up and sharing

Table 13.1 Preparation of participants

No preparation of mentors or mentees (i.e. informal mentoring programmes)	Preparation through briefing sessions	Training for mentors only	Training for both mentors and mentees
Expect 10% of relationships to deliver significant learning. This 10% may be influenced by the participants' previous experiences of good mentoring practices	Where a programme relies solely on briefing, expect 30% of mentoring relationships to succeed, where mentors apply learning from other training.	Expect up to 60% of relationships to deliver successful learning outcomes for the mentee. The difficulty here is that mentors are prepared, but mentees – who should be in the driving seat in terms of what they want to achieve through mentoring – are more inclined to be 'led' by the mentor.	Expect up to 90% of relationships to deliver successful learning outcomes – for both mentor and mentee. This also enables both parties to have an appreciation of the different roles of mentor and mentee. Success is further enhanced where line managers have been briefed and feel informed about the programme.

Reproduced with permission from Clutterbuck, D. 2014.

Source: *Everyone Needs A Mentor.* 5th ed. CIPD (Chartered Institute of Personnel and Development), London.

understanding of the aims and objectives as a collective group. As we shall reveal below, there are key aspects of the mentor and mentee development that differ, so if you can get people together in one location, one option may be to kick start the sessions as a total group (e.g. at a lunchtime seminar) and then run workshops for the separate groups to enable focus on the specific aspects of the programme that are relevant to them.

Developing mentors

> I think it's critical that parental mentors get extra training beyond a standard mentoring skills session. The differences in dynamics of the mentoring cycle are quite significant, so it is about being aware of this and responding to it.
>
> (Sue Hughes, Royal Society of Chemistry)

The content for your training workshops should take into account your current provision and methods for preparing mentors for existing mentoring programmes. Does your organisation already train and develop mentors for other developmental programmes, for example? In which case, you may feel the best approach is to continue with a generic workshop for development of mentoring skills (for any new mentors or mentors seeking a refresher in terms of mentoring skills) and then to offer an additional workshop built purely around the context and content of your maternity/parental mentoring programme.

Suggested content for a mentors' parental mentoring workshop includes:

- The purpose of the mentoring programme
- Background to the programme (using data from surveys, research, feedback)
- Aims and objectives (tailored to your business)
- Your process for matching mentors and mentees
- Key models and frameworks:

  ○ The journey framework (Chapter 6)
  ○ Mentoring trajectories (development vs. parent mentoring, Chapter 5)
  ○ Defining mentoring (see p. 6)
  ○ Mentoring modes (e.g. e-mentoring – Chapter 8)

- Skills and qualities of effective mentors and mentees (Chapters 9 and 10)
- Practical tools and techniques (Chapter 18)
- If things go wrong (p. 96)
- Supervision and ongoing support/development (Chapter 16)
- Next steps

The key is for your workshop to be informative and participative. Naturally, some of the content will lend itself to being 'briefed out,' but as far as possible, the workshop should include a blend of factual information (for example, your business case research), with plenty of opportunity for exploration and discussion, practicing tools and techniques, and space for reflection and review in order to begin to build understanding of the role of a parent mentor.

Good practice! The person who opens your workshop makes an important statement to your mentors about the level of investment and business support for your programme. Perhaps your HRD or programme sponsor is supportive and would open the session? As part of the introduction, it is also useful to set out how the mentoring dovetails with wider agendas of people development, diversity and inclusion, for example.

Supporting activities for a mentors' workshop

Here we offer a number of practical activities you might find useful to build in to a mentors' workshop for parental mentoring.

Activity – 'It starts with me'

Background

In the previous chapter, we identified one risk of mentoring in this context where the temptation might be for the enthusiastic mentor to assume '*what I have done works*' as opposed to '*let's explore how you can create your own path*'. The key here is to build awareness of the diversity of experience by exploring the mentors' own journeys first and for them to have an opportunity to look back, reflect on their personal learning and to hear others' stories – each of which will be different, but no less valid.

Method

In recognition of the fact that each journey to becoming a working parent is unique, a useful way to open your workshop is to invite the mentors to pair up and discuss the following questions:

• How was my own journey out of work and return as a working parent?
• Knowing what I know now, what might I do differently?
• Who am I as a working parent?
• What have I noticed about the experience of others? (For a mentor who is not a parent)
• What do I hope to bring to this mentoring practice?
• What do I hope to learn from this experience of mentoring?

Allow about 10 to 15 minutes each way – they will have much to share.

Invite the group to share headlines from their paired discussion and post key points as they present.

As part of the debrief, ask the group:

• What are the collective themes coming across from this group?
• What have you noticed from listening to these stories and anecdotes?
• How might this impact how you approach your role as a parent mentor?
• If this group were a representative sample of working parents, what might be the implications of these insights for the business?

This opening activity offers a simple way to reveal the myriad of journeys and options open to parents as they navigate their way to working parenthood and may also begin to highlight the value of having an offline helping relationship in support of that journey.

We have run this activity many times with new mentors. Typically, the room comes alive with animated conversations and we remain surprised and humbled at the level of disclosure. Some may have had positive experiences of maternity leave and return, while others may have really struggled. For each party this often comes as a surprise! There comes a dawning realisation that the 'truth' of return and the 'ideal' work scenario have infinite possibilities and outcomes, and with that in mind the point to draw out is that their future mentee's journey, their expectations, ambitions and experience are very likely to be different from their own.

Activity – Changing focus

Background

Having outlined the different stages of the maternity journey, there is an opportunity for the mentors to reflect how priorities change at this time, using the framework shown in Figure 13.1.

Method

Using two different coloured pens (one representing work, the other representing baby or child), ask the mentors to draw two lines across the different phases of the journey, indicating changes in the focus on work and family or baby. Invite them to write a few words alongside the peaks and troughs to indicate what they represent and what was happening at that point.

Typically what is revealed is a rapid and sudden exchange of focus from work to baby at the start of maternity leave and the collision as the two priorities converge and subsequently compete on return to work.

Useful questions to debrief this activity might include:

- What do I notice from having completed this activity?
- How does this journey compare with others' in the group?
- How does the model resonate with my experience or observations of others' priorities as I/they navigated out of work and returned?
- What have I learned about my own or others' relationships with work and family?
- What do I want to take away from this?
- Taking a step back, how might this activity inform how I work with a mentee?

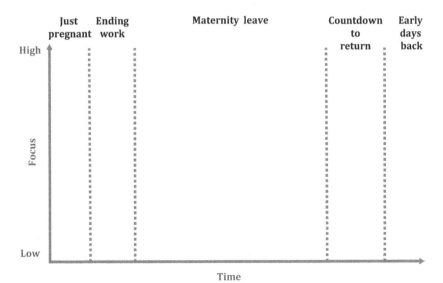

Figure 13.1 Changing focus.

Activity – Stepping through the journey

Background

This activity brings to life the journey framework (Chapter 6) and invites mentors to revisit the model in order to build understanding of the different stages. You may decide to add in Stage 1 (Early Pregnancy); however, we find that mentoring support typically (though not always) commences as the mother-to-be moves toward 'Ending Work.' Hence, this activity focuses from this stage of the journey onward.

Method

Ahead of time, prepare five circles on large pieces of paper (flip chart paper is perfect for this – or you could use coloured card). On each piece of card, place one of each the five stages as shown in Figure 13.2.

Place the different circles on the wall around the room and invite the mentors to step through the journey in sequence discussing:

- How is this stage different from what was before?
- What might be happening for a mentee at this point?
- What might be helpful in terms of mentoring support?

If numbers permit, you could have the mentors work their way around as one group, or you may decide to use two sets of circles to encourage maximum participation. This activity is best done sequentially (i.e. in order) so they have a sense of actually engaging with the journey. Debrief, sharing learning and insights.

Activity – Our experiences of mentoring

Background

As practicing mentors, we are all informed (consciously or unconsciously) by our experiences of being helped ourselves. This activity is a useful starting point to begin to consider what might be the core skills and qualities of an effective mentor by asking participants to look back and reflect on their own experiences of being mentored.

Figure 13.2 Five stages.

Method

Keep it simple – using A4 paper and pens or pencils, invite the mentors to draw an image that represents their experiences of being mentored previously. If this is a pilot programme, they may not have had formal maternity or parent mentoring, but may have sought out a work friend or colleague to act as an informal sounding board, or perhaps experienced mentoring as part of their ongoing development.

Questions to prompt thinking:

- What was your objective for this mentoring/helping relationship?
- What did those people do well as mentors?
- How did it make you feel?
- What was the impact?

Post the pictures on the wall and invite any comments and thoughts, pulling out key themes and observations. When you move on to build the role of an effective mentor, you have an opportunity to draw on these insights again. In this way, the framework for your parent mentors becomes an authentic collaboration, balancing the theory with the business' own language, culture and experiences in the room.

Activity – Contracting the relationship up front

Background

We know from experience (Chapter 6) that early mentoring agendas in this context can feel a bit flaky – for no other reason than the first time parent is yet to be convinced she needs any help and therefore isn't sure exactly what she wants to discuss. In contrast, the mentor may find themselves painfully aware of the scale of change ahead and wrestling with not going straight into advice mode.

The first conversation – meeting up, making early introductions and contracting the relationship – is critical. An opportunity to practice and 'voice' that conversation ahead of time may well pay dividends later, particularly around setting expectations of making time for mentoring, who is going to arrange the meetings and 'boundaries,' for example.

Method

Using the template on p. 45, invite the mentors to work in pairs and have a practice 'first conversation.' Give them a few minutes to prepare first with the following questions as prompts:

- How do you want to begin the conversation?
- What might be helpful to share about yourself as a working parent/mentor?

- What do you want to share about your role and expectations?
- What boundaries might crop up in this kind of mentoring?
- What are the watch outs – things you want to be mindful of?

Debrief as a group sharing learning and insights:

- What went well?
- What would you do next time?
- What builds do we want to make to the contracting model to make it work for us?

Activity – Bringing it all together

Background

Faced with a plethora of information, this activity brings the learning together from the workshop as a helpful one-page summary. It encourages mentors to firm up understanding of the different stages of the journey framework and within each stage, what they may want to do and how they might want to approach the mentoring support.

Method

Using copies of the blank template (Figure 13.3), invite the mentors to complete the sections based on what they have learned from the day. (Note, early maternity leave is not included in this activity because this is a time where work-based mentoring is superseded by the personal agenda of becoming a new parent.) If numbers are sufficient, you could divide the group into subsets, to complete a couple of sections each and then come back as a group to share the results. The objective is for them to be familiar with the journey framework, understanding that there are several distinct and recognisable stages, each of which has options in terms of approaches, content and practice. (It is also a useful framework for inclusion in supervision, which we explore in Chapter 16.)

Developing your mentees

Preparing your mentees ahead of the start of their mentoring relationship is just as important to the success of the programme, though the content will need some adjusting to be appropriate for the mentees.

Topics a mentee workshop could focus on include:

- Hopes and expectations for the future as a parent
- The purpose of the mentoring programme
- Aims and objectives

	Ending work	Countdown to return	Early days back	Moving forward
What's happening for my mentee				
Topics which may be helpful to explore at this point				
Tools which may be appropriate				
Mentoring modes (e.g. 1-1, text, email)				
Questions and prompts				

Figure 13.3 Mentoring support for the journey to working parenthood.

- Key models and frameworks:

  ○ The journey framework (Chapter 6)
  ○ Differing mentoring trajectories (development versus maternity mentoring – Chapter 5)
  ○ Defining mentoring (see p. 6)
  ○ Mentoring roles (What does a mentor typically do? Chapter 7)

- Qualities of effective mentees (Chapter 9)
- Matching mentors and mentees
- If things go wrong (p. 96)
- Getting started (expectations, key dates, next steps)

Again, the good practice approach should be to have a blend of information and participation with space for reflection, learning and networking. One of the advantages of these sessions is it raises visibility of them as a peer group of parents-to-be and for some it may open a new network of contacts and source of additional support in the workplace and while on leave.

Good practice! Invite one of your mentors and a mentee to join the session, and share learning and insights into being a working parent.

Ideas and learning approaches for a mentee workshop

Here we offer a number of practical activities and ideas you might find useful to build in to a mentees' workshop.

Opening activity – 'Awareness of breath and baby'

Background

We know from many conversations with mothers-to-be that the time in work immediately prematernity leave is often a frenetic period of closing down and finishing off. The net result is that often considerations of personal well-being, her baby and pregnancy are psychologically put 'on the back burner' during work hours. This opening activity invites the mentees to 'press the pause button' for a few precious minutes, opening your workshop sensitively and mindfully, by making space and bringing awareness of their pregnancy and baby into the room.

Method

Explain to the participants that you are going to open the session with some reflective (mindful) space. Adopting a mindful approach, they will be paying attention to the here and now, allowing them to just 'be' in the room with their breathing and baby front of mind.

Use the following text as a guide, taking appropriate time, pausing and paying attention to your pace and tone as you read.

Delivery tip: It is a good idea to use the present gerund (adding *'ing'* to your wording) throughout, as this really helps bring participants into the present and is invitational in tone.

'Awareness of breath and baby'

I'm going to invite you to make yourself comfortable in your chair, having your back straight, but not overly arched. Resting your hands on your lap. Closing your eyes or gazing at the floor with your eyes half closed and without actually focusing on what is before you.

As you're sitting there, beginning to notice your legs in contact with the seat, your hands perhaps feeling heavy and relaxed on your lap, your feet, toes feeling steady on the floor. Noticing your jaw, your shoulders – letting them drop a little – feeling any tension leaving you.

Now gently bringing your attention to your breath. Just breathing normally, breathing in, (pause) breathing out – the most natural thing in the world. Without trying to change anything, noticing *how* you breathe. Not thinking *about* the breath, but being *with* the breath.

Focusing your attention on your in-breath. Noticing how your breath feels as it comes in at the tip of your nostrils. Noticing any sensations there, any changes in temperature, any tickling, any other sensations.

When your mind wanders, as it surely will, gently bringing it back to the breath, using the breath as an anchor.

As you breathe in, saying to yourself, 'Breathing in'. As you breathe out, saying to yourself, 'Breathing out'.

Bringing compassion to yourself in the practice. Just breathing and noticing what is there.

And now bringing your attention to how your chest feels as you breathe in and out, how it feels in your abdomen as you breathe in and out.

And now bringing your attention to your baby in your abdomen as you breathe. Again, the most natural thing in the world. Breathing in, breathing out, noticing any sensations of your baby moving, (pause) or sleeping, (pause) safe, secure, (pause) waiting to meet you.

Just breathing and being with your baby

Again, gently bringing your mind back when it wanders and congratulating yourself for noticing your attention has wandered.

'Breathing in', 'Breathing out'. All is well, your baby is here with you…

(Pausing, silence for a few moments more)

….And when you are ready, gently coming back into the room

(Adapted with permission from the Awareness of Breath activity, Hall, L. 2013. *Mindful Coaching*, Kogan Page, London.)

Give the participants a few moments to feel 'back' in the room. Invite any reflections or thoughts from the participants as to how this activity made them feel. Explore the extent to which they feel able to bring a sense of pregnancy into the workplace right now. For some participants, this may be the first time they have felt able to relax and to simply 'be' with their pregnancy in a work context.

Activity – Hopes and expectations

Background

A helpful way to engage the mentees in the spirit of the workshop is to have them share hopes and expectations for the future, by building a vision of how they hope life will be for them as working parents. Following on from the mindful opening session, this activity works as a helpful bridge into the workshop itself and is a good way of introducing them to each other.

Method

Invite the mentees to take a sheet of paper and using a pencil or coloured pens if you have them, draw their hopes and expectations for the future as a working parent.

- What will that look like?
- What will they be doing more of/less of?

- Who is in the picture with them?
- Any concerns they may have?
- What might they be looking forward to most?

Invite them to pair up and share their pictures with a colleague, then as a group, invite the mentees to share any collective thoughts and insights.

Activity – Stepping through the journey

Background

This activity brings to life the journey framework and invites the mentees to begin to look ahead and think about what might be happening for them and help they may be looking for at different times.

Method

Ahead of time, prepare five circles on large pieces of paper (flip chart paper is perfect for this – or you could use coloured card). On each piece of card, place one of each of the five stages as shown in Figure 13.4.

Place the different circles on the wall around the room and invite the mentees to stand with each circle and have a discussion before moving to the next stage. Questions to prompt thinking:

- How is this stage different from what was before?
- What might I be doing/looking forward to/have concerns about at this stage?
- What might be helpful in terms of mentoring support?

If numbers permit, we suggest you have the group work its way around as one group, or have two sets of circles. This activity is best done sequentially (i.e. in order) so they have a sense of actually engaging with the journey.

Activity – Where to start

Background

We know that many mentees struggle with asking for help pre-maternity or paternity leave, principally because they are unsure of what lies ahead. Giving thought

Figure 13.4 Five stages.

to what help they may need where they are now and having this ready to share with their mentor offers a starting point. It may be that the mentor (from their own experience) has a sense of the level of change ahead, but it is for the mentee to have her own experience and to feel she has support from her mentor who understands new questions and agendas are likely to emerge as a new 'truth' of life postbaby begins to reveal itself.

Method

The first conversation to contract the relationship is an important one for mentor and mentee. It's about making connections, building early rapport and having some idea of what might be on the mentee's early agenda. For this activity, there is a simple template (Figure 13.5), which can be adapted to meet the needs of your business.

Mentee preparation	
Please use these questions to help you prepare for a first mentoring meeting. These are for your personal preparation in the hope they offer an opening framework for the conversation and begin to build the foundations for a positive mentoring experience.	
What do you hope to gain from this experience of parental mentoring?	
What will you bring to the relationship?	
What's helpful for your mentor to know about you?	
What would you like to know about your mentor?	
What are your strong points and yourbiggest needs?	
What questions are on your mind right now?	
Where do you want to start?	
What's the most important thing to discuss first?	

Figure 13.5 Mentee preparation template.

The preparation of your mentors and mentees is hugely important for the success of your programme. Hopefully, the topics and activities have provided some useful suggestions to make your mentee and mentor workshops interesting and engaging.

Good practice! In conclusion for this section, we leave you with the following considerations:

- Tailor your sessions so they are relevant to your business needs.
- Use your own research data, quotes and anecdotes to bring the context to life.
- Allow sufficient time for practical activities – the more practice the better prepared your participants will be.
- Build in individual reflection time and shared discussion.
- If possible, have some time where mentors and mentees can come together (this can really help the matching process and early rapport building).
- Include different people in the delivery of your workshop, to engage participants and demonstrate the wider interest and influence of the programme.
- Be careful not to try to cover everything in a single session. Your participants will only have so much capacity for retention of information!
- Be clear with next steps, dates for the diary and key contacts for queries and follow up.

14 Preparing your line managers

My colleagues were supportive but appropriate cover hadn't been put in place while I was away and they felt adrift during my period of 8 months' maternity leave. I had people getting in touch, sending emails and expecting that I would be able to respond. My female boss, who is single and has no children, did not empathise with my situation.
(Director, Russell Group University)

In addition to preparing mentors and mentees, the importance of preparing line managers should not be underestimated and having a mentor supporting the mother-to-be does not allow line managers to abdicate their responsibility. Our experience indicates they are frequently the deal breakers for a positive – or negative – experience of returning to work, fundamentally because they broker the return itself and these are high stakes conversations. Equally we find many line managers uncertain, worried about what they should and should not do, what they can and cannot ask, and poorly prepared for supporting an employee through parental leave and return to work.

Line managers often don't understand or know returners are struggling.
(Sue Hughes, Royal Society of Chemistry)

In development mentoring, there are three people central to a mentoring relationship. These three players operate in a form of triumvirate; three interconnecting relationships working within the context of the organisation:

- The individual employee/mentee
- Their line manager
- The mentor (offline support)

The concept of a triumvirate has an alluring simplicity, suggestive of a neat balance of three parties – two supporting and one being supported (Figure 14.1).

In a maternity/parental context, the interplay between the three is more complex as indicated in Figure 14.2.

Though all three parties operate (initially) within the organisation, the **mentee's** physical presence and focus shift *away* from the organisational context pre-parental leave, *to* an external/familial focus during leave, with considerations of *both* internal

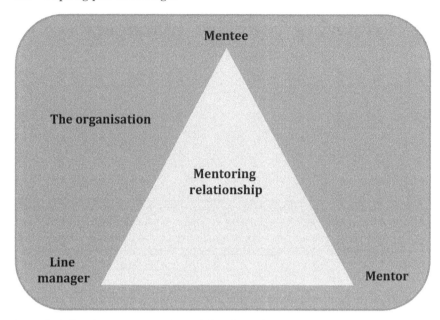

Figure 14.1 Development mentoring and three key roles.

and external contexts on their return to work. In contrast, the **line manager** focus is typically – and understandably – characterised by an internal/organisational focus in the interests of maintaining work-based deliverables and objectives. The **mentor** – by the very nature of their experience as an employee and parent – straddles both contexts. Mentors will typically be from a different business function from that of the line manager and mentee to minimise risk of conflicts of interest. Appropriately then, there is no requirement for connection (i.e. dialogue) between mentor and their mentee's line manager.

Without preparation and explanation, the potential for conflict is significant because the mentoring operates outside the day-to-day working relationship with the line manager. Understandably, they will wonder what conversations are taking place, why their colleague feels the need to take time out of an already packed agenda pre-start of parental leave and what is actually being discussed. Therefore, a key part of setting up your mentoring programme is outlining the purpose of the mentoring, exploring roles and responsibilities, including that of the line manager, so all are clear as to good practice for support and development in this context.

Table 14.1 attempts to draw a distinction between supportive actions and responsibilities of a mentor and line manager in a maternity/parental mentoring relationship as well as those of the employee/mentee over this time period.

The task of taking an employee through her formal rights and entitlements and the business' provision for maternity/parental leave will typically fall to a member of the HR team as opposed to a line manager. That being said, line managers do

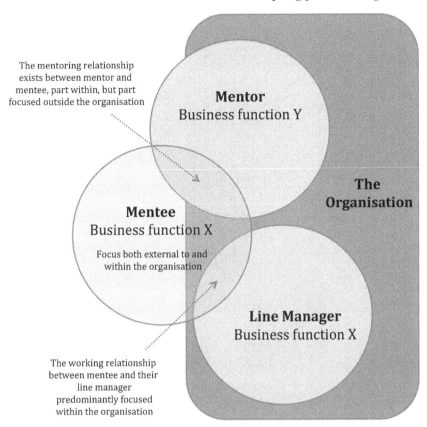

The mentoring relationship exists between mentor and mentee, part within, but part focused outside the organisation

Mentor
Business function Y

The Organisation

Mentee
Business function X

Focus both external to and within the organisation

Line Manager
Business function X

The working relationship between mentee and their line manager predominantly focused within the organisation

Figure 14.2 Parental mentoring and three key roles.

need to be familiar with the legal imperatives and guidelines surrounding maternity and parental leave, since they are the ones having conversations and coming to agreement with the returning employee.

It is also extremely important to raise awareness of the concept of unconscious bias with line managers, recognising the strength of their own biases and being conscious of the risks associated with bias in this context. Beliefs relating to career, family and gender roles are often at the heart of people's personal values, which – if left unchecked – can generate unhelpful expectations and assumptions and affect the working relationship and trust between a line manager and his or her direct report.

So how best to prepare your line managers? With input from learning and development and/or diversity and inclusion teams, our suggestion is to run bespoke workshops for line managers. These sessions could be jointly led by a member of the HR team (for legal and procedural considerations) and the programme manager.

Here we offer suggested outlines for each of these sessions:

Table 14.1 Actions and responsibilities

Line manager	Employee/mentee	Mentor
Be clear and agree on development goals and performance targets for completion/handover before leave commences and again post-return (asking rather than making assumptions)	Agree on development plan and performance contract with line manager	Help mentee to integrate work and career goals with personal goals outside work
Agree on and diarise a best estimate timetable for start of leave and return to work	Agree on separate mentoring contract with mentor	Agree on individual parental mentoring contract with mentee
	Keep line manager informed of key dates and commitments, e.g. expected week of childbirth, date for commencement of maternity/parental leave, ante-natal or related appointments	Diarise key dates and contact points for the mentoring
	Share key dates with the mentor	
	Responsible for organising mentoring sessions	
Arrange and recruit maternity replacement cover as appropriate	Plan for handover and contingency	Challenge mentee's thinking and assumptions
Agree on handover plan and priorities		Support mentee's thinking and preparation in relation to their handover plan as appropriate
Conduct review and/or performance appraisal before leave commences	Request and prepare for performance appraisal, seeking feedback from stakeholders and team as appropriate	Encourage mentee to manage expectations and relationship with her line manager
Mindful of the health and well-being of the colleague about to go on maternity leave, e.g. complete risk assessment (UK), review working hours and practices and discuss with the colleague as appropriate	Mindful of own health and well-being	Help mentee to prioritise health and well-being particularly in the lead up to start of maternity leave
Agree on communication content and how best to keep in touch while on parental leave (e.g. monthly emails, visits to work, home visits, keep in touch days)	Give thought to what might be helpful communication from the team and mentor while on maternity/parental leave	Keep in touch with offline updates of company activity and news as agreed
Actively keep in contact, demonstrating interest, inviting the colleague to team events, meetings and activities they have said they are interested in (acknowledging they may not always have headspace and it is their choice whether to respond to the contact/invitation)		

Give appropriate recognition – perhaps a piece of work or project has been successfully completed for which the colleague has been a contributor, in which case this is an ideal opportunity to get in touch with positive feedback and recognition Prepared and available for discussions relating to a return to work	Give thought to return to work solutions (full time, part time, reduced hours, perhaps a phased return) Plan for the return to work conversation	Be a 'sounding board' for ideas, suggestions and conversations. Help the mentee structure and be effective in the critical conversations she needs to have with her line manager, team, key customers The mentor's role remains offline throughout and is not intended to act as a representative for the mentee in return to work discussions with her manager
Organise reintegration/return to work plan for the returning colleague, e.g. 1. The basics of desk set up, phone, laptop updated, equipment ordered 2. Handover documents summarising relevant changes, business plans, papers, team meetings and key diary dates ahead 3. A plan for the first week, with meetings arranged, welcome back lunch, team buddy and scheduled one-to-ones 4. Prepare the team and colleagues for her return to work (one of the issues that frequently comes up is the need to leave on time – usually for child care reasons, so there may be a team adjustment to be made)	Draw up their return to work plan, building in contingency as appropriate Manage business' expectations of personal availability and time limitations – e.g. start and finish times, access and availability outside working hours	Support mentee's return to work plan, and explore anticipated changes to ways of working as a working parent and how to table these
Plan for a career conversation 6 to 9 months post return, which focuses attention on progress since returning and future ambitions	Request a conversation which is a forum to explore developmental goals and ambitions short term and longer term once they feel ready	Support preparation for conversations regarding future/longer-term career goals

*Workshop 1: Good practice for closing down
and keeping in touch*

1   Check in:
    • Share current experiences and challenges managing maternity/parental leave.
    • What questions are on their mind to have answered in the session? (Revisit these at the end to check they have been covered)
2   The formal context:
    • Legal provision for maternity and shared parental leave (e.g. time off for maternity/shared parental leave, antenatal care, salary payments, holidays, bank holidays, keep in touch days).
    • Business guidelines and policies for parental leave (many organisations offer enhanced provision over and above minimum legal requirements).
3   Unconscious bias:
    • Introduce and outline the concept of unconscious bias.
    • Raise awareness of unconscious bias in relation to maternity and working parents, exploring mindsets, individual assumptions and discussing illustrative scenarios, e.g. what myths and assumptions are there in relation to working mothers? What assumptions are there about working fathers? (Is there a difference in relation to gender with these questions?) What beliefs are evident around part-time working? How might these beliefs affect the way someone is supported through maternity and return to work when those choices conflict with our own values?
    • What action can be taken to minimise bias?
4   Mentoring support:
    • Aims and objectives
    • The maternity journey (Chapter 6)
    • Roles and responsibilities (p. 114)
5   Case studies:
    • Do your homework with HR and the legal team that support them to create a number of business relevant case studies that illustrate the kinds of issues that typically come up in your organisation when managing maternity/parental leave. These might include managing handovers, requests for flexible working, reduced hours, changes in line manager, organisational/team structure changes, employees on track for promotion, for example.
    • Use real (anonymised) examples of employees taking parental/maternity leave in the organisation returning with different scenarios for line managers to explore.
    • How would they handle these situations?
    • What do they need to be mindful of?
    • What questions should they be asking?
    • A reminder; if in doubt, consult HR for advice and guidance.
6   Good practice as a line manager:
    • A supportive, caring and thoughtful line manager makes all the difference. Use the group to work up their own outline of good practice in this

context, e.g. helping plan for close down and handover, being considerate of health and well being (particularly in the latter stages of pregnancy), taking an interest, sharing their own experiences as appropriate, agreeing the plan for keeping in contact.

7 Check out:
   • Outstanding questions
   • Key learning
   • Individual actions

Workshop 2: Good practice for supporting returners

1 Check in:
   • Share experience to date (keeping comments and examples non-attributable)
   • Questions/concerns on their mind for the session
2 Recap:
   • The maternity journey
     ○ What may be happening for the colleague as they consider their return?
     ○ Transition and return to work in the context of the change curve
   • Unconscious bias (revisit the concept in relation to return to work choices, for example)
3 The return to work conversation:
   • Effective preparation
   • Anticipating questions and requests
   • Consideration of any changes in the business or employee's role
   • What if…? (brainstorm scenarios and ideas)
   • Support for the conversation (e.g. HR team, procedures and policies)
   • Following up
4 The return:
   • Creating a robust reintegration plan
   • Planning week one
   • Handling emotions
   • Balancing the needs of the individual with the needs of the business
   • Making reasonable adjustments (e.g. to start or finish times for the first few weeks)
   • Positive support and feedback
5 Check out:
   • Any outstanding questions
   • Key learning and actions

Once set up, these sessions work well in small groups, where attendees have the opportunity to participate and share insights, learning and concerns. Good practice is for these to be a 'must attend' session. The return on investment should become evident in the reduction of HR case load and legal costs often associated with the poor handling of returns to work.

Case study

Good practice insights into the role of a supportive line manager

From the employee's perspective

My line manager, a man with three teenage children of his own, singlehand-edly made my maternity leave (and return) both an enjoyable and construc-tive experience. I was a late starter to motherhood at 37 years of age and worked as a Head of Department in a large corporation. There's never a right time to be absent from work for an extended time, and I certainly felt anx-ious about this in the lead up to my first baby's due date. About 2 months before my leave was due to start, I found out that I had a new line manager, someone who had been in a more senior role than me for the same time as I had been at the organisation. He was a breath of fresh air. With his help, we recruited my maternity cover externally and she started 3 weeks before I left. The final few weeks were quite intense but I left feeling things were in rea-sonably good order, which was important to me – after all I was coming back to this job and this team. I wanted my departure to be positive for all of us. I knew of other colleagues who had started maternity leave without having anyone to handover to so I felt fortunate to be able to do so. It then took me about 3 months to disconnect completely and enter the zone of maternity leave where all that mattered was my baby and work seemed far away.

The one person I kept in regular touch with, and who kept in touch with me, was my line manager. We caught up face-to-face only twice, away from work, for a coffee around the 3 and 5 month mark. Those were rich, relaxed conversations where he would openly keep me updated and get my thoughts on things. He also forwarded me critical emails, always with the precursor: "if you're interested; ignore if you're not". It felt like he was looking out for me and wanted me to return. One of our conversations focused on expected changes to my role. He wanted to sound me out about how I felt about them. It essentially involved me taking on a larger remit even though he knew I wanted to return 4 days a week. He managed to convey both his confidence in my ability to do the job, whilst also making me feel I had the freedom to negotiate how this might work.

I returned to work after 8 months, which felt right for me. After I had been back a few weeks, I got an email from him in which he expressed how much he wanted me to succeed in both my job and being a mother. He asked me to tell him if I ever felt I wasn't succeeding, and he would help me find a way. It was an email he never had to send but it meant a lot to me. After 6 months back at work, I went full time and after 15 months I went on my second maternity leave. I had exactly the same experience, returning this time after 10 months and once again met by more thinking around growth in my role. At the point I returned from my second leave, my line manager had managed to help my career grow as if I had never been absent.

I believe I became a better employee after motherhood. I focused more on the stuff which mattered, was more productive with my time, more empathetic with my team and colleagues, and more pragmatic with my decisions. In many ways, with my line manager as a mentor, having kids was hugely beneficial for both my personal and professional development.

Senior Manager
BSKYB

From the line manager's perspective

I always took the fundamental view that most roles can be done 4 days a week by a determined person, so that was my starting point. My experience of returning mothers was that they are even more determined to be efficient and productive in their work because they have a very good reason to prioritise (their kids!)

My default position was that maternity leave provided *opportunity* for all rather than threat (e.g. stepping up, deputisation, etc.) if you *chose* to view it positively.

Employers who make it a good/progressive experience for parents of young children have a great retention hook for these employees because so few employers do – and these employees know they have a good thing going!

Line Manager
BSKYB

15 Ending well

In Chapter 5 we explored each of the different phases of a parental mentoring relationship. This chapter considers the final stage in more detail; identifying a point of closure, winding down the mentoring relationship and formally saying goodbye as mentor and mentee.

Research (Clutterbuck and Megginson 2004) tells us the way in which this stage in the relationship is managed has a significant impact on how each party subsequently views the mentoring. A well-managed final meeting, where participants have the opportunity to review what they have achieved, consider next steps and agree on a formal conclusion to the mentoring, is viewed much more positively than a relationship that has been allowed to drift and fizzle out. Without closure, there is uncertainty and a sense of something left unfinished.

Sometimes there is a reluctance to acknowledge that the time has come to let go and endings can *'creep up on us and catch us unprepared'* (Batista 2014). Letting go can be a challenge for the mentee and equally for the mentor, particularly where there has been a degree of emotion shared and much personal disclosure along the way. It may also be that the nature of the relationship is changing and becoming more of a mutual friendship, with meetings more akin to an informal catch up and chat over coffee. In any event, there comes a time where there needs to be an end to things to allow each party to move forward independently. As Laurent Daloz so beautifully puts it:

> The trip belongs, after all, to the traveller, not the guide and the mentor has her own promises to keep.
>
> (Daloz 1999, p. 18)

The conclusion of mentoring then is an opportunity to step back and take a critical look at the work undertaken; the lessons learned, evaluation of the goals and initial objectives, what should be recognised and celebrated as well as acknowledging perhaps where things didn't always go as planned.

Good practice for ending well includes:

- Ending the mentoring by way of a final review meeting and tabling this as such with the mentee. (There should be no surprises, with both mentee and mentor in agreement they have reached this point in the relationship.)
- Sharing responsibility for the final review, since both mentee and mentor have been learning through their work together.

- Discussing any questions around dependency where a mentee (or mentor) might be concerned with how they will cope without the support.
- Agreeing if and how they might want to keep in touch in the future.
- Celebrating achievements and acknowledging how far they have come.
- Thanking each other and marking the occasion. It can be as simple as a coffee or working lunch. The message is to agree to do something that feels appropriate.
- For the mentee, thinking about future plans, career focus and building new support networks.

Recognising the signs

You can expect the end of a mentoring relationship in this context to vary each time for each mentoring pair. Unlike many leadership or management development programmes, parental mentoring has no fixed point for conclusion nor 'graduation sign off'. The journeys out of work and return, as described by parents, are unique to each individual and their circumstances, and it may take anything up to 6 or even 9 months from their return to work for someone to feel 'truly back' and ready to step away from the mentoring support.

A session cancelled and not rebooked will remain on the mentee's to-do list and becomes an awkward reminder of something unfinished. Maybe the original goals have been achieved; they are back at work, busy and in a good place. Unconsciously perhaps the support is becoming less important. Contrastingly, perhaps the mentee appears stuck and dependent on the mentor for advice and guidance.

So it is important to be tuned in for any signs that the relationship is changing and that things may be drawing – or need to draw – to a close (Figure 15.1).

Good practice is for the mentor to be alert to changes at a number of levels:

- Firstly, changes within the individual mentee. Typically there will be a shift in the mental frame of the mentee, moving from **survival** mode (in the first few days

---

- A positive shift in the mental frame of the mentee, from surviving, to coping, to managing and being more autonomous
- The focus of the mentee (as evidenced in what they bring to the mentoring sessions, for example) has shifted, from the immediacy of the present, to the near future, to the longer term
- Changes to the pattern and frequency of meetings
- Increasing gaps between mentoring sessions
- Successive meetings cancelled without scheduling replacements
- Little or no preparation for a mentoring meeting, in which case the conversation drifts in search of an issue
- The relationship begins to feel constrained
- A sense of dependency where the mentee is looking to the mentor for answers rather than come up with their own solutions to issues and challenges

Figure 15.1 Signs to look out for.

in particular where the pattern of this new life is yet to be established), to **coping** (as they begin to bank time back in work and establish a functioning routine that connects work with home and baby) through to **managing** (where they are planned and organised, more in control and the picture of life as a working parent has come together as a coherent whole). Within sessions and conversations, the mentor may also notice the focus of the mentee also shifting, from the immediacy of the present, to the near future and ultimately to the longer term.

- Secondly, the mentor may need to pay attention to how they are working with their mentee. Faced with an emotional parent struggling to feel good about being back at work and miserable because she is missing her baby, an enthusiastic mentor (with all the knowledge of how it was for them) may find their default mode is to offer advice, which if offered repeatedly over time risks creating dependency and a mentee who in turn looks to them before working a solution out for themselves. *'You've been there before me – what did you do and therefore what should I do?'*

- A mentor may also need to draw attention to changes in the simple mechanics of the relationship itself and speak to their mentee where they notice something is different, asking perhaps: *'I notice we've not met for a few weeks now and I don't seem to have a date for our next mentoring session in the diary. How are things going since we last met? How are you? I wonder if we're coming towards a close in our work together and with that thought, perhaps it's time to book in a final review session?'*

Case study

Endings

There were clear signs that indicated the mentoring was drawing to a close; things had started to lapse, the time between our meetings had started to grow bigger, and in contrast to early conversations, she came with her questions already worked through and answered. It was also the first time she cancelled a session and I had to chase her for a next meeting.

I really struggled to tie her down to the closing session. There was a sense of not wanting to acknowledge the end had come, but it had.

Sue Hughes
Mentor
Royal Society of Chemistry

A final review

So what makes for a helpful closing session? One mentor sent an email asking for advice on additional things to cover when closing down her first maternity mentoring relationship. An extract from her note reads as follows:

I was intending to explore where we started and where we got to, what worked well, what strengths she used through the process, how she would go about managing her maternity again if this was something that may happen, plus our relationship; what made it work so well, any improvements, and what she had learnt about herself.

These were insightful and useful questions to ask of her mentee. What was missing from this request though was the voice of the mentor herself; what were her own reflections on the mentoring? How did she feel about the work they had done together? What had she learned about herself through the process of mentoring another? What did she want to say to her mentee? Responsibility for ending should be a shared activity. Both parties are well placed to offer insights and reflections though from different perspectives.

Ending mentoring well requires shared preparation, so to get the best from this meeting, good practice is of course to offer some questions and ideas ahead of time so both mentor and mentee have the opportunity to reflect on what was, before moving to thoughts of what might be next. As the mentee grows in confidence and becomes less dependent, considerations of what comes after the mentoring and the mentee's plan for continuing to build their support networks are critical to moving the focus forward and on from the mentoring.

Figure 15.2 offers a framework of questions for discussion between mentor and mentee.

For the programme itself, there is an opportunity to create a joint record of the relationship and lessons learned. Anecdotal records, from within the organisation and which reflect its language and culture, are an invaluable resource, offering thought for future mentoring pairs and also as reference points for the participants

The mentoring relationship	How did we work well as a mentoring pair? Have we achieved what we set out to do? What's changed? What successes do we want to recognise? What shall we thank each other for? Where is this mentoring relationship now?
Learning for us and for the business	What have we learned about ourselves through the course of our work together? What surprises did we encounter? What might we want to do differently another time? What messages and quotes[1] do we want to share with the wider business in support of other returners and future parental mentoring partnerships?
Next steps	What are we each taking forward? Do we want to keep in touch? If so, what will that look like? For the mentee: • What does the future look like for you as a working parent? • What is your next step? • What support will you need to do this? • How will you access that support?

Figure 15.2 Questions for a final meeting.

themselves; for the mentor who may go on to mentor another returning parent and for the mentee who may become part of the next cohort of parent mentors.

Looking back

Pinning busy mentees down to a final session can be quite a challenge, particularly where they have returned to a bigger role or are on reduced hours and feel under pressure to deliver more and perhaps in shorter timeframes than before. Equally mentors are busy people too. It requires commitment from both mentee and mentor to get to the end point. The value of what can be achieved through a good ending is shown in the following commentary from a mentor:

Case study

A mentor's perspective of ending well

Quite honestly, I didn't know the value of that session until I'd done it. You get a real sense of what you've achieved through the process. It was also a chance to share what I personally took from the mentoring and what I was proud of. The session was surprisingly emotional – for each of us at different points in the conversation – but we were both left feeling really buoyant. Rather than let things fizzle out – it gave another boost of energy and positivity. Moving forward, we have ended the mentoring formally and agreed to meet for lunch occasionally and as mutual friends rather than as mentor and mentee.

Mentor
Royal Society of Chemistry

Further reading

For more information on David Clutterbuck and David Megginson's research around 'endings', see 'All Good Things Must Come To An End' in *The Situational Mentor* (Clutterbuck and Lane 2004).
A brief, but informative perspective on endings is also offered by Ed Batista (2014), in his Harvard Business Review article 'The Art of Saying a Professional Goodbye', in which he offers five simple principles for managing the process.

Note

1 Are we in agreement to share these with the programme manager?

16 Supervision

An essential element of your programme

The initial workshop to prepare your mentors and mentees represents an important first step in setting out ambitions and early practice for your programme and its participants. Following this, it is then over to individual mentoring pairs to get started and begin to navigate their way forward as a working partnership. This is only the beginning, however, and we know from experience that the chances of successful learning outcomes and positive mentoring relationships are greatly increased where there is a planned schedule of dates and follow up activities designed to support the continued development both of your mentors and the programme itself.

The importance of having a plan in place is reinforced by the particular trajectory of parental mentoring relationships as explored in Chapter 5. The mentoring gap that coincides with early days of parenting (which may be anything from a few weeks, or even 3 to 6 months) typically results in mentees dropping off the radar with the corresponding effect of disconnecting mentors from the programme and risk of loss of motivation, confidence and skills despite any upfront investment you may have made at the outset of the programme.

Of course it's also worth reiterating the unpredictable nature of the individual biological timescales of any group of mentees approaching maternity leave. Mentees in this context come forward at different times according to their own agendas and timeframes. There is no guarantee of early matching and start of mentoring prior to their leaving work if they don't feel the need for it. Some may not request mentoring until they have finished work or even delay seeking support until they physically walk back though the door and into work.

> I've always loved my job and felt positive about the workplace. Yet on that first day coming back, I pushed the door open and for the first time I had to really think about stepping into the office and it was horrible. I'd never felt that way before. I didn't like feeling like it. It was about 2 months in before I felt brave enough to ask for help and say; this isn't right, this isn't me.
>
> (Mentee, Royal Society of Chemistry)

So with staggered points of entry into mentoring, having time in the diary where mentors can get together, irrespective of where their mentee is on the journey, (and at what point the mentoring has commenced), helps keep energy in a mentoring programme and builds the foundations of a learning community for the mentors. Their mentee may not be at the same stage as another; however, there are always insights and points to note for future reference in a spirit of shared learning and growth.

The utility room

In his book *Supervision in Action* (2012) Eric de Haan offers the utility room as a metaphor for supervision; '*a sort of intermediate space between the work in the garden and full participation in family life*'. Somewhere '*we wipe the sweat from our brows and the dirt from our faces, wash our hands, look at ourselves in the mirror and get ready to become an ordinary person again*' (p. 1). In the context of an internal mentoring programme where work is only one email or one meeting away, supervision represents a much-needed reflective space between the day-to-day work agenda and their role as a mentor. It is a place to pause, where the mentor can reflect on their practice, think about conversations, bring questions, concerns, observations, conundrums and integrate new learning in order to grow and move forward.

> Sometimes when a mentee says something, it triggers something in your mind as a parent and you remember feeling like that too. I think it was a real challenge not to go too far with sharing by saying 'I felt the same way' or 'I did that'. It was a real learning point for me, to know when to share the experience and when to pull back from it. There was a lot of self-learning and self-awareness in the process.
>
> (Mentor, Royal Society of Chemistry)

For the programme owner, supervision sessions are also an opportunity to gain a high level view of your programme in relation to:

- The working practice of the parent mentors
- Any gaps in practice or knowledge across the group that may need to be addressed
- Ethical concerns or considerations
- Any aspects of the programme design that may require attention

In the early stages of one mentoring programme, for example, it was apparent that the level of initial contracting had been weak. Mentors were struggling to establish learning objectives and, in some cases, even get time with their mentees who felt they had 'impossible diaries' with no gaps in the weeks immediately preceding the start of parental leave. Though contracting had been a key element in the initial workshop (for both mentees and mentors), this had been lost in translation and the supervision session was a prompt to the programme owner to work with the group to create a new framework for contracting, also confirming that while mentors may sometimes be required to be a bit more proactive prior to the start of someone's parental leave, responsibility for the mentoring should remain with the mentee and it was the responsibility of the mentee to arrange and turn up to sessions.

The discussion and establishing a new template gave a number of mentors courage to revisit ways of working and recontract the mentoring with their mentees.

Supervision is also beneficial for the organisation in that it may raise awareness and reveal new issues and themes that may have wider implications for the business' policies, procedures and working practices. These may be issues that might not have been obvious before. For example, in one situation (despite a clear policy on flexible working) the HR team was unaware that a returning employee had real concerns about whether the company would really accommodate her with flexible/part time working when she returned.

A definition of supervision

Through ongoing practice and research, we have developed a definition for parental mentoring supervision, which incorporates a sense of shared support, learning, improving knowledge, practice and considerations of safety for all participants. This is critical in the context of maternity mentoring where a mentor needs to be conscious of his or her level of expertise.

> A collective space for reflection and sharing of experiences, to build confidence and develop effective and ethical practice, while keeping the safety of mentees and mentors front of mind.

With this definition in mind, we suggest three underpinning functions for supervision in this context:

- **Development** – encouraging learning and growth in parent mentors through increased self awareness and skills development
- **Quality** – ensuring parent mentors are practicing in a consistent and appropriate (ethical) way
- **Support** – encouraging and supporting parent mentors with clear space and a network of diverse support

Figure 16.1 offers a summary of this central aspect of mentor development, with key functions and suggested practices as an integrated approach to supervision.

Practical suggestions for supervision review sessions

Supervision of mentors can be conducted on a one-to-one basis; however, with larger numbers of mentors, group supervision reviews may be the most efficient way forward for an internal programme. It is important to consider who will be leading supervision sessions and if they need any additional development or help in order to do their job effectively. In the early stages of a programme, this 'lead mentor' may well be the programme manager or an external provider with experience of supervision in this area.

For internal mentors, there is always a tension in the immediacy and demands of work-based agendas, so it is important that supervision review sessions are:

Development	Planned schedule of supervision reviews and up skilling sessions
	Sharing of individual issues and practice for discussion and exploration
	Skills development sessions (on related topics, e.g. confidence, boundary management, advice giving, tiredness and balance, unconscious bias)
Quality	Opportunity to practice skills at supervision review sessions
	Appoint a nominated lead mentor for supervision reviews
	Clear contracting for supervision sessions
Support	Group supervision reviews (with one-to-one supervision in exceptional circumstances as required)
	One-to-one peer support (connect established mentors who may be able to support less experienced/new mentors)
	Business sponsor led reviews (bi-annually)

Figure 16.1 Functions of supervision.

(a) proportionate to the mentoring conversations and (b) seen to be helpful and add value to the mentors.

The EMCC (European Mentoring and Coaching Council) references this in its guidelines for supervision (www.emcc.org). Lis Merrick and Paul Stokes' 2003 research also noted, '*Mentors tend to be volunteers who are mentoring for a very small part of their working time and tend to have busy and stressful day jobs. In contrast to professional full-time coaches, selling the benefits of mentor supervision to part-time voluntary mentors can be harder*' (Bachkirova 2011, p. 206).

So with busy people in mind, while at the same time recognising the value of bringing your mentors together regularly, good practice is to have variety in your approach – to offer a balance of skills input and space for exploration of individual issues and concerns.

It's helpful to suggest questions ahead of a review meeting in order to be able to make the most of time within the session itself.

Example preparation questions

- **Your mentee** – Where are they right now in terms of maternity/parental leave and return?
- **Your practice as a mentor** – What is working well/less well?
- **Themes for the business** – What are the recurrent themes and topics you are hearing as a mentor?
- **One thing on your mind** you'd like to bring to the review session for exploration, help or to raise awareness

Contracting for supervision reviews

As with any coaching or mentoring relationship, good practice is to contract the intended ways of working with the group. In this way, everyone is clear as to their responsibilities and the aims and expectations. A suggested outline for a first session in which you contract supervision with the mentors is shared in Figure 16.2.

Procedural
The practicalities of parental mentoring supervision reviews
• How long do we expect to work together as a group?
• If a member of the group is unable to attend, who will volunteer to bring them up-to-date?
• How often to we want to meet? And for how long?
• What is realistic – in terms of diaries and in proportion to the mentoring? (e.g. quarterly reviews?)
• Who might we need to inform/seek agreement from in order to attend these review sessions? (i.e. managing expectations of our teams and line managers for them to be aware of any additional time commitments)
• Where will we meet in order to talk freely?
Boundaries
Outlining the limits of supervision reviews
• What are the boundaries to our group review meetings?
• What issues should we take elsewhere?
• How will we know when issues are outside our agreed boundaries?
• How will we preserve the confidentiality of our mentees and our discussions?
Working alliance
Sharing mutual expectations and building trust
• What do we want the goals of this (supervision) group to be?
• What is the purpose of the reviews? (Share your definition of supervision and functions)
• Are we all in agreement with that?
• What are our expectations and concerns for these sessions?
• How will we balance the needs of the individual with that of the group?
• What a good (supervision) review session looks like
Session format
The nature of the supervision
• How do we want to work together to get the most benefit from these sessions?
• How much individual focus can we expect?
• What are we expected to prepare before these sessions?
• Who will take notes?
Organisational context
Ethical and business considerations
• What is the business' expectation of these sessions?
• What are our ethical guidelines? (e.g. corporate code of ethics)
• What will happen to collective themes?

Figure 16.2 Contracting for supervision reviews.

Source: Adapted with permission from Hawkins, P. and Smith, N. 2006. *Coaching, Mentoring and Organizational Consultancy – Supervision and Development*. McGraw-Hill, Open University Press.

Follow on supervision reviews – a suggested outline

Depending on the business culture and availability of mentors, you may only have an hour and a half to 2 hours for a supervision review meeting. So with time at a premium, good practice is to spend the first few minutes contracting with the group at the start of each session and then to remain mindful of how the time is being used in practice.

Figure 16.3 offers an example outline for a supervision review meeting, using Hawkins and Smith's (2006) **C.L.E.A.R.** model as a framework.

The listening/exploring/learning part of a supervision review will naturally take up the volume of time in the session. The challenge is how and what to explore in ways that keep the reviews fresh and provide mentors with space and opportunity to participate – both as learners and peer supporters for each other.

Good practice! For ideas of *'what'* to explore, supervision sessions can be structured around a series of different focus points. Hawkins and Shoet's (2000) '7-eyed model' of coaching supervision is a recognised and established approach to supervision, which invites consideration of relationships from seven differing perspectives:

1   The coachee/mentee
2   The coach/mentor's interventions

Contracting
- What do we want to achieve as a result of this review session?
- What is within the scope of this session? (Boundaries)
- How do we want to work together today? (The amount of time, blend of one-to-one and group discussion, mentoring practice)
- A reminder of the central importance of maintaining confidentiality (for example, not disclosing individual mentee names, retaining discussion within the review)

Listening/**E**xploring
- Individual issues and questions

Action
- What do we want to take away from this session?
  - For ourselves as individuals
  - For X (as lead mentor)
  - As learning for the business? (broader context and collective themes)
- What might be the next steps?

Review
- How well did we meet our expectations?
- How did we work as a group?
- How could we improve this process for next time?

Figure 16.3 Outline for a supervision review session for parental mentors.

Ideas for 'how' you might explore issues

Each mentor has 5 minutes to outline and set the scene for an issue/question they want to raise. Note the lead mentor acts as timekeeper as well as facilitating discussions. After the context has been set, the group may take one of two approaches:

1 Having outlined their issue, the mentor hands over discussion of the subject matter to the wider group for them to raise questions, perhaps offer insights, suggestions, and discuss. In this scenario, the mentor (with the issue) does not take part in the discussion. They may remain part of the group, but will observe, listen and take notes as appropriate. They then have an opportunity to comment at the end of the discussion.

Or

2 Having outlined their issue, the mentor remains with the group and the group question and explore the issue with them. Again the mentor has the opportunity to comment and reflect learning at the end of the discussion.

Both approaches also afford an opportunity to see mentors' listening and questioning skills in action.

Depending on the number of attendees, you may find it helpful to split mentors into smaller discussion groups in order to give everyone an opportunity for airtime.

3 The relationship between coach and coachee/mentor and mentee
4 The coach/mentor themselves
5 The relationship between supervisor and coach/mentor
6 The supervisor's reflection
7 The wider context of the organisation

Taking learning from a BBC case study (Coaching at Work: January 2007), which indicated the full 7-eyed process can be lengthy if applied to each supervision topic, it may be helpful to take a pragmatic approach and focus on a condensed approach initially, which can be reviewed or extended as supervision progresses.

Figure 16.4 offers a condensed summary, which may be helpful as an initial approach for early supervision sessions.

Note, some of these perspectives call for sensitive facilitation on the part of the supervisor, relying on trust in each other with this level of disclosure and a reminder of the need for confidentiality.

Focus	Questions
1 The mentee	• What stage of the journey is your mentee at right now? • What have you noticed about your mentee? • What are they bringing to mentoring? • What are they not bringing?
2 Tools and approaches	• What tools and approaches are you choosing to use in your support of your mentee? • Why have you selected these? • What has been the impact? • Was there anything else you could have used? • What might have been the impact of these?
3 The relationship	• How would you describe your relationship with your mentee? • What's going well in your mentoring relationship? • What aspects of the relationship are working less well? • How are you contributing to this?
4 Staying safe	• How are you? In your conversations with your mentee, what feelings and reactions have been prompted in you? • What are you learning about yourself from this process of parental mentoring? • What more support might be helpful?

Figure 16.4 Content suggestions for supervision reviews.

Source: Adapted from Hawkins and Shoet's (2000) 7-eyed model of supervision.

Skills development for mentors

Given the nature of mentoring in this context, it is important to build in specific sessions that up-skill the mentors in terms of their own knowledge and understanding of related and relevant subject areas.

Such topics might include:

• **Frameworks for mentoring conversations** – For novice mentors, having a couple of models in mind such as the Three Stage Process (Garvey in Megginson and Clutterbuck 2009) and GROW (Whitmore 2009) can help provide a structure to conversations with their mentees. This could be a session in which the models are explained and mentors divide into pairs and practice their skills with current issues of their own.

• **Advice giving** – As mentors they come to the relationship with a level of experience, as a fellow employee and for many, as a parent too. It is useful to have a session that uses different scenarios to explore when it may be helpful to offer advice or when to hold the space for a mentee to work though questions or concerns for themselves. Questions to ask mentors could include: *What are* *the circumstances in which we find ourselves giving advice? What are the pros and cons of giving advice? When might it be unhelpful to offer advice to a mentee?*

- **Postnatal depression (PND)** – This is a type of depression experienced by some women after having a baby. It affects around 1 in 10 women and can also affect new fathers too. The timing for PND varies, but it is quite possible that someone returning to work postparental leave may be suffering from PND. A programme of this nature should have access to professional advice about mental well-being and mental illness in order to raise awareness of possible warning signs, and how and when to make referrals for specialist help. (For more information, www.nhs.uk/conditions/Postnataldepression www.nct. org.uk/parenting/postnatal-depression)

- **Boundary management** – Boundaries should be referenced in the initial contracting conversation between mentor and mentee (see p. 45), but how do we know when we have met a boundary? What kinds of things constitute boundaries that may be beyond the mentoring support? What is the recommended approach when this happens? Practicing conversations to enable mentors to experience and vocalise this in a safe space first is really useful.

An analysis of what might be appropriate in terms of content for these skills sessions will be best done locally by the programme manager and in conjunction with the mentors as questions arise through supervision review sessions. You may need to enlist the HR or L&D teams to help with design and preparation of content.

Emerging themes and questions

There can be no definitive list of what parent mentors bring to supervision sessions; however, we offer a brief insight into examples of issues gleaned from conversations with mentors from within different organisations and some thoughts in response to the issues raised:

> As a mentor and also as a parent, I have all this knowledge and sometimes I feel my own 'stuff' gets in the way.

Typically – though not always – mentors in this context are themselves working parents. This has the advantage that they are likely to be in a position to have empathy for the journey of another, having experienced their own transition and return to work, but correspondingly this experience may also prove to be a distraction for them.

As noted in Chapter 6, in the halcyon days pre-first baby, most mothers-to-be are busy in work mode and in blissful ignorance of what lies ahead, the blurred infinity of parenthood obscured by an all-consuming agenda to close down work well. For a mentor, their journey to working parenthood may have been smooth, or may have been traumatic. In any event, there is a wealth of knowledge, advice and 'stuff' many mentors find they want to bring to the table, often at a time when their mentee is simply not ready and doesn't need to hear it.

Contrastingly, a mentee may come to a conversation actively looking for advice and direction from someone who has been there before; *'What would you do/should I do in this situation? How did you manage it? What do you think?'* The decision to take a more directive approach, or to offer personal insights and share your own experience demands thought and sensitivity, and a healthy acceptance that the experience shared may not help, nor the advice taken up. The extent to which sharing our own personal experience is appropriate and helpful can change from conversation to conversation, which makes this an interesting topic for discussion both in your start-up workshop and also in subsequent supervision sessions. In practice, remember no two experiences are ever the same and with echoes of Daloz (p. 120) the journey belongs to the mentee after all:

I'm not a parent, so can I mentor effectively in this space?

We explored the value of 'difference' in mentoring matches in Chapter 12 and with this as a principle of good practice, it would be entirely appropriate to include as wide a pool of mentors as possible. They are after all within the organisation and have currency of knowledge, skills and experience. The key point here is concerned with your selection criteria for mentors including their motivation for participating in a parental mentoring programme. For example, you may want to ask the following question of all your prospective mentors: *'What do you hope to bring to this particular mentoring space?'* The initial workshop, built on by supervision review sessions where mentors get together from a diverse range of backgrounds, together with ongoing/bespoke development activities are all important preparation methods for equipping mentors to work well whatever their background or experience:

There was a poor relationship with the line manager, which overtook the agenda. I felt the panic of the ticking clock. The conversation felt unfinished and I came away feeling I left it in a bad place.

This comment was made by a new mentor in a group supervision review session. She seemed deflated by her inability to get to all the other issues, which she felt needed discussion before her mentee finished work. As the mentor, she felt distracted by the urgency of the wider agenda, whereas her mentee had her own critical issue to explore. Mentoring someone for the first time in this space can be difficult, for the inexperienced (but enthusiastic) mentor keen to stick to a plan, knowing there is so much to discuss and get through. There are perhaps two issues that could be explored in supervision with this example; firstly, one of structuring a mentoring conversation within a limited timeframe, perhaps revisiting GROW or the Three Stage Process and, secondly, how to liberate the mentor from the burden of her own knowledge in order for her to go where the mentee needs her to be – which on some occasions may indeed mean a conversation ends without resolution at that point. Encouraging reflective space in the time following a mentoring session can be as valuable to a mentee and mentor in terms of learning and resolution of issues:

> I had a really difficult return – I felt myself wanting to rescue her.

Our experience of recruiting working parents as mentors is that even though they may be supremely busy, there is a passion to help other working parents which secures their interest and commitment. At one induction workshop, we took time to share people's stories of maternity leave and return and one theme became clear; it was apparent that for a number of mentors, their own experiences of returning to work were still very much an issue for them. They brought real emotion into the room when sharing their journey (we had tears in the opening icebreaker) and their motivation for being a mentor was fundamentally around helping someone to have a more positive return to work than their own. The concern here rests with the real possibility of transference and that their mentee may encounter similar difficulties which might reopen issues and make it difficult to disassociate from their own journey. This is echoed in the earlier quote where the mentor is feeling the need to 'rescue.'

These kinds of issues require extreme sensitivity on the part of the supervisor – to enable a voice to be heard without inviting a tide of collective despair across the group. Group supervision offers an opportunity to explore patterns and themes common across the mentoring pairs, some of which may need to be raised with the senior leadership team from a strategic HR perspective.

Further reading

As referenced in this chapter, Peter Hawkins and Robin Shohet's book *Supervision in the Helping Professions* (2002), offers some valuable models and frameworks for supervision. In particular, their book explains and illustrates the complete Seven-Eyed Model of Supervision. It also offers chapters on group supervision, which may be of most relevance to an in-house mentoring programme where groups of mentors come together for supervision reviews.

The nature of supervision should change as mentees grow in experience and practice. Lis Merrick and Paul Stokes[1] (2011) offer a progressive framework for supervision in mentoring programmes, which takes account of increasing levels of mentor skills as supported by differing forms of supervision (Figure 16.5).

For additional information relating to supervision in the specific context of maternity, Jennifer Liston-Smith[1] (2011) shares expert insights into her work as a supervisor of corporate external maternity coaching across a number of organisations between 2005 and 2010.

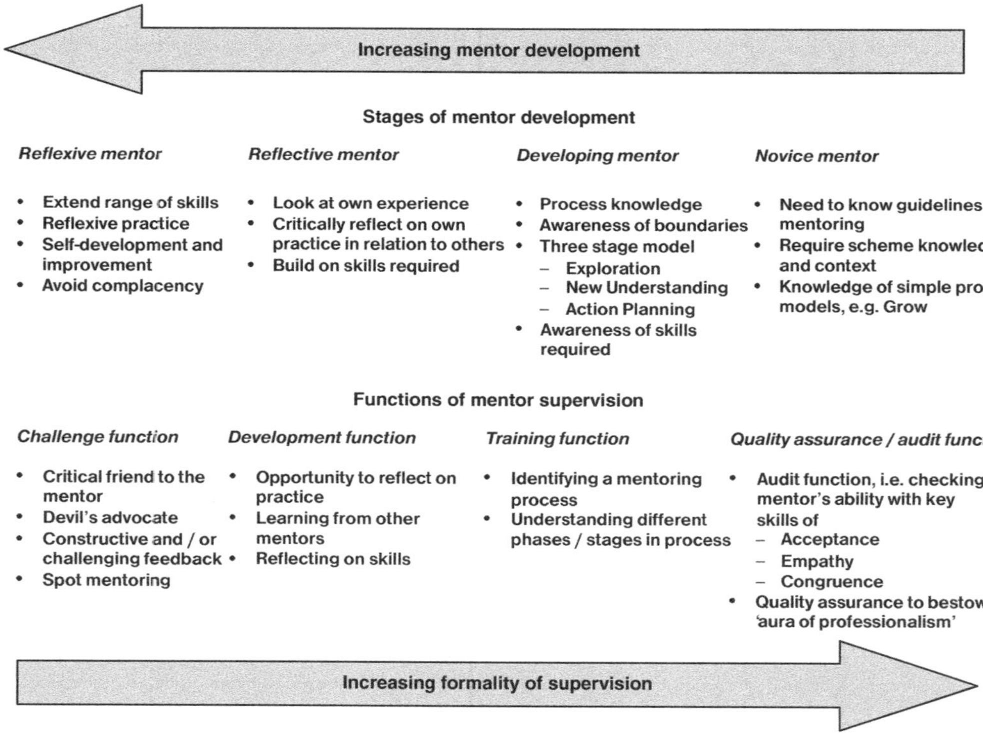

Increasing mentor development

Stages of mentor development

Reflexive mentor
- Extend range of skills
- Reflexive practice
- Self-development and improvement
- Avoid complacency

Reflective mentor
- Look at own experience
- Critically reflect on own practice in relation to others
- Build on skills required

Developing mentor
- Process knowledge
- Awareness of boundaries
- Three stage model
  - Exploration
  - New Understanding
  - Action Planning
- Awareness of skills required

Novice mentor
- Need to know guidelines for mentoring
- Require scheme knowledge and context
- Knowledge of simple process models, e.g. Grow

Functions of mentor supervision

Challenge function
- Critical friend to the mentor
- Devil's advocate
- Constructive and / or challenging feedback
- Spot mentoring

Development function
- Opportunity to reflect on practice
- Learning from other mentors
- Reflecting on skills

Training function
- Identifying a mentoring process
- Understanding different phases / stages in process

Quality assurance / audit function
- Audit function, i.e. checking mentor's ability with key skills of
  - Acceptance
  - Empathy
  - Congruence
- Quality assurance to bestow 'aura of professionalism'

Increasing formality of supervision

Figure 16.5 A schema for mentor development.

Source: Reproduced with permission from Merrick, L. and Stokes, P. 2011. Supervision in mentoring programmes, in *Coaching and Mentoring Supervision – Theory and Practice*. Bachkirova, T., Jackson, P., and Clutterbuck, D. (eds.). Open University Press, McGraw-Hill Education.

Case study of one-to-one supervision

Helen came to supervision worried about her mentee.

In their post-return conversations, Helen noticed how tired and drawn her mentee Suzanne appeared, sometimes almost dropping asleep in the relaxed atmosphere of the sessions. Prior to her second maternity leave, Suzanne had been identified as a rising star, full of confidence and fresh ideas. She radiated energy and was regarded as the one to have on a team. During their second session, Helen felt she should draw attention to the change in Suzanne, and explore what was happening and what could be done to help. It soon became apparent that Suzanne was doing all the necessary childcare as well as running the household, whilst her husband (who also worked for the company) was concentrating on his work and career. Suzanne had poured out her worries; lack of sleep, concerns about her marriage, worrying that her husband hadn't wanted another child so soon after their first, worrying that he wasn't getting enough attention from her. The floodgates had just opened and soon she was crying. Helen was very calm throughout all this, allowing Suzanne simply to talk and being sympathetic but not taking sides. They had agreed to meet again quite soon after this session, Helen feeling that Suzanne needed a lot of support.

Helen then came and poured all this out to me as her supervisor, showing her concern for Suzanne, wanting to get involved with her marriage and trying to work out how she might broach the issue with the husband without betraying any confidences. The "pouring out" in the supervision session was a parallel of Suzanne's conversation with Helen, which to me was a hint to beware of parallel process. Sometimes the work between the mentor and mentee parallels what is happening for the mentee, sometimes it is between the mentor and the supervisor (sometimes even both).

I asked her about her mentoring contract with Suzanne – what had they agreed to work on? Helen looked a little thoughtful and said they had agreed to work on Suzanne's future development and how she could continue with her career plans, whilst taking care of the family. "So the focus is on her career and her work?" "Yes". "And what about our contract?" "To support and challenge me in my mentoring." "So how can I best do that?" "By helping me to mentor Suzanne appropriately."

I could have chosen to explore why Helen had had her buttons pressed by this story; what in Helen's own background this had triggered, but at that stage as the supervisor, I decided I needed to model and mirror being true to our contract, rather than following other paths, as yet not contracted for. We therefore worked on ways of getting Suzanne in touch with her strengths, to bring back her confidence. Helen had been caught by Suzanne's helplessness, rather than her strength, but by working with

Helen to get in touch with her own strengths as a mentor, she was able to see how she might support Suzanne likewise. The marriage wasn't part of her work with Suzanne, but she did the right thing by enabling Suzanne to "dump" her worries at the time, and maybe she could suggest to Suzanne if there was a repeat situation, starting a pattern, that she and her husband might discuss it, find other support; but equally, that 'dumping' might have been all that was necessary for Suzanne to see she needed to do something different.

This example case study illustrates the value of the supervisor as an independent party able to offer a different perspective when the mentor finds themselves overwhelmed and drawn into an issue. Note also that the supervision work here was concerned with creating space to explore the mentor's work and emotions – not an alternative forum to solve their mentee's crisis.

Kate Pinder
Supervisor
Pi-Affirm

Note

1 Both of these accounts are to be found in *Coaching and Mentoring Supervision, Theory and Practice,* edited by Tatiana Bachkirova, Peter Jackson and David Clutterbuck (2011).

17 Evaluating parental mentoring

Having set up and established a parental mentoring programme, it is important both for the business and for you as the programme owner to understand the extent to which you are achieving what you set out to do and to demonstrate that the multiple investments of people, resources, time and money have been worthwhile. As we saw in Chapter 11, good practice is to design a programme with the end in mind, setting out clear objectives and measures of success. The more specific you can be at the outset in terms of your objectives and outcomes, the more confident you can be about what you are reviewing and the positive impact it has had.

Success for a parental mentoring programme should therefore be set in the context of its original aims; for example, to offer mentoring as a strategic support to improve the experience of employees returning to work post maternity or parental leave. Knowing whether your programme has been successful is bound in multiple perspectives; at a personal level with the experiences of mentees who, it is hoped, have found mentoring helpful in making their transition to working parenthood, for the mentors in service of their preparation and learning and what they have noticed in their mentee, and for the line manager and broader business in seeing talented people return more engaged and staying to continue their career.

Approaches to evaluation

Kirkpatrick's (1967) model is frequently referenced as a good practice framework for evaluation. He proposed four levels of evaluation as follows:

> *Level 1 – **Reaction** – the thoughts and feelings of the learner*
> *Level 2 – **Learning** – the transfer of knowledge and skills*
> *Level 3 – **Behaviour** – the application and demonstration of learning in role*
> *Level 4 – **Results** – the effect of the changes in behaviour to the organisation*

Originally designed for evaluation following a training intervention, the Kirkpatrick model lends itself to a 'moment in time' approach to evaluation. When applied within a mentoring context, however, accounts from programme owners, mentors and mentees indicate parental mentoring relationships rarely begin life as one identifiable cohort or group intake. As we know, these relationships start at different times and different points on highly individual journeys. They are characterised by dramatic changes in tempo and focus, with learning as something that is emergent and on-going, and from an evaluation perspective, do not lend themselves to a set date for completion and subsequent review as a single group output.

Overlaying this picture is an extended timescale. Mentoring in this context, as previously noted, is a slow burn. A single parental mentoring relationship can span anything from 12 to 18 months from commencement to close (subject to statutory and employer policies for paid parental leave, local norms and expectations around leave and return to work) and also taking into account the health and well-being of the individual returner. This gives an indication of the length of time simply to get to Level 1 of the Kirkpatrick model.

What to evaluate

A helpful model for what to measure is shown in Figure 17.1 and illustrates a focus on both the *structures and processes* you have in place and *outcomes* of the mentoring from the perspectives of the individual mentoring relationships and the programme itself. By considering each of these areas you should achieve a balanced view of what impact your programme is having. Note any measures will need to be specific to your own programme's aims and objectives; however, we offer some suggestions for measures (some short term and others longer term), which could include the following:

The Parental Mentoring Programme	
Structures/processes	**Outcomes**
Recruitment and selection criteria for parent mentors	Improved retention of returners
	Career progression and promotion of returners
Recruitment of mentees	Engagement levels post return to work*
Preparation and on-going skills development of mentors	Improved perceptions of work–life balance*
Preparation of mentees	Performance and appraisal ratings of returners
Completed mentoring relationships	Reduction in sickness absence statistics of returners
Failed relationships	Reduction in occupational health costs
	Gender balance at senior levels
The Mentoring Relationships	
Structures/processes	**Outcomes**
Matching process	Expectations met
Numbers of mentoring relationships	Goals achieved
Length of mentoring relationships	Challenges overcome
Number of meetings/level of contact at different stages of the parental leave and return to work	Confidentiality maintained
	Future career ambitions clarified
Confidentiality	
Rapport	
* It may be possible to attribute a measure to these points where questions relating to these topics form part of an employee engagement survey, for example.	

Figure 17.1 A framework for measurement of a parental mentoring programme.

Source Adapted from Clutterbuck, D. 2014. *Everyone Needs A Mentor.* 5th ed. CIPD (Chartered Institute of Personnel and Development), London.)

A word of caution before reaching for the calculator. In the desire to apply a monetary 'return on investment' (ROI) and demonstrate a programme's value to the business, we may sometimes find ourselves tempted to extrapolate the data to prove a point, yet there is unlikely to be a simple correlation between mentoring and any one of the above measures. Inevitably, there are many factors that may influence someone's decision to stay with a business, their levels of engagement, their decision to apply for promotion, their attendance record and level of performance ratings, for example. Without someone expressly sharing their intention not to leave the business as a direct consequence of the mentoring, it would not be an easy task to strip out all the other variables in order to quantify the specific contribution made by the mentoring support. Add to this the fact that mentoring is inherently a confidential relationship between two individuals, and the business of return to work is a very personal journey with no guarantee of disclosure for the purposes of evaluation.

Key to any statistical analysis is having a baseline against which to make comparisons, in an effort to identify where parental mentoring may have contributed and helped to make a difference. One way of doing this might be to compare data for employees where mentoring support has been in place with employees who have returned without mentoring support. As a programme progresses over time, there may also be an opportunity to make year on year comparisons against your own initial measures and start point.

Case study

An opening benchmark – Asda

Following the initial launch of maternity mentoring in Asda, I designed a questionnaire to understand more about colleagues' experiences of maternity and return to work. I surveyed a complete year of maternity returners in the home offices in Leeds, an example copy of which is shared in Figure 17.6. A 64 percent return rate (from a respondent group of 87), revealed a rich source of data (relating to commencement of maternity leave, duration of maternity leave, working arrangements on return, perception of confidence pre- and post maternity, for example) and anecdotal insights (e.g. thoughts on what helped/hindered returns to work, intentions to stay and perceptions of future career with the business). The survey itself and subsequent report provided an opening benchmark position for the MumtoMum mentoring programme.

Nicki Seignot

A credible piece of evaluation balances statistical based insights and commentary with anecdotes/stories from across the population involved, which add context and bring the figures to life. Numbers are useful and helpful to strengthen your continued business case, however, our experience has shown that it is often the stories people remember and which get repeated.

When to evaluate

Our suggestion is to have a plan for evaluation which encompasses reviews at the end of mentoring, and also has mechanisms for reviewing progress along the way.

At an individual relationship level, and timescales aside, it is of course important and appropriate to have an end (summative) review of the participants' perspectives on what has been achieved when a mentoring lifecycle has reached its conclusion. Given the nature of staggered starts to parental mentoring and lengthy time frames, there is an equally appropriate expectation that there will be some form of on-going (formative) evaluation in order to get a broader view across the programme as a whole.

For the programme manager, this is a way of tracking progress with the programme, finding out which aspects are working well, what might need changing or improving, getting a current view as to how relationships are progressing, and being able to deal with any issues in a timely manner in order for the programme to grow and move forward.

For influential sponsors and stakeholders, on-going evaluation also offers a way to keep them in touch with and supportive of your programme. Without this, stakeholder interest may wane and in the intervening gap, questions may be asked about a programme's relevance, where there is little or no information that makes the connection between the programme and the issues and challenges you set out to address in the first place. Klasen (2002) echoes this with her warnings of '*short attention spans*' of executives '*especially when compared to the excitement of a new initiative*' (p. 294). Managing expectations in terms of what they can expect and when is key. This can be particularly important where a programme needs further investment, or has been piloted and requires senior level commitment to fund a larger scale roll out, for example.

Who to involve?

To maximise learning and insights, any evaluation and review of your programme should have input and feedback from as broad a range of people as possible, including:

- Parent mentors and mentees themselves
- Line managers of returners
- Peers and direct reports of returners
- Key stakeholders (e.g. HR business partners, learning and development team)
- Business sponsor(s)
- Champions and steering group members (where you have one set up)
- Programme administrator
- Programme manager/owner

While responsibility for the plan and approach to evaluation needs to sit with the programme manager, our recommendation is to involve others in the process too. Ask for time with your programme sponsor, members of your steering group, and the HR team and invite them to join you and lead a focus group, for example. They have an interest in finding out how the programme is working, and hearing feedback and anecdotes first hand can be extremely powerful. While maintaining a commitment to confidentiality, the retelling of these stories gives working parents and your mentoring programme an authentic 'voice' and builds interest and awareness across the business.

Good practice! Being mindful of busy diaries, it is a good idea to be clear as to the amount of time involved and to have an outline structure and questions for their sessions prepared in advance. (Find a volunteer/programme administrator to help with the nuts and bolts of coordinating attendees and booking a room.)

You may decide to seek external support for evaluation from an external provider. This has the benefit of an independent perspective with depth of expertise, readymade tools and experience of evaluation. This is of course subject to the funds you have available and may be something you want to consider budgeting for at a later stage as the programme gathers pace and volume of participants.

Case study

Evaluation using an external resource

As a consultant at Coach Mentoring Ltd I have provided an outsourced evaluation service for many clients including multinational companies, universities and professional bodies. The main benefits to an organisation of outsourcing this function are:

- They lack internal resources to undertake the evaluation.
- They require guidance on what and how to evaluate.
- They want an unbiased and dispassionate external viewpoint.
- Participants may be more open in what they report back to an independent consultant.

I can also support them with interim check-ins at regular intervals to check that relationships are up and running and to find out if they need more support or up-skilling training throughout the relationship. This helps to ensure that by the time you come to your final evaluation, you should have few surprises or failures as these will have been identified and resolved early on.

For the final evaluation, I support organisations in compiling the questions in line with a programme's original aims. These questionnaires are usually either a short word document sent by email, or an online survey that compiles the results at the end. There should always be some open text boxes to allow participants to provide feedback in their own words, and it can also be

(Continued)

a good opportunity to ask both mentors and mentees if they would like to mentor in future programmes.

Where I support with telephone interviews, I send an introductory email to participants outlining how long I need and asking them to suggest a suitable time for me to call. Whilst being more time consuming, telephone interviews can uncover a lot more about a mentoring relationship than a questionnaire, especially if you have built a good rapport with the interviewee. It is also easier to understand any issues in a conversation by being able to ask questions and delve deeper. If appropriate, and in agreement with the interviewee, you may also need to escalate an issue to the programme manager.

From the questionnaires and telephone interviews I provide a written report outlining the positives and negatives to the programme, along with recommendations for future programmes, if required. This report is often used when we support them in setting up and delivering their next mentoring programme, taking into account any recommended changes.

Jacki Mason
Operations Manager and Consultant
Coach Mentoring Ltd

Methods of evaluation

Good practice for evaluation is to have a broad range of methods to obtain data, some of which should be quantitative (e.g. as evidenced through statistical analysis of a series of measures) and some qualitative (e.g. more in depth, sharing individual insights, commentary and anecdotal feedback). Here we consider some of the methods open to you:

- **Questionnaires** – These can include a blend of quantitative and qualitative questions and are easily distributed at the end of a workshop or webinar with questions tailored to the specific target audience. The benefit of this approach is the potential to secure volume of feedback, though it is worth noting that questionnaires tend to produce high level results as opposed to detailed insights and feedback.
- **Interviews** – These can be conducted on a one-to-one basis (with mentors, mentees, line managers, stakeholders, etc.), or perhaps with mentoring pairs, using a series of prepared questions focused around the areas you want feedback on. As an evaluation method it is time consuming but the end result is a rich insight into individual experiences and also an opportunity to go deeper with questions or get clarification if needed.
- **Focus groups for evaluation** – It is always good practice to get groups of similar participants together during the course of a mentoring programme. A facilitated discussion around key questions will deliver a depth of insight across a particular group, e.g. mentors, mentees, line managers. The shared conversation also gives momentum to the programme and reinforces networks and

connections across these different groups. Again, having an opening structure of questions ahead of time focuses the discussion.

Table 17.1 offers an outline plan for evaluation of a parental mentoring programme, offering suggestions for what might be measured, methods of collecting data, target audience(s), timings and suggestions for who may support and/or lead a particular activity.

Practical examples of evaluation tools

The content for your programme's questionnaires, interviews, focus groups and measures for statistical analysis will be driven by your programme-specific objectives. However, there is always value in having access to examples of documents in order to help with creating your own tools and frameworks. Cranwell-Ward's (2004) practical examples and case studies are particularly helpful in sharing best practice approaches to evaluation questionnaires. For the purpose of parental mentoring, we also offer a number of example templates as follows:

- A mentee questionnaire (post completion of mentoring) (Figure 17.2)
- Mentors' focus group with semi-structured questions (Figure 17.3)
- Returning mentees' focus group (Figure 17.4)
- A line managers' focus group (Figure 17.5)

Post-evaluation – what next?

The critical point of evaluation then becomes the follow up; what needs to happen as a consequence, by when and by whom. Klasen (2002) is clear on this point; '*The evaluation should not be a static "post-mortem" report, but should be a dynamic set of recommendations and actions to enhance the programme further and build on the success of mentoring in the organisation*' (p. 309).

The key outputs being:

- What have we learned?
- What will we keep doing/stop doing/build on and improve?
- What were some of the unanticipated outcomes? (i.e. What did we discover that we didn't expect to?)

Have a clear communication plan for how you intend to share these outputs, actions and headlines and who needs to know. An annual summary report gives you a metaphorical 'line in the sand' to showcase the programme and can be revisited each year to celebrate success, measure progress and set objectives. Updates via your existing communication structure (e.g. functional meetings, steering groups, mentoring intranet site, network meetings, internal blogs) keep the programme on the agenda as a live activity and one that is making an ongoing and very current contribution to the business.

Table 17.1 Outline plan for evaluation

What to measure	Suggested method	Target audience(s)	Timing and frequency	Who can lead/support this?
Statistical Measures • Returns from maternity/shared parental leave • Retention figures (e.g. up to 12 months postreturn) • Promotions • Engagement • Work–life balance • Performance and appraisal ratings • Sickness absence statistics • Occupational health costs • 360° leadership surveys (Analysis of mentored returners versus nonmentored returners)	Statistical analysis from management information (MI)	n/a	Annual analysis	HR/learning and development/with access to MI Feedback given to programme manager
Impact of initial workshops to prepare participants • Mentees • Mentors • Line managers	Questionnaire (to capture reactions, learning and commitments)	Mentors mentees, line managers as appropriate	On completion of each session	Programme manager
Impact of up-skilling development workshops for mentors	Questionnaire (to capture reactions, learning and commitments)	Mentors	On completion of each session	Programme manager/lead facilitator
The mentoring relationships Feedback relating to the individual mentoring relationship, rapport, timescales, outcomes and impact	Questionnaire	Mentees Mentors	On completion of a mentoring lifecycle	Programme administrator With results fed back to programme manager

Mentors' perspectives • The matching process • Mentoring relationships • Working support • Outputs • Learning for the mentor • Learning for the business • Mentor development and support	Focus groups (with semi-structured interview questions)	Mentors	6 monthly	Facilitated by sponsor/steering group member/HR and the programme manager
Mentees' perspectives • Experiences of the transition • Preparation for mentoring • The process and relationship • Outputs and learning • Future focus and thoughts on career • Learning for the business	Focus groups (with semi-structured interview questions)	Returning mentees	6 months after return to work	Facilitated by sponsor/steering group member/HR and programme manager
Line managers of returners Impact of mentoring on return to work, performance and levels of engagement	Focus groups (with semi-structured questions)	Line managers	6 months after return to work	Programme manager or HR business partners
End of year report Capturing insights, learning from across the above activities and recommendations for actions moving forward	n/a	Stakeholders, sponsors, HR, steering group	Annual	Programme manager with support as appropriate

Example Mentee Questionnaire

We'd appreciate your feedback on your mentoring experience. Your responses will be treated in confidence and collated with others to help build our understanding and awareness of how the mentoring is working in practice to support colleagues in transition to working parenthood.

The mentoring process	
How many times did you meet with your parent mentor?	
Including your maternity/parental leave, how long has your mentoring relationship lasted?	
Did you periodically review how the mentoring was working?	
Has there been a clear and positive ending to the formal mentoring relationship? What did that look like?	

At what stages in your transition to working parenthood has the mentoring been most helpful and why?			
Ending work	Maternity leave and countdown to return	Early days back	Moving forward as a working parent

The mentoring relationship				
Questions	Strongly agree	Agree	Disagree	Strongly disagree
I felt well 'matched' with my parent mentor				
I felt confident our discussions were confidential				
My mentor demonstrated appropriate listening and questioning skills				
My mentor offered appropriate advice and direction when I needed it				
My mentor helped me find my own solutions to challenges				
My mentor kept me 'in touch' while on maternity/parental leave				
The contact I had with my mentor was appropriate for what I needed				
Mentoring really helped my return to work				
I would recommend mentoring to others on parental leave				
I have built confidence through the mentoring support				
I have improved my performance though the mentoring support				

Figure 17.2 (Continued)

I understand better what my personal priorities and career ambitions are				
I feel confident about my future career with the business				
Overall thoughts				
What have you gained most from your mentoring relationship?				
What improvements would you suggest?				
What advice would you have for future mentors/mentees?				
Any further comments you'd like to add related to the mentoring and/or your experience of returning to work?				

Thank you for your feedback

Figure 17.2 Example mentee questionnaire.

Parent mentor focus group	
(Semi - structured questions to prompt discussion)	
Focus area	**Opening questions**
Their mentees	• What did you notice about your mentee and the journey she took? • What topics and challenges did she bring to your sessions? How did this change over time? • What words would you use to describe your mentee's return to work? • What do you think your mentee has gained from her experience of mentoring?
The working support	• What was the impact of parental mentoring on your diary? • How well prepared were you for this form of mentoring? • What else would have been helpful? • What tools, ideas and approaches did you choose to use to help your mentee? What was the impact?
The relationship	• How would you describe your relationship with your mentee? • How well 'matched' did you feel? • What's gone well/less well in your relationship? • How did you close the mentoring? • Where is the relationship now?
You (as mentors)	• What have you learned about yourself from participating in parental mentoring? • What have you personally gained from mentoring in this space? • What would you choose to do differently in your next mentoring relationship?
The organisation	• What can we learn as a business from this form of mentoring? • What improvements would you suggest? • What value does mentoring at this point in someone's career bring to the organisation?

Figure 17.3 Parent mentor focus group.

Mentee focus group	
(Semi-structured questions to prompt discussion)	
Focus area	**Opening questions**
You (the mentees)	• How would you describe your journey to working parenthood • How prepared were you for the mentoring? • To what extent have you achieved the objectives you agreed at the outset? • What changed?
Your mentor and relationship	• How would you describe your relationship with your mentor? • How well 'matched' did you feel? • What's gone well/less well in your relationship? • How did you close the mentoring? • Where is the relationship now?
Outputs	• What do you feel you have gained from your mentoring relationship? • How has mentoring helped you re-engage with work and career? • What will take the place of this mentoring for you as you move forward?
The organisation and the future	• What do you think the business can learn from this mentoring programme? • What improvements would you suggest? • What advice would you give to future parents in terms of mentoring support at this point in someone's career?

Figure 17.4 Mentee focus group.

Line Manager Focus Group	
(Semi-structured questions to prompt discussion)	
Focus area	**Questions**
You	• What are the questions on your mind when a colleague announces they are pregnant or requests shared parental leave? • How well prepared were you to support your direct report though maternity / parental leave and return? • What else would have been helpful?
Your direct report	• How did you keep in touch with your colleague? • How did you support their departure and keep in touch with them while on leave? • How did you support their return to work? • What was the biggest challenge in terms of their return to work? • When they returned to work, how long did it take for them to get up and running?
The mentoring	• How did you encourage them to make the most of the mentoring opportunity? • To what extent do you feel the mentoring support has helped their return to work? • How do you feel the mentoring supports/conflicts with a line manager's role during this time?
The organisation and future	• What value does mentoring at this point in someone's career bring to the organisation? • What do you think the business can learn from this mentoring programme?

Figure 17.5 Line manager focus group.

Experiences of maternity
(A baseline study)

Before your maternity leave
1. Which department/function did you work in?
2. What job level were you when you took maternity leave?
3. Where did you go for help and advice about your maternity leave?
4. How close to your due date did you commence your leave?
5. On a scale of 1–4 (4 being easiest), how easy was it to 'close down' work?

Your maternity leave
6. Did you ask to keep in touch with the business while on maternity leave?
7. How did you keep in touch?
8. What sources of support were most important to you as you prepared to finish work, took parental leave and on your return to work?
9. What additional support would have made a difference to you?
10. How long did you take off work?

Returning to work
11. On a scale of 1–4 (4 being smoothest), how would you rate your return to work?
12. What helped your return to work?
13. What hindered your return to work?
14. What had changed for you?

Working arrangements on return
15. What was your preference for work solution on your return?
16. What position did you actually return to?
    - Same job, full time
    - Same job, full time (flexible hours)
    - Same job, reduced hours
    - Same job, reduced hours and job share
    - Different job, same level, full time
    - Different job, same level, reduced hours
    - Different job, same level (job share)
    - Different job, reduced grade, full time
    - Different job, reduced grade, reduced hours
    - Different job, reduced grade (job share)
    - Other (free text)

Future ambition
17. How do you feel about your future career path with the business?
    - Unchanged – on track for promotion to next level
    - Still want to progress
    - Continue in same role
    - Continue at same level/grade, but different roles to broaden experience
    - On hold right now – happy at this level right now
    - Don't know
    - Other
18. What are the contributing factors to your thoughts on your future career?

Looking back
19. What are the top three lessons you have learned about combining work and parenting?
20. What would you do differently if taking maternity / parental leave again?

Figure 17.6 Example survey.

18 A mentor's toolkit

A key aim of this book is to provide accessible resources for mentors working with mentees on their journey to working parenthood. With that in mind, this chapter offers a number of tools and techniques, which mentors may find helpful at different times and with different mentees. The tools are offered in a spirit of guided practice. Some are more complex than others and we have attempted to indicate this by way of a number adjacent to the title of each one; from 1 – at its most simple, to 3 for more complex tools for experienced mentors and coaches. The challenge is for mentors to be aware at all times of the boundaries of their own competence.

Good Practice! Where a mentor is new to a particular tool, our suggestion is to test run and work through the tool with themselves in the position of mentee first, then to take time afterward to reflect on the experience considering:

- What was the learning for them personally in using this tool?
- What were the insights?
- What actions do they want to commit to?
- What might they want to do differently, or be mindful of, when using this with a mentee?

It's also then extremely useful to practice with a colleague or another mentor willing to give feedback in terms of what worked well for them, what didn't work, and what might be improved on. In this way, the mentor becomes more familiar with the tool and with its introduction, setup and application.

Setting up and exploring buy in are essential precursors for using any tool or technique. The invitation is to help address an issue or challenge by means of a different method or perspective, trusting in the exploration and ambition for new understanding and learning for the mentee (and the mentor). Remember also that an invitation may or may not be accepted!

For a programme manager, introducing and practicing different tools and techniques could be an agenda item for a mentors' supervision session or a topic for a separate up-skilling session with your mentors. Our experience of working with new mentoring programmes indicates the importance of having a planned schedule for the on-going development of your mentors beyond the initial workshop. With busy day jobs, internal mentors inevitably have a limited capacity for retention of knowledge, so additional workshops (even if run over lunch times with the added promise of sandwiches and time for networking) are a helpful way for tools to be introduced, explored and practiced in pairs or small groups. In this way mentors are encouraged to build their skills and practice and in doing so, begin to create their own personal library of tools to draw on when the time feels right.

For each tool, our approach is to:

- Outline the context and underpinning concepts
- Indicate at what point this may be of most help
- Offer ideas and suggestions for using the tool in practice

Massively difficult questions (1)

Great questions are at the core of a powerful mentoring conversation. Asked at an appropriate time and with sensitivity, they are an invitation both to explore – and sometimes challenge – ideas, assumptions, or concerns in a trusted and confidential space. With this in mind, using the journey (Chapter 6) as a frame of reference, we have developed a series of parent focused Massively Difficult Questions (MDQs) that mentors may find helpful to refer to and also to add in some of their own, in an effort to create a personalised bank of great questions.

What makes them MDQs? You will notice most of the questions open with an enquiry using 'Who,' 'What,' 'When' and 'How' in an effort to encourage the mentee to pause and reflect, perhaps thinking at a deeper level than otherwise they might. When we're introducing the concept of MDQs, a question we often ask internal mentors is this; '*When you're mentoring someone, how does it feel to be in a position of asking and not telling?*' Therein lays the challenge! For new mentors in particular, it is important for them to be consciously asking open questions when their default mode might typically be to ask closed questions, e.g. 'Have you thought about …?' or 'Have you tried …?'

As ever, it's helpful to have your mentors practice using these, since we often find novice mentees will note a question, and in the actual delivery rephrase it as a closed question, with the risk that it is more likely to limit the mentee's response as opposed to opening up thinking and new ideas.

Note we offer no questions for early maternity leave itself. While every new parent will always have endless questions on their mind, this stage of journey will be at capacity concerning life as a parent to a new baby and has no requirement for a work-based agenda and mentor.

Ending work

1   What gives your life meaning now? How do you expect that to change?
2   What are the things you're most proud of having achieved?
3   What are you good at that's got you to where you are? (You'll have these skills when you return to work.)
4   Who do you want to connect with before you leave work and why?
5   Who do you want to keep in touch with during maternity/parental leave?

  6 How are you preparing the team for your maternity/parental leave?
  7 What support are you getting/do you need from your line manager? From others?
  8 What's stopping you from asking for their support?
  9 What do you need to complete before you can leave with a clear head?
 10 What's not going to get finished?
 11 How are you prioritising your own health and well-being right now?
 12 When do you give yourself permission to be pregnant at work?
 13 What are you looking forward to most?
 14 What do you fear most?
 15 What are your biggest concerns about finishing work?
 16 What does success look like for you?
 17 Looking ahead, how do you imagine life as a working parent?
 18 What assumptions are you making?
 19 What will life be like at its best?
 20 What are your hopes and expectations?
 21 What sort of a parent will you be?
 22 Describe your support network outside of work
 23 How will you make sure that you maintain sufficient connection with your professional identity?
 24 How will you keep growing intellectually?

Countdown to return

  1 What skills and experience are you bringing back to work?
  2 How have you changed and grown as a person?
  3 What are the choices in front of you in relation to work?
  4 What's the uncomfortable truth about returning to work?
  5 What would your ideal work role look like?
  6 What do you want to ask for?
  7 What do you need to do to be ready for the return to work conversation?
  8 What questions do you want to ask your manager/the business?
  9 What skills do you want to hone before you go back to work?
 10 What will you be wearing for your first week back?
 11 How are you preparing for your first day back at work?
 12 What contingency have you built in?
 13 What are the nonnegotiables for your return?
 14 What might be the pros and cons of part-time or flexible working?
 15 What might be the pros and cons of full-time working?
 16 What compromises are you prepared to make?
 17 How will you negotiate for what you want?
 18 What is holding you back from asking for what you want?
 19 If you could have what you want from work, what would it look like?
 20 What would a smooth return to work look like for you?
 21 What is the impact of your decision?

22 What do you want to be known for when you return to work?
23 What are the biggest derailers you will have to face going back to work?
24 What will your morning routine need to look like?

Early days back

1   What's the best thing about being back at work?
2   What are the priorities?
3   What's changed?
4   Who are the people you rely on in work for support or help?
5   Who are your cheerleaders? What are they saying?
6   What do you get from being at work?
7   How do others see you now that you're back?
8   How has your network changed – within work and outside of work?
9   How do you feel others' expectations of you have changed? What will you do about this?
10 What are the changes in your expectations of yourself now?
11 Who are the people you believe are judging you? What do you believe they are saying?
12 What would the confident you do here?
13 What would you achieve if you weren't afraid?
14 What's gone well this week?
15 How are you organised?
16 What could work better – and how?
17 What short-term goals can you set yourself? (Personal or work related)
18 What will it take for you to feel back on track? What does the 'track' look like now?
19 What's the most important thing to you about being a working parent?
20 What compromises have you had to make?
21 How will you reconnect with your professional network now you're back?
22 What does a 'good enough' parent look like?
23 What boundaries could you put in place to help balance work and home?
24 What help do you need at home/outside work?

Future focus

1   What's your ambition for the future?
2   What's your greatest fear?
3   What do you want to be known for?
4   What are your short-term and longer-term career goals?
5   What is your first next step toward those goals?
6   What one or two things could you do to build your confidence in moving forward?
7   How will you access support for your next step?
8   What changes do you want to make to your professional network?
9   How have your work and home networks changed?

10   How are you maintaining and building each of these networks?
11   Who makes life possible for you now?
12   What have you learned about yourself through this transition?
13   If you were to do it all again, what would you do differently?
14   What advice have you got for your past self?
15   What values are important to you? How have these changed?
16   What changes would you like to make to demonstrate these values consistently?
17   If this journey were a metaphor, what would it be and why?
18   How do you recognise and reward your own success?
19   What are you most proud of?
20   What strengths will you draw on as you move forward?
21   How can you use your experience to 'pay it forward' and help others?
22   What are you doing to ensure you continue to grow and develop as a leader?
23   What does support look like from here for you?
24   What would you ask yourself if you were a mentor?

A vision for a new world (1)

What is it?

Visioning is a technique frequently used in coaching and mentoring for goal setting. As we know, the time immediately pre-parental leave is frequently occupied with all things work related: rescheduling tasks, closing down activities, handing over projects, people and issues. Mentoring conversations are an opportunity to pause for a moment, to take a wider perspective (beyond the immediacy of closing down work) and to look further ahead to new goals and a different life, which will inevitably incorporate both work and being a parent.

The output of this activity is a visual manifestation (perhaps a drawing, an image or a vision board with many images) of their goals, hopes and aspirations for life as a working parent.

When might it be helpful to use this with a mentee?

This is a useful activity early in the mentoring relationship and before the start of parental leave, as you begin to explore early agendas and ambitions with a mentee. There needs to be an acknowledgment that the reality of experience (i.e. becoming a parent for the first time) will bring with it fresh perspectives and the potential for changes in thinking. Once a mentee has returned to work, it is useful to revisit this 3 to 6 months in, to explore how life is in practice, what might they still want to do toward the original vision, what they might wish to amend or build on knowing what they know now.

Suggestions for this in practice

This activity will need thinking time and space on the part of the mentee as guided by the mentor. Consideration should be given to the location for this activity, i.e. finding a space where they can feel relaxed and any distractions are kept to a minimum, e.g. external noise, the potential for interruptions and, in particular, personal visibility if your meeting rooms have glass walls and are next to a busy corridor.

Introduce the activity to the mentee, explaining the approach and ensuring you have their agreement to proceed.

This next part is led by the mentor and is not intended to be a dialogue at this point. The idea is for the mentor simply to talk slowly through their own adaptation of the points below, pausing at times for the mentee to 'be there' in their mind's eye.

Invite your mentee to close her eyes for a few minutes and step into the future, imagining herself in 12 months' time asking:

> How different will life be in comparison with where you are now? What are your hopes for life at its best – as a parent, for your home life, your future career? When thinking of your return, what will life be like for you as a working parent? What will you be doing? How will you be feeling? If you're feeling positive and excited, what is it that's making you feel that way?
>
> Talking through the start of a working day; it's morning, you're waking and greeting your baby, getting ready for work, getting your baby ready too, perhaps your partner or a relative is there to help or the baby may be going to a nursery, then you're travelling on to work, going through the doors at the main entrance and greeting colleagues, exchanging stories, phones are ringing, keyboards tapping, you're in your first team meeting back…

As you talk through the scenario, from your knowledge of the environment, introduce specifics in the story that are relevant to her particular working environment and which engage the senses. There might be a particular individual on reception everyone greets as they come in to work, there might be the smell of freshly brewed coffee as they walk past the café, etc.

Having led with these thoughts, invite her to open her eyes when she is ready to be back in the room. Then invite her to explore in more detail what she would like life to be in 12 months' time. What would success look like? The idea is to include anything that inspires and motivates her in relation to her future life. For example, she might want to focus on the following areas; the new baby, herself as a parent, her partner, home life, friends, her career, finances, health and well-being.

Having given this some thought and discussion, the opportunity is to make a visual record. You might simply have a blank sheet of paper and pencils available for the mentee to sketch out some early thoughts and ideas. Then invite her to complete it in more detail in her own time away from work with a view to sharing at your next meeting if she wishes. The onward discussions can focus on the plan – how will she get there, what needs to happen, what might be some milestones to recognise along the way?

Some mentees like to use this as an opportunity to create a vision board. This can be a blend of drawings, images cut from magazines, photographs, quotations – anything that resonates and feels relevant to them. For mentees who prefer a digital approach, there are websites such as www.pintrest.com or www.visionboard.me for example, that offer a wealth of images and quotations to create an online vision board. Alternatively, there are also numerous smart phone apps available to download which they may prefer to use.

Having created their vision, the invitation is to share it perhaps with a partner and then to place it somewhere visible and accessible as a reminder of what they want to accomplish. Of course, a digital copy or photograph also enables them to have this with them wherever they go.

Either side of the line (1)

What is it?

For a mentee struggling in the vortex of close down and endlessly busy, this is a simple, but effective tool to help her differentiate and sort through the volume of things that '*must be done before I go*' acknowledging that some tasks or projects will extend beyond her leave date, since the business is going to carry on without her. The focused action of tabling all the activities she has on her mind and stepping back to look at the total picture can be liberating and a timely prompt to seek support if appropriate. It is also an opportunity for the mentor to explore with their mentee the extent to which the things to be done before she finishes work are all work related (e.g. tasks, projects, team) and not focused on the individual (e.g. completing a performance review with her line manager, agreeing to a communication plan for keeping in touch).

When might it be helpful to use this tool with a mentee?

This activity is designed to help a mentee prioritise tasks and activities before she finishes for the start of maternity/parental leave.

The idea in practice

For this activity you will need a piece of flip chart paper, coloured pens (red, orange, green) and plenty of Post-it notes:

- Start by inviting your mentee to write down on separate Post-it notes all the things she has to complete before the start of her leave. (She could do this as prework before a mentoring session.)
- Invite her to make a note of any personal actions that she wants to complete, e.g. having a 1-1 with a key sponsor, or performance appraisal with her line manager (having her performance documented is an opportunity to finish on a high as well as provide a useful start for returning conversations).
- Having made a note of her tasks, ask her to prioritise each of these on a scale of 10 (most important) to 1 (least important).
- Next ask your mentee to rate each of these tasks in terms of progress; i.e. *red* – not started/in crisis, *orange* – part completed, *green* – on track for completion.
- Move to the flip chart paper and draw a vertical line from top to bottom, indicating this line as the start of parental leave.

- Now invite your mentee to stick her Post-it notes on the sheet, starting with her most important tasks until all Post-it notes are on the page.
- Step back and pause to look at the total picture

Key questions you might ask in support of the model/framework

- What do you notice as you look at what needs to be done before you finish work?
- Which of these tasks could you delegate to someone else?
- Who could that be?
- Which are the tasks occupying most of your headspace right now?
- What do you need to do to move these forward specifically?
- Whose help can you enlist?
- What stops you from asking for support?
- What could be moved to the other side of the line (i.e. handed over)?
- What's not going to get done?
- If you were the mentor in this situation, what advice would you have for your mentee?
- In support of a positive close down, what insights/actions will you share with your line manager?
- What do you want to take away from this activity?
- How are you feeling right now?
- The flip chart is for the mentee to take away. Alternatively, she may want to take a photograph for future reference.

Powering the network (1)

What is it?

This activity focuses on the personal networks and relationships that support an individual both in work and outside at home, across a period of parental leave and return. Networking is one of the activities that tend to slide down the to-do list finding itself deprioritised in favour of more pressing work-related tasks.

Typically when one thinks of networking one thinks of it in the context of someone's profession or work environment; establishing and building relationships with people that you can offer something to and who in turn have knowledge, experience, influence and may be helpful at some point in the future. With the prospect of being away from work for an extended time, there is value in connecting with people before the start of a period of parental leave, nurturing those contacts, for advice or maybe even making tentative explorations for future roles and possibilities.

Outside of work, the principles of establishing and building relationships are just as important, particularly for the new mother separated from work for the first time and about to go through a life-changing experience. A community of support around a new mother (e.g. partner, family, friends) can make a real difference to the experience of maternity and is also a factor in reducing the potential for postnatal depression. The same can be true for a father taking extended parental leave, finding himself isolated at home with a small baby and few male peers to connect with for shared support and friendship. (See our case study on p. 191.)

Case study insights

New networks

Before my first child, most of my waking hours and activities were concentrated on or around work; either I was in work (full time hours, weekends and more), thinking about work (emailing, planning, preparing), shopping and sleeping (in order to be ready for work), and socialising at work and with friends from work. My home was a monument to being at my best for work. I couldn't imagine life without it. In an instant, maternity leave changed all that and brought with it a whole bunch of people closer to home, many of whom were career women on maternity leave like me. How did I find my new network? With my bump (and later baby) I went to antenatal classes, parenting groups, met other parents at play groups and in the park, signed up for exercise classes, chaired a local charity, offered help and in turn was helped. We laughed, questioned endlessly and shared learning, each making our own unique journey to working parenthood. Nineteen years later, the friends I made on maternity still meet, only now it's all about universities and young adults leaving home (and that's a very different book!)

Nicki Seignot

With a bicycle as a metaphor for a balanced and well-maintained network (at home as well as at work), this activity encourages focus on closing down connections and why and how to build new connections while on maternity and parental leave.

When might it be helpful to use this tool with a mentee?

This activity is designed for use pre-parental leave and then on return to work to notice what has changed and what actions may now be useful.

The idea in practice

Set the scene for the activity in your own words using the notes above as a guide. For this activity it helps to have a visual image of a bicycle at hand. Open by exploring the idea of a bicycle as a metaphor for the journey to working parenthood asking:

- What ideas come to mind?
- What might the different component parts represent? (Seat, handlebars, wheels, the spokes, breaks, etc.)

- Whose bike is it?
- What direction is it taking?
- What terrain is the bike going to encounter?
- What will help get the bike to its next destination?

Step one: Draw two large circles on a piece of A3 or flip chart paper representing the two wheels on a bicycle and invite the mentee to write her name at the centre of each wheel.

On Post-it notes, invite the mentee to write down the names of key people in her work/professional network she wants to connect with before she finishes work.

Ask her to place the Post-it notes around her name on the first wheel, according to how important she feels those individuals are to her. If they are really important, then put them close to the centre and if less so, then toward the edge of the wheel.

Write a number next to each name on a scale of 1 to 10 (10 being high) on the quality of the relationship she has with that individual.

(Notice the relationship between how important they are and the quality of the relationship.)

Step two: This step is to focus on her network outside work. Repeat the process as described above for the second wheel, except ask your mentee to write down names of people outside work who will be a means of support and friendship during the forthcoming months.

Step three: Invite the mentee to describe the support networks in front of her and make a note of anything that springs to mind. You may choose to explore each wheel using the following questions as a starting point:

Key questions you might ask in support of the model/framework

In support of your professional network:

- If you only had time to meet with two people before you finish work, who would they be?
- What makes them your priority?
- What do you bring to those relationships? (Do they need to be reciprocal?)
- What messages do you want to get across?
- How might they support you while you are off?
- What have you done so far?
- Why is this difficult?
- Where are the easy networking opportunities? (e.g. business meetings, briefing sessions, lunches, forums.)

In support of building a network away from work:

- Who are the key people in your network at home/outside of work?
- What do they offer you?
- How do you contribute to these relationships?

- What do you bring to, as well as need from, your network?
- What's missing from this network?
- Where are the opportunities to connect with other new parents taking maternity or parental leave? For example, antenatal classes, exercise classes, play groups, local networks such as the National Childbirth Trust (NCT).
- Which online communities could offer you support and guidance?
- How might your social media network be of value to you at this time?
- How do you expect your network to change over the forthcoming months?
- What aspects of your network are working well?
- What needs attention?

Coming back with confidence (1)

(A letter to my future self)

What is it?

A word frequently expressed by individuals in conversations post return to work is confidence. In the lead up to return and early days back, individuals can find themselves questioning the relevance of their skills and currency in the workplace, and find their confidence diminished. As noted in earlier chapters, the nature of the transition is such that there will be natural peaks and troughs in confidence and motivation. The aim of the mentoring is to create a safe space to voice this aloud and in doing so, support someone to feel more confident.

This activity invites a mentee to look to the future with confidence, by completing a personal audit of her achievements and strengths, and think about new skills she might develop and bring back to the workplace as a result of her experiences and learning during maternity leave. It is about creating a positive frame of reference for her return, reconnection with work and her professional identity.

When might it be helpful to use this tool with a mentee?

This activity is best completed before the start of maternity/parental leave and then revisited with the mentee once she has returned to work. The letter acts as a positive reinforcement and reminder of what she brings to the workplace and what she has achieved as well as the potential for new learning in the months ahead.

The idea in practice

Using the questions below, the idea is to invite the mentee to write a letter to herself which documents her successes and performance pre-departure while at the same time projecting forwards to future skills. There is no requirement for her to share the letter with anyone. Having written the letter, the mentee simply seals the envelope and gives it to her mentor for safekeeping. Caught up with multiple agendas and then an extended period of time away from work, a mentee will often forget about the letter until it is placed back in her hands on return. It can make for a positive opening conversation at a time when she may be feeling low and unsure.

Four questions that make up the content of the letter

- The things I'm most proud of having achieved.
- What I'm good at that's got me here today (I'll still have these as core skills when I return).
- What I've got to look forward to coming back.
- What I know I'll get even better at, as I juggle new priorities, e.g. planning/ organising.

Mentee insights from use of this tool

Though I didn't realise it at the time, this has been such a useful activity for me. Three months in, I still have my letter in my handbag and if I have a bad day at work, I get it out and remind myself of all the good things I have in place and more.

(Mentee, Asda)

Of all the tools, this was the one I procrastinated over the most. But as I got into it, it was like giving myself a motivational team talk. I wrote quite a light-hearted letter that enabled me to draw on the things that were fundamental to me, my beliefs and my context. My issue on return was a lack of self-belief. I'd been away so long and I'd lost my confidence. My letter listed all the strengths I had before I had my son and all the new strengths I was bringing back. When I analysed it, I was more organised (getting ready and on time for work with a small toddler in tow), I was more confident than before (making decisions for myself and my family) and I was more self-aware (things had changed but so had I). Mentoring guided me on the journey.

(Mentee, RSC)

Stars in a night sky (1)

What is it?

This is a discussion exercise with the objective of exploring and identifying what has changed in or for an individual through their maternity/parental leave and the impact (positive and less so) of having a baby and being a parent within the context of work and career.

The inspiration for this tool was prompted by a chapter within Kate Figes' book *Life After Birth* (2008), in which she talks openly and honestly about some of the wonders that come with parenthood, and also some of the more challenging elements, in particular the physical changes associated with motherhood:

> Every woman who gives birth needs an extensive period of adjustment to come to terms with the irrevocable changes to her body so that she can more easily

accept her role as a mother. There are billions of tiny lights glowing inside each one of us, and it can feel as if the effort it takes to produce each child is so great that it extinguishes a few of those lights for ever. We can live perfectly well without them, but that does not mean that we do not need time to mourn their loss. (p. 22)

I have since extended this metaphor, adapting Figes' 'tiny lights' into stars in a night sky. The metaphor of stars seems to me to have an association of light, positive energy and new possibilities. There is something about placing these lights in the context of a night sky, where the stars shine visibly and exist as part of a wider universe – a space without boundaries and endless opportunities for exploration and discovery. Parental leave represents an amazing learning experience. Life will never be the same once you have a child, some of our stars may disappear, but when we take time to pause, to look up, our sky reveals a myriad of new stars; new skills, new experiences, new motivations, which can shine new light and guide us on the next stage of our journey.

When might it be helpful to use this with a mentee?

This exercise is probably most useful for someone either on countdown to return, or in the early stages of returning to work after maternity or parental leave. The metaphor seems to be most useful where someone is struggling with confidence and questioning the relevance and currency of their skills when returning to work. In this context, the stars relate to an individual's skills and motivations.

Some examples of skills developed on parental leave might include:

- Time management, multitasking and prioritisation
- Dealing with change
- Resilience and self-motivation
- Emotional intelligence
- Coaching and listening
- Creativity
- Empathy
- Networking
- Communication skills
- Influencing skills
- Project planning and organising
- Financial management
- Crisis management

Typical examples of motivation might include:

- Work–life balance
- Doing the right thing for my family – it's more than just me now
- Security
- Responsibility for another
- Presenting the 'me I want to be' in the workplace
- Making sure I, and others, value the 'New Me'

The idea in practice

Introduce and explore the metaphor with your mentee. With an image of a night sky to prompt the conversation, invite your mentee to identify her own 'night sky' through a series of open questions:

- Which stars have dimmed for you through this journey out of work and return?
- What will it take for them to shine brightly again?
- When might that be?
- What could you do to reignite those stars?
- Which stars have gone out forever?
- How does this feel?
- Which new stars have since emerged?
- How do they add value in the context of work?
- What might others see in your night sky?
- How does this feel?

You could invite your mentee to plot these either on a sheet of paper or perhaps as a series of Post-it notes on the wall. It is a great way to encourage them to take a step back and look at what they have in place and then to reflect on the learning.

Insights from use of this tool

The star exercise made me really think about what new things I had learnt or could do now. I started out only seeing the negative stuff – loss of confidence, feeling out of touch, my body being a different shape – but the star exercise made me realise that many of the challenges that come with parenthood had also brought with them a new skill set that was applicable at work and not just at home. A really useful and practical approach – I love my new night sky!
(Head of Department EDF Energy)

Our thanks to Kathy Denton for this contribution. Kathy is an Executive Coach and EMCC senior Practitioner. She is also a Chartered Psychologist (Occupational) and Associate Fellow of the British Psychological Society.

The first 30 days (1)

What is it?

The first few weeks back revolve around a series of demanding and simultaneous priorities. At work, for example, it's about getting to grips with changes within the organisation, understanding the requirements of a new job, or changes to the previous one, there may be a new line manager to meet and get to know, changes within the team, and more generally a desire to get back in and up to speed as soon as possible.

At home, the priorities are about establishing a routine for the (now) working parent and her baby. Mornings have a new urgency with an extended pre-work task list (of feeding, dropping off at child care, navigating traffic, arriving at work probably later than was the case previously). The end of day appears earlier than before (pick up time may be non-negotiable) and evenings are a much-wanted window of time with the baby and preparation for the next day (i.e. baby food, milk, bottles, clothes). It's not surprising that many returners' initial experience of combining work and parenting feels overwhelming and a whirlwind of tasks they have yet to master.

With this as a backdrop, there is something powerful in applying the 'progress principle,' i.e. paying attention to the progress that is being made every day, however small that progress may be. A 2011 *Harvard Business Review* (HBR) article by Teresa Amabile and Steven Kramer ('The Power of Small Wins'), shared research findings relating to the power of small wins for employees in terms of their levels of motivation. In the article they reference a 1968 issue of *HBR* in which Frederick Herzberg asked '*One more time: How do you motivate employees?*' Forty-three years later, their 2011 research findings were consistent with Herzberg's 1968 message; '*People are most satisfied with their jobs and therefore most motivated when those jobs give them the opportunity to experience achievement.*' The hypothesis was that the mechanism underlying a sense of achievement was about '*making consistent, meaningful progress*' (p. 4).

Applying the same principle to returners struggling to feel truly 'back,' identifying progress – however small – may be central to helping someone begin to feel more positive and confident about themselves and their contribution at work as well as at home.

When might it be helpful to use this tool with a mentee?

This activity is designed for the time period post return to work.

The idea in practice

Invite your mentee to share how she is feeling/managing the return to work and her sense of progress as a working parent. Introduce the tool in your own words, using the information above as an opening guide.

In a spirit of recognising and encouraging progress, ask your mentee to email, send a text or message you each day for the next 30 days with one thing she has achieved (big or small, at home or work) that she wants to share with you. Remember, home and work are uniquely intertwined from this point onwards, so achievements from one or the other sphere are equally appropriate in this context. Stuck for ideas? It may be useful to invite her to start by reflecting on the previous day or noticing something about the present day.

Some questions to prompt ideas might include:

- What's gone well today?
- What am I proud of?
- What have I achieved?

- What impact does noticing this have on me?
- As a mentor, it is good practice to
- Respond to each small win and personally acknowledge the achievement.
- Keep a log of the notes as they come in.
- At the end of the 30-day period, collate the achievements into one document for your mentee.
- Share the document with her, exploring the nature and balance of achievements (perhaps noticing how many are work related, how many are home or family related).
- Invite your mentee to reflect on what's changed over that period and her sense of progress.

Mentee insights from use of this tool

This is an activity I don't want to forget. Coming back, I felt like the world had changed. I was unsure who I was and what I was doing. I just wasn't feeling like myself – the professional self, the confident self, the 'I know what I'm doing' self. In an effort to help rebuild my confidence, we focused on small wins and my mentor asked me to share something I felt I had achieved every day for 30 days.

I found I really looked forward to it and it became a highlight of my day. It could be work related, a presentation or project milestone achieved, or something at home like making a really nice home cooked stew for the family.

She responded every single day. It cemented our relationship and I discovered I had an awful lot going on in my life that was really good.

(Mentee, RSC)

The change curve as a framework for a transition to working parenthood (2)

What is it?

The change curve is based on a model researched and developed in the late 1960s by Dr. Elizabeth Kubler-Ross who proposed the concept as a means of understanding and coming to terms with terminal illness. Her model indicated five distinct stages: Denial, Anger, Bargaining, Depression and Acceptance. She went on to propose that application of the model could be extended to any dramatic life-changing situation.

In a business context, the change curve (Figure 18.1) has since been adapted many times (a recent online search for 'change curve' revealed 39.6 million results) and is frequently used as a framework for leading organisational change; helping an organisation and its employees understand more of the process they go through in relation to significant change, the potential impact on productivity and motivation and with that in mind, how to expedite as smooth a transition as possible.

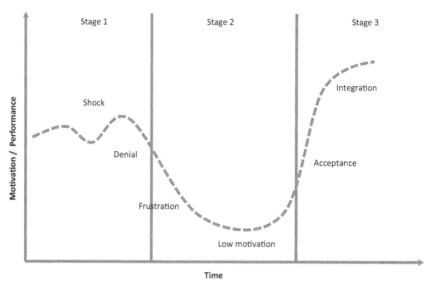

Figure 18.1 The change curve.

Figure 18.2 offers an interpretation of how the change curve might look in the context of maternity. Becoming a parent is a life-changing event, with predictable fluctuations in confidence and motivation at different points of the journey. Most notable is the indication of a 'roller coaster' shaped trajectory. Clearly, there is no set formula for change – the peaks and troughs are not rigid nor for specific time periods and each individual will experience the change associated with leaving work, becoming a parent and returning, in a way that is unique to them, their particular circumstances and motivations.

Coming back to work presents enormous challenges and incremental change on top of experiencing the transformational change associated with becoming a parent. The message of the change curve is that it gives the individual a framework and language to validate the emotional peaks and troughs of this experience, which ultimately move them forward. The mentee can take heart from the fact that many of these journeys follow a pattern.

When might it be helpful to use this tool with a mentee?

The change curve can be used as a tool pre-maternity, to raise awareness and generate thoughts of how they might want to approach their maternity leave. With a supportive mentor, they have space to begin to think about their personal journey, how they might recognise where they are at any given point and correspondingly at what points help may be of most value.

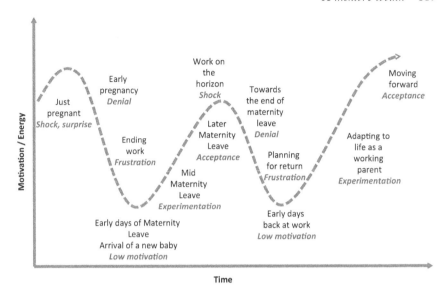

Figure 18.2 The 'double' change curve of maternity.

For the returning mentee, it is a useful way to look back at their journey to working parenthood and reflect on the highs and lows of the experience, perhaps contrasting how they anticipated things would be with the reality of their experience. This can be particularly useful if a mentee is back at work and 'stuck', struggling to move forward.

The idea in practice *(pre-maternity leave)*

Open by establishing your mentee's knowledge and understanding of the change curve as a concept. You might choose to draw a visual image of the change curve (or perhaps there is a version you already use within your organisation), explaining the different axis, peaks and troughs and changing dynamics of the different stages.

With the change curve as a visual guide, invite your mentee to revisit some recent examples of change, exploring a recent piece of change that she felt went well and was a positive experience, and correspondingly a piece of change that she viewed as a less positive experience:

- What were the differences between the two experiences?
- Where are you now (on the change curve) in relation to those examples of change?
- What help was needed/did you receive at different points?

- What did you learn about your ability and willingness to deal with change?
- What are the factors that sustain you and help to get you through change?

Invite the mentee to look to the future for a moment and draw a rough sketch of her anticipated change curve for maternity adding markers/events and comments where relevant:

- In the context of your maternity/parental leave, what is your understanding of the change you're embarking on?
- What stage in the process do you think you are at right now, here, today?
- How do you anticipate moving though the different stages?
- What help is there to support you to get back into flow if you feel stuck at any point?
- How helpful is this as a concept in terms of the journey ahead for you?

The idea in practice *(post maternity leave)*

Invite your mentee to draw out her journey to working parenthood on a blank copy of the change model, indicating different stages and changes in direction with notes or images as appropriate:

- Talk me through the journey as you've drawn it.
- What comes to mind as you look at the complete picture?
- How does your experience contrast with what you anticipated pre-maternity leave?
- Where are you now on the curve?
- What is needed to help you move to the next stage and move ahead now?
- If this journey represents a pattern (and hope for the future because we can be confident in making progress), who are the people you could seek out for advice or guidance who have been there before you?
- What are the changes ahead you want to be mindful of?
- What have you learned about yourself through this period of transition?
- What do you want to take away which may help with future change?

Learn/exploit/coast model (2)

What is it?

A model for working parenthood focusing on re-engagement with work in the context of new demands on their home life.

When might it be helpful to use this model with a mentee?

Approaching return and early days of working parenthood. This is a model to encourage dialogue around an individual's return to work choices.

The model explained

People need an appropriate balance of **learn/exploit/coast** in their work if they are to remain engaged and at the right level of positive stretch and learning. That balance may change radically according to circumstances.

In the context of new parenting, for example, women frequently report loss of confidence relating to their work-based skills and abilities while on maternity leave. With this in mind, some returners may find it helpful to be in **coast – exploit** mode for a period as they restore their confidence, refamiliarise themselves with job roles, re-establish networks and begin to feel they are succeeding in making a contribution at work.

With increasing confidence, and time back in role, they may then begin to seek more stretch in work to stay interested and motivated, thereby emphasising **learn and exploit**.

Work, however, is just one half of the equation. Remember, the work context is uniquely interlaced with the domestic context for a returning new parent. Pre-baby, home life could be deprioritised in favour of work and career. Post baby, there is a new urgency and heightened significance to the home context, which can't be deprioritised as it once could. As a new parent, she is in **learn** mode: surviving on broken nights' sleep, preoccupied with considerations of contingency (babies are frequently ill in early days at nursery), trying to keep up with the constant change associated with a developing baby or toddler and working to establish new patterns and ways of living.

As the model suggests, a level of certainty in terms of what's known and expected in work (emphasising **coast and exploit**) may be hugely helpful to the returning employee already stretched to capacity on the domestic front (emphasising **learn**).

That is not to say the take up of a brand new role or next level promotion on return to work is automatically unhelpful. Simply a flag to note they are likely to be in maximum learn mode in both contexts, and to think about what additional support may be needed in order to flourish.

The value of the **learn/exploit/coast** model seems to be that it gives a language around which returning parents can have a dialogue with themselves and their colleagues about how they phase their re-entry into full on working mode in a way that is mindful of the total context.

Suggestions for using the tool in practice

Draw! Using a pen and paper, build the up model (Figure 18.3) to introduce the concept step by step, using the explanation above as a guide.

Step 1: Start on the left-hand side drawing the axis and two arrows indicating the levels of learning (from least to most).

Step 2: Draw the WORK sections next, with the boxes representing the three theoretical work options and differing levels of learning for each one.

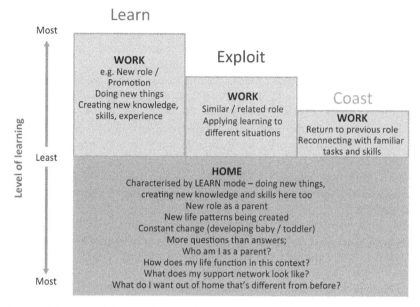

Figure 18.3 Learn-exploit-coast framework.

Step 3: Explore with your mentee how these relate to her return to work options. You could invite her to overlay and note these options on the model, so it becomes a working document for her.

Some opening questions might include:

• What are the options for your return to work?
• How might they look in the context of this model?
• Where are these in terms of your level of 'learn' and transferrable skills for each option?
• What are the business' expectations for your return? (e.g. the business is expecting me to return to a next level role, since I was on track for promotion when I left)
• How is this different from your expectations?
• How do you feel about this?
• What would your ideal return role look like and why?

Step 4: Draw the HOME section on the model (which underpins all return to work options) and invite the mentee to populate this with things on her mind relating to home:

- What are the biggest challenges facing you at home as you return to work?
- What do you need to do to address these?
- What help do you have in place?
- What other help do you need?
- When will you know you have addressed these?
- To what extent is home a significant factor in your return to work solution?

Step 5: Step back and consider the choices for work and home as one complete picture.

- Are there other considerations you want to add to the model?
- On a scale of 1–10, how would you rate the level of learn for you across each area?
- What is your ideal return to work option?
- What makes this your best solution right now?
- What are you prepared to compromise?
- What are you not prepared to compromise?
- Who do you need to have a conversation with next?

Step 6: Invite the mentee to reflect on learning and consider next steps.

The Thinking Environment™ (3)

What is it?

The Thinking Environment is a powerful framework that supports people to think for themselves and to challenge the assumptions that might stop them from achieving all that they would like to. The approach was pioneered by Nancy Kline, a leading thinker in the world of leadership development and coaching. She has published several publications on the Thinking Environment including the ground-breaking books *Time to Think* and *More Time to Think*.

This is an incredibly easy approach to understand but it can be incredibly challenging to master for mentors as it often challenges the assumptions that are made by both mentor and mentee about who is the 'expert' in the room. This can be especially challenging when the mentor is emotionally engaged in the content of the session or feels that they can establish credibility through providing advice. The Thinking Environment puts the independent thinking of the mentee at the core of everything it does.

When might it be helpful to use this approach with a mentee?

This approach has particular relevance when working with a mentee who is preparing for maternity as well as when helping someone to think about her return to work.

The idea in practice

The Thinking Environment provides a framework for your mentee to truly think about what is most important to her during all stages of her maternity journey and to challenge any assumptions that might limit her thinking in relation to her role as a mother and leader and how she can navigate her return to work with ease.

The approach puts the independent thinking of the mentee at the core of all discussions, enabling each individual to identify the specific solutions that will best suit her unique and individual needs. The approach is underpinned by 10 particular behaviors or 'ways of being' with your mentee that allow her to think for herself. These are called the Ten Components of a Thinking Environment:

The ten components at a glance

- **Attention** – Listening with palpable respect, interest and curiosity, and without interruption.
- **Ease** – Being at ease and free from internal rush and urgency.
- **Information** – Ensuring that we have a full and accurate picture of reality; making sure that we have the facts available and where necessary overcoming denial to help people to move forward.
- **Incisive questions™** – Removing untrue and limiting assumptions and replacing these with true and liberating alternatives to liberate our thinking.
- **Equality** – Everyone's thinking matters, regardless of status, current knowledge or experience.
- **Encouragement** – Moving beyond comparison with others and freeing ourselves from the need to compete – championing diverse ideas.
- **Diversity** – Welcoming difference and divergent thinking because they add quality to everyone's thinking.
- **Appreciation** – People think well when there is genuine acknowledgment of their positive qualities.
- **Feelings** – People need to express feelings appropriately in order to continue to think well.
- **Place** – Ensuring that the (internal and external) environment tells people they matter so that they can relax into thinking.

Key questions you might ask in support of the model/framework

The first question that is always asked is, '*What would you like to think about and what are your thoughts about …* (for example, *your upcoming maternity or parental leave?*') In the presence of the 10 components and your uninterrupted, generative attention, this simple question can ignite your mentee's thinking.

When needed, this is followed up with, '*What more do you think or feel or want to say?*'

Only after the mentee has had sufficient time to fully explore her own thoughts and ideas would we ask her to specify '*What more would you like to achieve in this session?*' giving her full ownership of what in particular she would like to focus on specifically during the session.

If the mentee appears to be blocked or is making assumptions that are limiting her thinking, we might follow up with, '*What are you assuming that is stopping you from achieving this (inserting their stated goal in their words)?*' or '*What are you assuming that is making you feel a lack of ease?*'

Insights and feedback from having used this with clients

We have found that it is often the untrue and limiting assumptions that women make about themselves; their roles as mothers and leaders and their future at work that can really limit their thinking. The Thinking Environment can really support both mentors and mentees to identify and replace these limiting assumptions with more liberating alternatives thereby enabling themselves to move forward.

Case study

The thinking environment

Justine had not worked full time for 5 years and had 3 young children at home. Her previous role before children was as a senior marketing manager for a large bank, a role she was exceptionally good at and really enjoyed. Whilst she had enjoyed her time at home, she needed now to return to work both for financial reasons as well as for her own development and sense of professional identity. She wanted to return to a part-time role which would allow her to use her skills and continue to develop her career. Her husband worked full time.

The key untrue assumptions that she identified included:

- That my skills are no longer relevant
- That I have nothing to add
- That I won't be able to get a role part time which is also interesting and uses my brain
- That my CV has huge gaps since I went on maternity leave
- That everyone else has developed since I left
- That I have a fuzzy head now
- That I will have nothing to talk about at interview
- That I don't really know what I am doing anymore
- That people will think I am not committed as I will have to leave to pick the children up

Her key untrue and limiting assumption during one of her sessions was that '*my skills are no longer relevant*'. When asked if this was true and what her

(*Continued*)

reasons were, she could see that this was not true. Her alternative liberating alternative was that *'I have all of my previous skills, plus I am more focused and motivated than ever'*. With this alternative she was then able to identify the ways in which she wanted to present herself, the kinds of roles that she was interested in and the type of organisation that she most wanted to work for.

Since returning to work 3 years ago, Justine has been identified as 'key talent.' She has been put on a leadership development program and has been promoted twice. She currently works 4 days a week, one of these from home.

Sophie Stephenson

Our thanks to Sophie Stephenson for this contribution. Sophie is a qualified Time to Think® Coach, Facilitator and Consultant and member of the Time to Think Global Faculty (www.thinking-time.co.uk)

Systemic exercise (3)

What is it?

During my years working as an Executive Coach I have come to recognise that working one-to-one with clients it is important to look beyond the level of the individual and take a view of the whole system in which they operate. The aim here is to offer two simple practices, which may help your most experienced mentors to apply a systemic approach when mentoring working parents.

When might it be helpful to use this model with a mentee?

After a mentee has returned to work and is beginning to get to grips with new patterns of working and how these interface with life away from the workplace.

The model explained

A mentee's system is made up of a wide array of interacting elements that make up their life and includes personal, professional and organisational elements such as their family, their relationships at work and the culture they work within. A systemic approach takes some, or all, of these elements into account and recognises that when working only at the level of the individual, crucial information about the wider view may be lost.

As systemic facilitator John Whittington states in his book *Systemic Coaching & Constellations* (2010):

> However well an individual performs and aligns themselves with their values, motivations and goals, the hidden forces that act in organisational systems will affect and often compromise their individual skills, talent and performance.

A systemic approach recognises that there are hidden patterns and dynamics within someone's interacting elements (i.e. their system). By working systemically you can help them to gain awareness of these often unconscious dynamics and also gain access to information and resources in the wider system. Taking a systemic approach is vital when coaching or mentoring working parents as it is inevitable that their personal (i.e. family) and professional (i.e. work) 'systems' will be highly interdependent. It is often at the point of returning to work that working parents struggle most to recognise their value and success and can be left feeling overwhelmed and under-resourced in their life and work.

It should be acknowledged that the area of systemic interventions is vast and there are many different approaches, all of which could be valuable when working with individuals in a coaching and mentoring context.

The practices are based on the concept of *constellations*. A constellation is a practical intervention that creates a three-dimensional spatial model that can be used to illuminate new information and access resources. A constellation is often described as a living map as it creates a physical representation that externalises an individual's (often unconscious) image of their system. Constellations are useful to get someone out of their head and beyond rational thinking. They also can help them to access a larger and less entangled picture of 'their system.'

Suggestions for using this in practice

Exercise 1: Inner Resource *Mapping*

The first exercise is useful when a mentee is feeling unresourceful in her situation and can be used to support her with accessing and acknowledging her inner resources. It is best used in an environment where you can use the physical space around you with ease. It would also be helpful to have a pack of Post-it notes or pieces of paper for this exercise.

Step 1: Invite your mentee to stand and face toward something visual (flip chart paper, Post-it note on the wall, a chair, for example) that represents the situation or element (person, dynamic, belief, for example) that is creating the feeling of being under-resourced or ill-equipped.

Step 2: Ask your mentee to define the situation or element in a short sentence. Encourage her to take a moment to connect to her felt-sense of this situation, which effectively is asking her to get out of her rational-thinking based mode of operating. To do this, it can be useful to ask her to take a few deep breaths and get her to connect to the physical sensations in her body (to feel the weight of her feet on the floor, for example).

Step 3: After a little while ask her to reflect on what resource she needs most to support her in this situation. A resource could be an inner quality (e.g. courage, wisdom, calm) or it could be a mental, emotional or physical resource. This is about helping your mentee get clear on what resources would be of most value to her in this situation even if she doesn't believe she has access to it at the moment.

Step 4: Ask your mentee to write down this resource on a Post-it note or piece of paper. Then ask her to find a place for this piece of paper in the space around her. In constellation work the space around a person all has meaning and there will be a right place for her that only she will know.

Step 5: Slowly repeat this process until the mentee has identified all the resources that she needs and has found a place for them around her. It is common that she will end up with Post-it notes all around the room, under her feet, behind her, in her pockets and even stuck to her head!

Step 6: Ask her to take a 'tour' of each of her resources. This involves simply looking at each piece of paper or Post-it note, reflecting on what it is offering and acknowledging what needs to be said that would deepen contact and integration with this resource. For example, this might mean that she says, 'I see resilience now but didn't see resilience before.'

Step 7: It can be useful for the mentee to take a photograph of her resource map on her phone as well as keeping the pieces of paper as a reminder.

Exercise 2: External Resource *Mapping*

This exercise is useful when someone is feeling like they are isolated or feeling the sense that they have to be strong and shoulder the challenges of their situation alone. This is a trait that I've found in senior executives who return to work after maternity leave; feeling like they have to be strong and independent, having difficulty asking for help and using the resources that are there in their system.

Step 1: Invite your mentee to stand and face toward something visual (flip chart paper, Post-it note on the wall, a chair, for example) that represents the situation or element (person, dynamic, belief, for example) that is evoking the feeling of being under-resourced or ill-equipped.

Step 2: Ask her to define the situation or element in a short sentence. Encourage her to take a moment to connect to her felt-sense of this situation, which effectively is asking the mentee to get out of her rational-thinking based mode of operating. To do this it can be useful to ask her to take a few deep breaths and get her to connect to the physical sensations in her body (to feel the weight of her feet on the floor, for example).

Step 3: After a little while ask your mentee to reflect on the first resource she has around them in the system. This could be her partner/spouse, her parents, siblings, friends outside work, her boss, work colleagues, her HR business partner, to name but a few.

Step 4: Ask her to write down this resource on a Post-it note or piece of paper. Then ask her to find a place for this piece of paper in the space around her. It is useful to pay attention to the distance that she places the piece of paper and encourage her to give a sense of what direction the resource is pointing in. In constellation work the space around a person all has meaning and there will be a right place for her that only she will know.

Step 5: Slowly repeat this process until the client has identified all the resources that she has and has found a place for them around her.

Step 6: Ask your mentee to take a 'tour' of each of her resources. This involves simply looking at each piece of paper or Post-it note, reflect on what it is offering and acknowledge what needs to be said that would deepen contact and integration with this resource. For example, this might mean that she says 'I see you now, but didn't see you before.'

Step 7: It can be useful for your mentee to take a photograph of her external resource map on her phone as well as keeping the pieces of paper as a reminder.

Our thanks to Nicky Lowe for this contribution. Nicky is an APECS accredited Executive Coach. (See www.luminate-coaching.co.uk)

Case study

Self-esteem and the returning parent (3)

In my experience as an Executive Coach supporting mothers returning to work after maternity leave, the most profound work I do is often linked to self-esteem.

In most cases, it is widely accepted that self-confidence is likely to be impacted after taking time out to have a child. As a result there are many tactical tools and strategies that can be used to help minimise this impact, even before someone goes on maternity leave. However, in my experience, less attention is paid to self-esteem and even less is known about what we can do to help with this. I think it is probably important to start by defining what I mean by these two terms, which are often mistakenly used interchangeably.

Self-confidence is linked to how we experience ourselves in our external world. It is how we experience ourselves in relation to other people, situations and circumstances. Our self-confidence is situation specific; for example, I feel confident as an Executive Coach but put me on stage to perform in an opera and I wouldn't feel confident. At its most simplistic level, self-confidence is linked to *what we do* – our behaviour. As a result, confidence is like a skill, we can learn to become more confident at something. The more we do something the more our confidence grows.

Self-esteem is linked to how we experience ourselves in our internal world. It is based on our inner sense of value and self-worth and is less directly linked to our external situation or circumstances. It is based more on a subjective general emotional evaluation of our sense of worth. At its most simplistic level, self-esteem is linked to *who we are*. This becomes a more fixed concept in our mind that forms our identity. That is why parents are encouraged to link criticism to a child at a behavioural level not an identity level; "what you've *done* is naughty" rather than saying "you *are* a naughty child."

(Continued)

This case study is from one of my coaching clients which I hope will bring the concept of self-esteem to life and what can be done to support someone returning from maternity leave whose self-esteem might have been negatively impacted.

My client, a senior executive, had taken 9 months off on maternity leave to have her first child. I had been asked to support her as an Executive Coach to ensure her smooth transition back into a demanding role in a large corporate organisation. I started working with her 4 weeks after her return back to work. In our first meeting it appeared that she was coping well balancing the demands of her role with being a mother. Four weeks into her role she was feeling more and more confident about getting up to speed with people, projects and her deliverables. Her network was still strong and she was getting positive feedback about the impact she was having in such a short space of time. However, I didn't experience her as someone that was thriving being back at work despite her surface appearance and articulation of all being well.

Through our initial discussion my belief was that her self-esteem had been weakened from her extended time out of the business and also from her transition into becoming a working mother – which in itself is a new identity to come to terms with.

When working with someone on self-esteem, there is a model that I hold in my mind that I developed when reading a book that was originally written in the 1960s by a plastic surgeon Maxwell Maltz. In his book *Psycho-Cybernetics* Maltz describes the psychological impact he witnessed in his patients when he changed facial disfigurements. He often experienced his patients having sudden changes in personality and character by changing their physical appearance. His book is focused on the concept of self-image which he describes as follows; '*each one of us carries with us a mental blueprint or picture of ourselves.*'

What I've come to understand and believe in my work is that a person's self-esteem is influenced by two key concepts:

1   Self-image
    A person's self-image is the internal image they hold about themselves and the person they believe themselves to be. It is rarely an actual reflection of reality. This is due to it being influenced by many factors over their lifetime. Our self-image is made up of various factors including:

    •   Physical description of who we are; e.g. I'm a woman, I'm short, I have blue eyes, etc.
    •   Social roles we have in life; e.g. I'm a manager, I'm a mother, I'm a wife, I'm a daughter, I'm a football supporter, etc.
    •   Personal traits; e.g. I'm a worrier, I'm driven, I'm conscientious, I'm lazy.

2 Self-ideal

A person's self-ideal is made up of the beliefs, standards and expectations that form a perception of how they would like to be. This perception could be a loose image of who they aspire to be based on their goals and values or it could be a carefully constructed image by which they hold themselves to high standards.

As illustrated in Figure 18.4, the closer together (i.e. similar or consistent) these two concepts are, the higher a person's self-esteem is likely to be. However, the further apart and the larger the discrepancy between a person's self-image and self-ideal, the lower their self-esteem is likely to be.

When working with my client, I decided to explore this concept with her and started getting curious about how she perceived herself (i.e. her self-image). To do this, I used questions to elicit her self-image. Examples of these questions would be:

- How would you describe yourself?
- What five words would you use to describe yourself?
- How would you finish this sentence 'I am …'?
- How would you finish this sentence 'I am not …'?
- What are you most proud of about yourself?
- What are you most conscious of?
- What do you see when you look in the mirror?
- What do you criticise yourself mostly for?

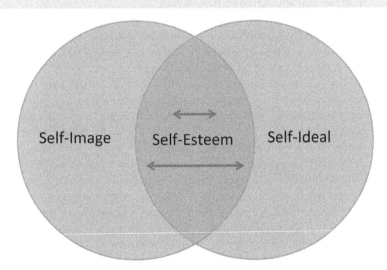

Figure 18.4 Self-esteem as a product of the relationship between self-image and self-ideal.

(*Continued*)

Through these questions I uncovered that she was holding an out-of-date and minimised self-image. For example, she hadn't taken into consideration all the amazing hurdles she had overcome as a new mother and the strength of character and resilience that navigating them demonstrates. Through questioning I was able to help my client realise the parts of herself that she hadn't acknowledged; for example, her strengths and achievements.

It is often useful to ask how other people would describe them (e.g. their partner, their colleagues, their parents) as this perspective often opens up more positive aspects of themselves as often other people can recognise things in us that we don't see in ourselves. Through our conversation, the ideals she was holding herself accountable to became apparent.

It is very common, in my experience, for high achieving executives to hold very high self-ideal expectations and standards. For example, my client talked about the common experiences of:

- Feeling guilty when they are at work, that they are not with their child and when they are with their child, feeling guilty about work.
- The struggle they are having coming to terms with the amount of time they can have with their child at the end of the working day.
- The feelings of guilt leaving the office 'early' to collect their child from childcare, when colleagues were still working in the office.
- The challenges of managing emails around the new demands of parenthood.
- The pressure they were putting themselves under to make home cooked food for their baby and family each night.

All of these challenges spoke to the unconscious standards and expectations that they had about themselves and about being a working parent. By exploring these standards and expectations, I could help my client to question how appropriate, how reasonable and how helpful they were for her. I invited her to write down these expectations and, where they were proving unhelpful, helped her to come up with more supportive and appropriate expectations. If the expectations were 'nonnegotiables' that she wasn't willing to let go of, I helped her come up with other strategies to help achieve them. This involved brainstorming options about how she could achieve the same outcome but with a different approach; for example, asking others for help.

The end result of this discussion was that my client had reframed and recalibrated her self-image and her self-ideal so that they were now more aligned. She had effectively updated her internal blueprint (Maltz). As a result, she was able to see and accept a lot more of her strengths and qualities. She also was kinder to herself on her self-ideal standards so that she was much less critical of herself for not meeting some unrealistic expectations.

Our thanks to Nicky Lowe for this contribution. Nicki is an APECS accredited Executive Coach (See www.luminate-coaching.co.uk)

Building good practice

We offer these tools and ideas as suggestions to build practice and enhance mentoring conversations with new parents. There are of course many additional resources that could be helpful to mentors in this context; see, for example, Megginson and Clutterbuck, *Techniques for Coaching and Mentoring* (2005) and *Further Techniques for Coaching and Mentoring* (2009). In a spirit of continuous learning, the invitation is to expand the portfolio, adapt, and invite mentors to create their own tools for parental mentoring and then practice, practice, practice!

19 Extending the maternity model to new fathers, same-sex couples, adoptive parents and more

The accounts and ideas contained within this book so far have been predominantly concerned with maternity. Research papers, articles, media reports and personal anecdotes all echo the sense of a fundamental uprooting and repatterning of life as the new mother navigates her way to early parenthood and return to work. Yet, are these issues and challenges unique to maternity? What of the uprooting and returns associated with new fathers, same-sex couples, and adoptive parents? Can the model for mentoring be extended? In the interests of building a diverse, inclusive workplace, the answer is an unequivocal yes. The transitions associated with becoming a parent absolutely affect new fathers, same-sex parents and adoptive parents.

In the UK, with the introduction of Shared Parental Leave in 2015, employers are increasingly moving toward inclusion and rebranding of programmes to family or parent mentoring. We note a number of our case study contributors are making this change; at the Royal Society of Chemistry, their Maternity Mentoring pilot has evolved into Parental Mentoring, CityMothers has become Cityparents, and Imperial College London launched their Parent Mentoring programme in 2016.

While the majority of parental leave continues to be women on maternity leave, these statutory changes are symbolic of the ambition to challenge gender stereotypes of the involvement of mothers and fathers in childcare and the benefits of shared parenting as a principle of good practice. Supporting new fathers so they can be confident in their new role is key to helping new mothers too. Avivah Wittenberg-Cox in her book *How Women Mean Business*, makes the case for taking a gender balanced approach to business practice concerning parenting: '*Companies will be able to retain and develop women as leaders only when they also allow men to be fathers. Companies welcoming women as full contributors and partners at every level in the workplace will make it easier for men to fulfill their responsibilities as parents. The same applies the other way round. Those which accept that men are full partners in parenthood will make it easier for women to fulfill their potential at work.*' (p. 254)

Add to this, the employee taking a sabbatical, a career break or ill health absence and in practice, mentoring someone returning from any form of extended absence from work can have a positive impact as they reflect on their transition out of work, to a different space with new experiences, personal challenges and opportunities for learning. In each of these circumstances, support for an individual's return is critical for exactly the same reasons as you might invest in maternity returners; to improve retention, engagement and fuel a more balanced talent pipeline.

That is not to take away from the diversity of these experiences. There will be issues unique to each situation and points of convergence. The power of mentoring lies in its central premise that puts the individual at the heart of the process. The mentee's emerging goals, questions, concerns and issues become the template for their particular learning journey and the mentoring relationship. The challenge for a programme manager is to have a ready pool of mentors with a range of experiences available to match to prospective mentees.

So what does our experience of mentoring maternity tell us about helping people in other circumstances where they too are absent from work for a period of time? Where do the similarities lie? What are some of the points of difference? This chapter offers insights into a range of experiences of extended absence and return to work through a series of illustrative case studies and commentary.

New fathers sharing parental leave

As noted earlier, in the UK, parents of babies born or children adopted after April 2015 now have the opportunity to take advantage of Shared Parental Leave (SPL). This change in legislation represented a significant move intended to give new parents greater flexibility and choice around who takes time off work and was a challenge to cultural and gender stereotypes of the role of mothers and fathers in early childcare.

So for a father considering shared parental leave, what might be some of the issues or concerns on his mind? These could include:

- Cultural attitudes and nervousness about approaching his employer to request time off (where perhaps it is not yet custom and practice for new fathers to take extended leave to care for a baby).
- The effect his absence may have on key projects, initiatives and his professional network.
- Being out of touch and disconnected from work for a period of time.
- Lack of external support networks with concerns around the possibility of domestic isolation.
- What this might mean for his next career move and senior sponsorship.
- Changing perceptions of his line manager and leadership team regarding his commitment to work.
- The implications of making future requests, e.g. flexible hours or changes to working practices in order to continue to support with childcare and family responsibilities post return to work.

For businesses actively looking to promote inclusion and family friendly working, the opportunity is there to challenge cultural attitudes and perceptions and find ways to encourage and support their pioneers. Our first case study is an extract from a Cityparents blog, and is a personal account of a father working part time and looking after his daughter 1 day each week. The message is clear; irrespective of gender, there are challenges for all parents when seeking to maintain a career on reduced (paid) hours (with all the assumptions from employers relating to viability of part-time working) while holding the space to be the parent they want to be. The question is whether the organisation recognises the opportunity (for the individual and itself) by improving practices around flexible working and offering offline support to work through just these types of issues and challenges. In this case, the risk is the loss of much needed talent and professional expertise.

Case study

James's blog: Falling asleep on the job...

I've come to the realisation that, unfortunately, my part-time working arrangements are not working. I notionally work a 4-day week in my profession and, on the fifth day, fulfil another job looking after my 2-year old daughter.

My weekly working hours are no fewer than my full-time peers; in fact they are generally more. And despite this I take home a reduced salary. That doesn't bother me though, if it means that I get to spend some quality time with my daughter. Unfortunately, however, that is not always the case. I invariably work until the early hours of the morning before my day off if, indeed, I manage to have that day off at all. And I invariably work late into the night on my day off once I've put my daughter to bed, and whenever I can over the weekend. I know that I'm not alone in making this complaint, and that I have it better than a great number of people but, quite frankly, I'm knackered.

Everything came to a head a few months ago when, on a couple of occasions, I fell asleep at home when I was supposed to be looking after my daughter. It's become clear to me that the sacrifices I'm making both at home and at work are not really paying off. So I thought that I'd have a look around to see whether there might be an alternative environment within which my part-time working arrangements could succeed.

The fact that I currently work a 4-day week has not been an impediment to other law firms being willing to meet with me to discuss other opportunities. However, when it comes to the offer stage, firms invariably stipulate that they see the particular role on offer as full-time, not part time. I know that these firms have fee-earners currently working part time. These are, however, normally fee-earners who have trained at the particular firm. Recruiting laterally into part-time roles seems a rarity.

Overall, I've found the process quite frustrating. I know that, with the correct team working around me, I could make part time working a success. Perhaps that is the problem though. It depends on having a supportive team around you, and perhaps my desire to work part-time puts additional stresses on the rest of the team.

At the moment foregoing that extra time with my daughter and the ability to keep her off nursery for a further day, is something which I can't bring myself to agree to. But I know that it is not sustainable. And so I'm starting to look at other opportunities outside of the career that I've studied 4 years for, and practised for a further 8 years. I'm aware that this career has given me a lot, and that it would be a shame to have to give up something that I enjoy and, I believe, am good at. But at the same time, I know that giving up quality time in my daughter's life would be a far greater shame. And so I'll keep searching for that utopia of work/life balance, in whatever job that may be.

James is in his early 30s and father to a beautiful 2-year-old girl. He now works 4 days a week at a City law firm, spending the fifth day of the week colouring, playing dolls with, and looking after, his daughter.

See more at: www.cityparents.co.uk/Blog/Cityfathers/293.htm#sthash. TG50WZev.dpuf

In our next case study, we hear from a professional couple employed by two large UK businesses who offer insights into their experience of shared parental leave. What is noticeable from their account is:

- Their equal commitment to their family, work and careers
- The value of a father having protected time with the new baby
- The benefit SPL offered the returning mother, able to resume work with a clear head and focus on the task, secure in the knowledge that her baby was in safe hands

Case study

Shared parental leave (UK)

The background

Our second child was an unexpected bonus with almost a 6-year gap after having had our first daughter. By the time she came along, my husband and I were both well established in senior roles, but with different employers. We have both always worked full time although we're able to manage our working hours and support each other when one needs to travel/stay late so we can cover our childcare needs.

The decision to share parental leave

James and I are on an equal footing in our careers and salaries and in addition, my employer offers a generous incentive for women to return after 9 months of maternity leave. So financially it made more sense for me to come back

(Continued)

at the point when statutory maternity pay stopped. Also, I had enjoyed a full year off with my first child and really wanted my husband to have some of what I had experienced. It was also important to us that she had a complete year at home before starting full-time childcare. The statutory changes in parental leave had happened since the birth of our first daughter, so we were keen to make the most of that.

Discussions with employers

James: I think my manager knew what the law allowed in terms of extended leave but was still surprised when I said I was going to take advantage of it. That said, she was completely supportive and positive about the opportunity it would give me to spend time with both my daughters. The HR team were really well informed and able to talk me through the process. I was taking 3 months off work, which isn't really long enough to merit getting someone in on a fixed-term contract to cover. We worked things out within the team though to make sure my role was covered. The whole team was actually in a state of flux at the time (I was coming to the end of a secondment) and so my manager and I sat down and worked out who would cover which elements of my role while I was off to make sure the job still got done.

Parental leave – the transition away from work

Sue: As a woman, this transition is pretty much determined for you. There's not much time or capacity for thinking about work once you've given birth and are dealing with the demands of a new baby. The challenges are far more acute in the return to work.

James: I had the easy end of the maternity leave. Isobel was 9 months old by the time I took my share of the time off. That meant she was pretty easy to look after and good company. I had no problem adjusting to life outside work. And it certainly helped me to clear my head of all work thoughts/worries and to relax in a way I hadn't for a long time. That's healthy and helped me on returning to work too.

The actual return

Sue: Unfortunately my return to work was pretty awful. I had no role to return to, no team and a different line manager. However, given my relative seniority and a strong network, I fought for the situation to be resolved and with some senior advocates managed to find a role, which was right for me and challenged me in all the right ways. As a mentor myself, I was aware of the likely emotional impacts of a return to work and was much better equipped to deal with this side of things following my second return to work.

James: I had no need for formal support. I had a supportive manager and a great team. I was just straight back into the swing of things – but I'll never forget the time I had with the girls.

Looking back

Sue: This decision was the best I ever made in my career. My return to work was difficult but never in relation to worrying about Isobel as I knew she was with the best possible carer. Seeing how she and James built their relationship in that 3 months and the sheer amount of fun that they had in that time was amazing and took all the pressure off me. All businesses should be actively advising colleagues to explore their options on parental leave.

James: It was a fantastic opportunity and I'm incredibly glad I took it. I know we're lucky to have been able to do this. Not many fathers feel able to do the same.

Our shared view. Employers should do everything they can to build awareness of SPL. There's still a long way to go to change attitudes and stereotypes.

While it is early days for Shared Parental Leave in the UK, other EU countries have had gender neutral paid leave in place for a number of years, with the aim of sharing the allowance more equally and seeing increasing numbers of fathers taking leave as a consequence; Sweden, for example, offers 480 days of parental leave with each parent entitled to 2 months of nontransferrable benefits (1).

It is reported that close to 90 percent of fathers take paternity leave at an average of 7 weeks (2). Germany offers working mothers and fathers equal entitlements and grants parental leave of up to 14 months (1) and Iceland has a 3-3-3 system of 3 months leave for each parent with the remaining 3 months shared (3).

There is a wealth of information and commentary to be found on the web. A number of links to recent press and web articles concerning shared parental leave are listed below:

1   www.newjurist.com/shared-parental-leave.html
2   www.economist.com/blogs/economist-explains/2014/07/economist-explains-15
3   www.theguardian.com/lifeandstyle/2015/apr/04/shared-parental-leave-new-era

What impact does this shared provision have in practice? Our next case studies are accounts from 3 parents in different European countries; a father taking parental leave in Denmark, a mother's perspective on sharing parental leave in Germany and a father's experience of paternity in Norway, all of which emphasise the value and importance of an inclusive approach to parenting.

Case study

Shared parental leave in Denmark – a father's perspective

According to EU research (see www.europa.eu), Danish parents are amongst some of the EU's most successful in balancing work and family responsibilities. The Danish Policy on families is designed with the starting principle of 'dual-earner' families and the system supports equal rights between men and women.

Mothers are entitled to 4 weeks of maternity leave before the expected date of birth and 14 weeks of maternity leave after the birth. Fathers are entitled to 2 weeks of paternity leave within the first 14 weeks after the birth. Significantly each parent is entitled to 32 weeks of parental leave.

Thomas was working as a Head Chef in a restaurant in Århus, Denmark and requested parental leave from his employer. Here is his perspective on the experience:

'At first, they were a bit against it, but we reached agreement and I got 26 weeks on full salary. I had no challenges finishing work. The parental leave was a good time and I had the privilege to watch my daughter's first 26 weeks at close hand. In terms of going back to work, I simply returned as if I hadn't been away. I didn't feel the need for any help, since I had kept in contact with my colleagues during the leave. It has been a great experience. In terms of the relationship between career and family, I have learned that NOTHING is more important than family…'

Case study

Shared parental leave in Germany – a mother's perspective

I'm French, though I live and have worked in Germany since 2003. I have two children (a girl aged 6 years and a boy aged 1.5 years old). In Germany, it is much easier to stay for several months at home and receive sufficient money from the government to take care of the children for at least 12 months without the need to work 'outside' (i.e. in employment.) For both children, I shared my maternity/parental leave with my partner 50/50. We took 14 months of parental leave of which we had 2 months together.

I think this has had, and will continue to make, a real impact on our understanding in terms of what it means to take care of children in daily life. My children have experience of a balanced parenting model, where it is quite normal to go to Daddy or Mummy for most of their needs (cuddles, handicraft work, sport, going to bed, eating, washing, etc.) I'm convinced that sharing parental leave is one of the most important foundations for a happy family and work life.

Senior Manager at PayPal

Case study

Paternity leave in Norway – a father's perspective

As a new parent, I felt that my life changed radically. Fortunately, the professional support system was good and effective. As a father I had 8 weeks' paternity leave, and my employer was very positive and flexible with this. While waiting for my turn to go on leave, I had positive expectations as how wonderful it would be, to be home with my new baby boy. In practice, I was in for a disappointment caused by my insecurity in the new situation and missing my workmates.

I realised that most men do not take the up the possibility offered by the state to take paternity leave. Consequently there were no postnatal groups for fathers, and to join a group only with women was out of the question I felt.

For me, I found enjoyment in the daily walks with the pram, and the opportunity to visit family and grandparents during the day. Eventually I got in contact with other fathers in my situation via Facebook, and that resulted in lots of shared trips and meetings. In spite of this, I felt socially isolated during the days, which I spent taking care of the baby and doing domestic work. In the evenings I did some work in order to feel connected with my workplace.

I loved going back to work again, to resume contact with my colleagues and to enter a structured day. Since our child has now a place in kindergarten, both my wife and I could go back to work. My experience was that my employer was very supportive when I returned to work. I was allowed to leave work without questions if I had to pick up my son from the kindergarten when he felt poorly. In Norway, as a parent with small children, you have the right to more sick leave days than other employees.

Looking back, it was a very positive experience to be home with a very young child. I bonded with him in a very deep and strong way. Your relationship with your child is formed during the first years of life, and I think it is of utmost importance for the child to bond with both mother and father.

The arrangement in Norway with paternity leave is very good, and in combination with kindergarten, family services and other public services this enables you to manage both your role as a parent and as an employee.

All in all, I will say that Norway is a great daddy country!

Manager within a public sector organisation

Adoptive parents

The decision to adopt a child can be made for a variety of reasons and there are set criteria for who may adopt a child and a rigorous process to follow before approval for adoption can be confirmed. In the UK currently the approval process typically takes around 6 months after which the applicant(s) can then be matched with a child for adoption. As with maternity provision, when someone takes time off to adopt a child, or have a child through surrogacy arrangement, they may be eligible for Statutory Adoption Leave and Statutory Adoption Pay. There may also be eligibility for Shared Parental Leave.

So in much the same way as someone may take time off for maternity or a father may take time off for parental leave, someone adopting a child will appropriately take leave from work to care for their new son or daughter. It follows therefore that many of the challenges in terms of close down, keeping in touch, planning for return and choices around return are also relevant in this context. However, given the particular circumstances for adoption, there may be specific concerns and challenges of which a mentor may need to be aware.

Some of the work-related issues that may be of concern to an adoptive parent may include:

- When and what to share with their line manager, employer, and team
- Managing expectations of the business in terms of timescales from approval to adoption once a child has been matched
- Dealing with emotions, frustrations and barriers through the process
- Challenging assumptions and stereotypes
- Helpful terminology for a new identity (e.g. referring to a mother as opposed to an adoptive mother)
- External support networks
- Keeping in touch during adoption leave (as with early maternity leave, there is likely to be limited or no contact for the first few months after the child arrives, for reasons of attachment and bonding)

Our next case study offers insights into an adoption leave.

Case study

Becoming a parent via adoption

My career has always been very important to me. Over a period of 20 years, and through a series of increasingly complex roles and project teams, I succeeded in becoming a director of a large blue chip organisation. I remain very proud of this.

On a personal level as a married couple, our intention was always to start a family; however, following treatment for breast cancer our dreams of becoming parents took a different direction. We decided to investigate adoption and whether we would be suitable candidates. This is a very challenging time as there are so many difficult routes to explore before adoption becomes the solution. As much as the child has a process to follow, so do adoptive parents. It is a soul searching time as you are presented with case studies of children who come forward for adoption and the challenges you will face as their prospective 'forever family'.

At this stage the conversations are between the two of you as partners and no real discussion is needed with any other parties at that point. I did however begin to question aspects of my job role and the potential impact of having a child even at this early stage in the process. We always wanted as young a child as possible, which meant one of us would have to give up work for a period of time to care for our new child. As I was the higher earner, it was not automatic that it would be me who would give up work.

We were assigned an experienced social worker who supported us throughout a lengthy and extensive application process. Early on in the process, the request was made for an employer reference which was done discreetly and in confidence by the HR team. At that point we were not ready to be open about our plans to our wider teams, nor did we want our respective line managers to be concerned with contingency planning for an adoption leave before we had had official sign off.

We finally met our first child a year and a half from the start of the application process.

In the UK, the point at which you are required to inform your employer of your intention to adopt is when the matching certificate has been issued. The challenge then is that adoptive parents can be matched with a child within 4 weeks. (Contrast this with maternity, where the majority of women are able to share their pregnancy with their employer once the initial 12-week period has passed, thereby giving them 4 to 5 months' notice of the start of maternity leave.) As a director, this would not have been realistic in terms of my role and responsibilities. So in the interests of the business and doing the right thing, I informed my line manager once we knew we were approved to adopt a child. Approval and then matching can take between 6 weeks and a year.

Privately the questions we had on our mind included:

- Considerations of work and career. How we would manage if one of us was to step out of work? What would the impact be?
- Which of us would take time off?
- What was the difference between adoption leave and maternity leave?
- What did we need to share with our employer in terms of time commitments for training courses, introductions and phased handover from foster parents?
- What messages did we want to communicate – to reassure our employers of our commitment to the business, but also to indicate a shift, a rebalancing of life and our future commitment as parents to our forthcoming child?

In fact, my employer was very supportive and good discussions were had about what was happening and next steps. Our little girl arrived with us after just 10 days of introductions. She was just 9 months old and we were delighted. The change was immediate – to go from managing a team and

(Continued)

working full time to being a mother in a matter of weeks, with both physical and emotional challenges as I transitioned into a new role as a mother for the first time. Work quickly became a very distant memory.

There is always a worry when you take leave of absence from a business after so many years' service. Away from the workplace and on adoption leave, I wondered:

- What will I do in a year or 9 months' time when my leave ends?
- What will have changed?
- Will I want to go back?
- What will happen to my child if I go back?
- Do I have time to give the role now I am a parent?
- Can we afford for me to be off for longer?
- Who is looking out for me in work now I am not present at the table?
- Could my role work part time?
- Is my boss understanding enough to support me?
- Who will support me when I go back?
- Who do I talk to about all these questions I have?

While the journey to becoming an adoptive parent is very different, I have a sense these questions are as typical for an adoptive parent as they are for someone returning from maternity or parental leave. A supportive mentor within the organisation would have been a powerful means of support to me at this time.

In fact, my career journey has since taken a whole new direction as I now embark on setting up my own business. It fits with the timings and needs of both my adopted children at this moment in time. Adoption is a delightful, wonderful and rewarding gift to be given and has given us so much joy as a family.

Thoughts a business may like to consider

- Where you have a parent going through the adoption process, there is value in having a professional expert in to share information about adoption with a view to understanding what specific support may be most helpful at different times.
- Understanding the timeframes associated with adoption and potential impact on the business when planning for cover and handover, for example.
- The emotional roller coaster of the journey for the individual going through the adoption process from approval to matching.
- Is there a mentor available to support in your pool of mentors?
- Connecting with other adopting parents within the organisation can help and open a new network of support.

Same-sex couples

Deciding to becoming a parent within a same-sex relationship also brings questions and choices; whether to foster, to adopt, to involve donors and or surrogates – as well as considerations of caring responsibilities and continuation of work and careers. Our next two case studies offer insights into the challenges associated with gay professional couples becoming parents firstly through international surrogacy and secondly through adoption. What becomes apparent from these accounts is:

- In the first case study, the emotional journey undertaken through a complex surrogacy process
- Both surrogacy and adoption processes occur in parallel with busy work schedules requiring time and flexibility on the part of the individuals and their employers
- The essential value of support for new parents – both in work and in the community
- The challenges of making the transition to being a new parent and combining this with work and career are there irrespective of gender
- Life alters and priorities change fundamentally when you become a parent again irrespective of gender

Case study

A new family through surrogacy

We have two-year-old twins by means of a surrogacy arrangement. As parents we are both senior professionals; I am a lawyer and a partner of a private high street firm with a City background, my partner is an academic and senior psychologist in the National Health Service.

As a gay couple embarking on surrogacy, we had less options open to us than a lesbian couple might in terms of becoming parents. In my experience, very few lesbian couples opt for surrogacy unless they are unlucky, and the process of pregnancy and giving birth in a lesbian relationship in many respects simulates heterosexual parenting, i.e. typically both partners are together during pregnancy, one partner gives birth and the provision for maternity leave, care and support is in place. Gay couples simply don't have the biological option of pregnancy, and have to go abroad to have their children. In our case we went to South Africa.

Support is vital during a surrogate pregnancy taking into account the geographical distance, different cultures and socioeconomic backgrounds. It takes a huge amount of effort and can be very stressful financially and emotionally. I wanted to be part of the journey and the procedure and went to South Africa four times during the pregnancy. The first scan was priceless, however, there were emergencies (and of course you can't always be there)

(Continued)

doctors, lawyers and courts to contend with. By the time the twins arrived I was shattered.

Once the twins were born I had to be in South Africa for 3 months to complete legal arrangements. Being self-employed I own half the law firm, so I had some flexibility, but as a lawyer if you don't do the work you can't bill the hours. My partner has a number of different hats, so it was very tricky for him to make multiple arrangements, coupled with the fact that his primary employer offers no entitlement to parental leave without a UK court order.

In South Africa, the legal process is slick; we had our first visit in December, received the appropriate court order in April, our surrogate mother was pregnant in May (using donor eggs) and by January we became the parents to our own children born of the surrogacy process, i.e. Parent 1 and Parent 2. Unfortunately, South African jurisdiction and UK jurisdiction don't dovetail with each other. In the UK, the surrogate mother who gives birth is still presumed to be the mother of the infant. There is a requirement for the UK courts to process a parental order, which means you are not legally recognised as the parents of your children in circumstances of surrogacy until the court says you are. We have been waiting for a year and a half for this (so far), which contrasts with an adoption order that gives you parental responsibility and the ability to then claim parental leave from that point.

It's a complex process. In terms of support, unless you've got someone to speak to who's got experience, you really don't know what you're in for and eventually you're in at the deep end. I found friends and family the best place to start. Moral support came from my sisters-in-law and various gay friends and couples in similar situations. Before the twins' birth I found a gay dad's group and met other professional couples who were also aspiring parents. Their experiences gave me encouragement, and inspiration knowing it could be done. One father worked for a large multinational organisation, which was amazing. He had 6 months paid leave, flexi time and because of the nature of Internet work, was able to work from home. In contrast, in my own work context, we are a small firm and not in a position to offer the same level of flexibility and support. The older lawyers wondered why I was doing this and since becoming a parent have never once asked about the children. It's a subject never broached which is disheartening.

When planning our family and life as a working family, we realised we had to be realistic about what we could do and set up our support system. We had a full time maternity nurse for 5 months, which helped immensely. She knew how to do everything! That being said, the early months were the toughest. I was working a full day and coming home to the twins needing three to four feeds each over the course of an evening/night and then going into work the following day to do a full day's work again. It was very difficult. I had a brilliant friend who is a grandmother of 14 children who supported us in the absence of close family (my mother is 6000 miles away). She was just the most wonderful person to have around. There were times when I hadn't slept for 4 days. She would come in and I could sleep for a few hours, knowing my son and daughter were being looked after. That kind of support goes a long way. Sleep gives you your humanity back.

As a couple, there are challenges in terms of decisions around parenting and who will be the primary carer. It may not be a 50/50 split. My experience is that gay couples tend to be similar level professionals; one may be a judge partnered with a brain surgeon, another a director with their partner perhaps a clerk in the House of Lords, so where they are more on a par professionally, there can be a struggle in terms of who gives up time and managing competing pressures and demands; *'I have to go to court'* versus *'I have a patient with Ebola.'* In our situation this was a full-time lawyer and full-time psychologist and we had to get our heads around that.

It sounds a lot worse than it actually was! The story is actually very positive and we now have two beautiful children of our own. As a teenager, the thought of being a gay parent was crazy. We've come a long way.

Case study

Same-sex adoption

Nick is a partner in a global law firm. He and his husband were approved for adoption both in the UK and US. They adopted a baby girl privately 5 years ago.

I was a partner in the UK branch of a law firm and the first openly gay partner to have a child. At the time (5 years ago), there was no provision for how an employer should deal with same-sex parents adopting a child. That being said, my husband and I were both fortunate to work for enlightened employers who were willing to be as accommodating as possible and asked us what we wanted. As a partner in the firm, I was entitled to take an extended sabbatical; however, it is a busy practice and so I requested 3 months' adoption leave. My husband is a psychologist and he was the one who stopped work in order to become the primary carer for our daughter. I recognise we're in a fortunate position to be able to do that; however, since she is an only child, we were keen to get as much stability as possible. He is home most of the time for her.

Looking back, I underestimated the extent to which you actually want to spend a lot more time as a family than you ever thought you would. I come from a generation of gay men, who went through life never expecting to become a parent. In my mind, I never really thought of, nor wanted kids. I just never contemplated it as a possibility. Having once discounted it, I am now happily married as a gay man and have an adopted daughter!

My experience has taught me that once you have a child, all of your priorities change and your perspective on life alters dramatically. I see that amongst straight colleagues when they become parents too. Pre-children, people in

(Continued)

jobs like mine find themselves working 14 to 16 hour days. Work is what drives you. It is all encompassing and there is very little time for a home life. Most people are over achieving nutters! Then suddenly the surprise is you've got something else which is as important and a bigger priority.

We now live in New York City, the drivers for the move to the United States being all about my daughter and her well-being. In the UK, we had very few friends with kids, whereas in the US, my husband has an extensive family network and we have lots of relatives around us all with children or grandchildren. If someone had told me 5 years ago we'd have modelled our life on our family and social circles, I would not have believed them!

We have very little formal mentoring in the workplace for parents. Typically I think it happens informally with discussions around practicalities, the shock of being new parents, how to adjust etc. As a law firm, there is an acceptance that people from different minorities need different forms of mentoring. I support the LGBT network here and globally there are opportunities for more senior gay lawyers to offer mentoring support. The partners need to recognise that not everyone is from the same mould and of course parenting is just another example of that.

Further information

The NHS offers guidance and further links relating to gay health, and having children at: www.nhs.uk/Livewell/LGBhealth/Pages/Havingchildren.aspx

Stonewall is the largest lesbian, bi-sexual, gay and transgender (LBGT) rights organisation in Europe. They have really helpful information on parenting rights, including adoption, fostering and surrogacy; www.stonewall.org.uk/help-advice/parenting-rights.

The P3 Network www.p3network.com offers a network of support specifically for LGBT parents, prospective LGBT parents and parents of LGBT children. They aim to offer support for social engagement, a forum for sharing experiences and positive role models for parents working in law, finance and professional services in 'the City' (London).

The career break/returners from extended absence

At a recent line manager workshop, we outlined the different stages of maternity and the role of the line manager in supporting the individual through this time of transition. In the subsequent discussion, one participant shared the fact that he had recently returned from a 6-month career break and that our description of maternity leave and associated challenges resonated with his experience of taking a career break. The challenges he described included:

- The pressure associated with ending, closing down and leaving everything 'in a good place'

- Dealing with the unknown, creating a new life away from work (the thing that had defined him previously)
- The fear of someone else doing 'your job'
- Questions and concerns relating to choices for what to return to and when
- The need to regain confidence coming back to work

In his words, "*It was like being on maternity leave without the sleepless nights or the trauma of going through pregnancy.*'

A senior leader within a large blue chip organisation, we share his experience of his 6-month career break and subsequent return to work. Where his comments resonate with similar stages and experiences within the maternity model, these areas have been highlighted in *italics.*

Case study

Career break

I'd been on this treadmill for the last 10 years and it all felt very linear. I was worried I was going to get to a certain point and look back and think 'What was all that for?' My wife had the idea we should invest £200 a month in getting a babysitter and going out for a meal every other Thursday. Even though it was money we hadn't got, we could find it because if we broke up, it would cost a fortune to pay the alimony, I would have to find another girlfriend, woo her (that would cost a fortune), and then I would have to find another house (i.e. thousands of pounds). So what is £200 a month when compared with that?

Here I was, pre a mid-life crisis trying to chuck in positive disruption rather than waiting for what I felt could be inevitable. I could sense bits of it coming. I was interested that when you leave school, and leave university, the only people you have regular contact with are in work and then there's your strained relationship with your other half. It's because you're tired, they're tired, the kids are hard work and you don't really go out with each other much. I could see where it was going.

In work, I'd reached that point where I knew something had to give. Because of the nature of my job, you never know quite what is going to appear until it appears. I just got to the point where I was beginning to be ground down by it all and I knew I needed to take a break.

Roller-coaster (from relief to paranoia). As soon as I told my line manager and the rest of the team, *it was like a load was lifted from my head because I knew I was going and there was a big adventure in front of me.* My line manager was brilliant – so supportive. *The downside of that though was that I started to think … he wants to get rid of me* and that's why he is so supportive! (In practice, he had spent 3 years abroad and had seen the benefit of being able to go away and reinvent yourself.) I was typecast and was probably getting to the point where there was nowhere else to go.

(Continued)

Building up to leaving, *I didn't want my legacy to be the man who walked out and left a load of problems.* That was quite a good burning platform! I left at the end of June and had a month before we went travelling. There was something about the physical handing back of the Blackberry with the little flashing red light. It was weird, like *my comfort blanket of importance:* that red flashing light meant somebody needs me and *suddenly nobody needed me.* All my male friends were working, so the only people I had interaction with from work were my female friends who were either on maternity leave and/or worked part time. I would be twitchy, feeling I should be doing something. It felt weird making the transition.

I did take the kids to and from school, but the day was so short! Before then, I would have been working when the Blackberry went on in the morning, (i.e. from half six and on the train) and suddenly there was none of that. I'd get the kids ready, take them to school, walk the dog, sit down to write, make a bit of toast and then it would be nursery pick up at half past twelve. I'd keep her occupied, and then it was half past three and time to get my other daughter. I volunteered for Help the Aged, learned how to be a radio presenter, and then we went travelling. *It was brilliant. Getting to know the kids and actually spending time as a family.* I was almost feeling guilty that I needed time to get to know my own children.

Planning the return was an emotional turmoil. I met my line manager in the October before returning in January. *I thought it was going to be one of those great meetings where he was going to tell me how much they were missing me.* But no there were changes ahead and it was all about him. Words to the effect of 'By the time you get back I might be gone and you might have a new boss and everything will be changed.' I wanted him to say 'Everything has fallen apart since you've gone' (it hadn't) and I can't wait for you to come back and of course, we will do everything we can to accommodate you.' I felt I had been shot through the heart. There might be unrealistic emotions going through you. It was just my pride getting in the way.

I needed to ask myself, *'Just what do you want to come back to?' and I needed to start making that clear.* Over a week, I wrote down everything I was going to want. I wanted to find a role where I could be celebrated for the things I am great at. *My godfather used to do a lot of management consultancy and helped me frame a conversation with my boss and senior leaders.* I was ready to come back. I had travelled, I had tried to write the book, I had got into research mode and I could see the opportunity. I found I was not constrained in the way I thought I was. *I was ready to go in and show them what I could do and I think that gave me the confidence to come back more on my terms.*

The first week I was back I heard someone say 'He's on fire, isn't he!' It was like I had my mojo back. *Those 6 months away had given me energy, a bit more confidence, and made it clear what I wanted and what I didn't want.*

Work/life balance is just non-negotiable. I want to be coming to work at a reasonable time in the morning, for me that is 8.30 a.m. not 7 a.m. and leave at 5.30 so I am home at 6.15. I manage expectations.

Looking back, my career break took the blinkers off. *All the things I learned in the career break I have since brought back into work with me.*

Senior Leader
Blue chip organisation

Long-term absence

An employee on leave of absence for health reasons can face many similar challenges as described by returning parents and career break returners. Feeling out of touch with current business plans and agendas, disconnected from peers and their previous networks can have a significant impact on someone's confidence and self-belief in terms of coming back to work. The difference in this situation is the health of the individual, which may have meant immediacy of departure (so perhaps no opportunity to 'close down' well) and may also have prevented them from keeping in touch. Aside from any occupational health provision, it follows that mentoring may also be helpful as a means of offline support to help someone regain confidence as they return to work. Mentoring in this situation has a requirement for clear contracting and goal setting, being clear where the boundaries are so as not to confuse this with any medical or therapeutic support.

Some of the specific issues that may be of concern to the individual returning after illness may include:

- Managing expectations of colleagues in work
- Conversations to request adjustments, or flexibility of working arrangements
- Confidence, personal resilience and capability
- Managing perceptions of others
- Ongoing and future considerations of health and well-being
- Future career choices

Bringing the learning together

With the ambition to extend the model for mentoring, we have prepared a visual summary (Figure 19.1) to give an indication of points of similarity and points of difference between various groups of individuals who may be away from the workplace for extended time including:

- New parents:

  - Mothers on maternity
  - Fathers taking shared parental leave

- ○   Adoptive parents
- ○   Same-sex parents

- •   Career break/sabbatical returners
- •   Returners from long-term illness

The topics shown are not intended to be an exhaustive list. Rather they are designed to illustrate what may be relevant and important to the particular individual. What becomes clear is the potential for overlap in terms of issues and challenges, some of which you can prepare your mentors for but also that there are inevitably going to be questions or concerns determined by a mentee's specific circumstances. For a programme manager, the key is to take an inclusive approach when it comes to sourcing mentors, aiming for a diverse range of backgrounds and experiences. It is also important to invest in specific up-skilling for mentors, to raise collective awareness by exploring topics such as unconscious bias in order to ensure they come to their mentoring relationships with an open mind. As these relationships progress, it is then about capturing learning and insights in order to build depth of experience and good practice for future mentors and mentees.

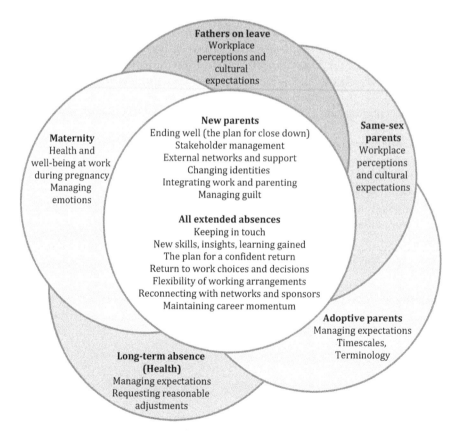

Figure 19.1 Extending the model for support across a range of extended absences.

20 Towards a research agenda for maternity and parental mentoring

There is a wealth of academic and formal research literature concerning gender diversity and the nature of women's advancement and progression in organisations; however, the message to the would-be researcher is to approach the subject area with caution and clarity of purpose:

> Prepare to enter the labyrinth...
> Even a cursory glance at the literature about women in management shows there is a great danger of meandering and digressing: the subject is so vast and hard to crack!
> Averil Leimon et al. *Coaching Women to Lead* (2011, preface)

Despite the volume of literature, there has been limited academic research into maternity coaching or mentoring per se and the specific contribution of these forms of support to a woman's personal development and engagement with her career as a working mother. In this chapter, we offer a number of brief insights from literature and an overview of two related research projects and marketplace practice. Finally, we set out a tentative framework for research in an ambition to build momentum and increase knowledge and understanding of the specific contribution of internal mentoring and coaching at this key transition point.

Current understanding

The overwhelming view from the literature is that women's career paths are complex and distinct from men's (Leimon 2011, O'Neil and Bilimoria 2005, Mainiero and Sullivan 2005, Wittenberg-Cox 2010). O'Neil refers to women's careers as '*embedded in their larger life contexts*' (p. 173) while Mainiero and Sullivan (2005) suggest women's career decisions are made through '*a lens of relationalism*' (p. 111), incorporating the needs of others (children, partners, ageing parents, and even friends). This stands in marked contrast to men who typically draw a distinction between career and family, and whose career decisions tend to be more linear and focused on professional goals (Mainierio et al. 2005, Wittenberg-Cox 2010).

If maternity is the metaphorical fork in the road that causes many women to '*off ramp*' (Hewlett 2005), then the interesting discovery is that this is frequently not the focus of discussion. McKinsey's report 'Women Matter' (2012) argues that the majority of debate and analysis of women's representation centres on senior positions, but '*what often goes unmentioned is the pipeline that feeds those positions*' (p. 7). They reference '*leaks and blockages in different parts of the pipeline*' indicating that '*finding ways to support women at a mid-career point, particularly where this converges with children would "reshape the pipeline"*' (2012, p. 2).

As noted earlier, within the report, McKinsey benchmarked the diversity programmes of 235 European companies. Their research indicated that the best performing companies had a '*critical mass of initiatives*' in place and that these initiatives were contained within a '*supporting ecosystem*' (p. 1). Sixty-three per cent of companies had at least 20 different initiatives in place as part of their gender diversity programmes. Within this list of initiatives were in fact a number of programmes – including coaching 'to smooth transition before, during and after maternity leave' (p. 23).

Related research

In 2008, Joy Bussell published a UK research article entitled 'Great Expectations: Can Maternity Coaching Affect the Retention of Professional Women?' Her paper looked at the specific issues encountered by a small group of high achieving professional women, combining work with having children. Bussell's research identified the value of coaching, the pressures and conflicts associated with the '*new dual role*' of the returning mother and suggested the transition to be more complex and longer than had previously been assumed. Her research indicated that issues were less about returning to work and much more about retention and the need for coaching support across a series of distinct transition points. With that in mind, the recommendation was for short-term and longer-term coaching interventions:

> Where organisations are seeking to retain, nurture and develop women at the height of their professional lives, coaching – both maternity coaching in the short term and executive coaching in the long term – offer a solution to the "brain drain" of professional female talent'. In her view, external coaching offered 'expert support' and was a valuable means of 'identifying and achieving their professional and life goals in an environment in which challenge, balance and authenticity are paramount.' However, Bussell also offered a warning: 'In isolation, where organizational culture and inflexible working policies prevail, maternity coaching can only offer a sticking plaster.

A later study by Claudia Filsinger (2012) considered the way maternity coaching influences women's re-engagement with their career. Filsinger found that maternity coaching influenced career re-engagement factors at an emotional level (for example, a perceived sense of value from the business' investment in them personally and also a positive influence on confidence), while also offering practical guidance (relating to decisions around working patterns and requests for flexible working, for example) and offered opportunities for longer-term career reflection. Finsinger found coaching '*supported women in finding the right quality and quantity of work appropriate for their experience and availability. This is an important foundation for achieving work-life balance, in particular for women who work part time, but also for faster re-engaging with career development'* (p. 53).

While internal maternity mentoring is not well publicised, external maternity coaching is now widely available and has been in place in the UK for over 10 years. Maternity coaching is a growing industry in the UK with a number of skilled and expert providers including Talking Talent, My Family Care, and Talent Keepers, who enjoy established long-term client relationships across a wide variety of organisations. In contrast with the two academic studies above, (where research samples were limited to a small group of women and based on legal firms), the size and range of clients has enabled these external providers to work with large numbers of returning mothers and in doing so, to develop evidence-based strategies in the context of volume of data, anecdotal accounts and case studies. Information and case studies relating to some of the client organisations can be found on their websites with additional information referenced in practitioner articles: Harrison (2008), Freeman (2008) and Sparrow (2006). Collectively, these make a powerful case for the value of supporting the transition to parenthood and return to work.

So the question for this publication is this: Does that support work best when it is offered from outside or from within an organisation? How does the nature of the support differ between the two? Is it a question of external versus internal support, or is there a place for a blended approach? Where is the evidence – other than simply cost – which makes the case to support the introduction of an internal mentoring programme?

The Ridler Report, which analyses strategic trends in the use of executive coaching, noted an increasing trend toward the use of internal coaches in its 2013 report. Seventy-nine per cent of the 145 participating organisations reported they were investing in building their internal coaching capability over the next 3 years. One of the principal reasons given was the belief that internal coaches understand their businesses better than external coaches. Cost efficiency was also reported as a significant driver in the growth which gave 'a wider population of managers and leaders access to coaching especially those who are not the most senior leaders' (p. 8). Subsequently, the Ridler Report 2016 reported a continuation of the trend toward internal coaching, with 70 per cent of the 105 participating organisations having internal coaching capability in place and 75 per cent expecting an increase in internal coaching over the next 2 years.

The top drivers of investment in internal coaching included:

- To make coaching more easily accessible when it is needed (81 per cent)
- To widen the availability of coaching to less senior executives who have not traditionally had access to coaching (73 per cent)
- To be able to coach more individuals for a given budget (64 per cent)

This may be of particular significance in the context of maternity where the volume typically occurs at middle to early senior levels of leadership. Interestingly, as we write this book, Ernst and Young (EY) have brought their Career and Family

Coaching in house for the first time. The EY Exec Coaching Team now provides 1:1 coaching for their senior managers, partners and directors and group coaching by webinar and 1:1 support for managers and below. This is delivered by the EY Talent Centre which also provides career coaching support to junior staff and hosts webinars for managers of employees going on maternity/parental leave. Additional mentoring support is also available through their EY Parents' Network. (See Chapter 3 for the EY Case study.)

Clearly not all businesses have the financial resources to secure the help of external specialists for the long term. If the Ridler Report is indicative of wider marketplace trends then perhaps momentum is building for internal support for new parents, making use of talent from within the organisation, who have experience and knowledge of the business and who, with appropriate support and preparation, can offer support as a long-term and sustainable solution for returning parents.

What is needed is currency of research which evidences the specific impact of internal support on the retention, performance and progression of professional women and parents more generally as they transition to working parenthood.

A research agenda

The issue of gender diversity and the impact of maternity remain crucial agendas for exploration and continued focus; however, the advent of shared parental leave also tells us there are implications for offering support to men as they work through the transition to fatherhood. While it may be early days for the UK, Scandinavian countries are much more advanced in terms of cultural expectations of shared parenting and take up of shared parental leave. What we have yet to discover is the extent to which mentoring can support returning fathers just as much as mothers and the nature of what gets brought to mentoring in service of a positive return and re-engagement with career. There is also a need to broaden the research and understand the differences across geographical areas and countries with different provisions and cultural expectations around maternity/parental leave and subsequent return to work and career.

Are you a business who has an internal programme for mentoring new parents already in place? Perhaps you are about to introduce parental mentoring for the first time? We invite you to be part of the emerging picture evidencing the experience and value of internal maternity and parental mentoring to organisations through new research. We are interested to understand more about the following areas:

- The drivers for the introduction of parental mentoring in a business

  - The nature of the business context
  - Any additional provision for maternity/parental leave (over and above statutory arrangements)
  - Volume of maternity/shared parental leave and attrition rates
  - The levels at which maternity and shared parental leave occur
  - Talent ratings of employees pre- and post leave
  - Levels of retention post return

- **The wider cultural context and constellation** of support that sits around working parents – positive indicators which support the agenda more broadly, e.g. blend of external coaching and internal mentoring, buddy systems for support, networks – formal or informal, circles, online forums and communities, line manager preparation and support mechanisms
- Learning from parental mentoring

  - Insights in relation to the transition
  - Levels of expenditure to set up and maintain programmes (e.g. external support at set up and/or additionally for supervision/ongoing development of mentors)
  - Benefits for the individuals, the mentors, the business
  - Challenges and difficulties
  - Supervision of internal mentors
  - The longer-term impact of parental mentoring on the gender balance of a talent pipeline
  - Recommendations and insights for other organisations

- The psychology of a return to work
- A systemic analysis of absence and return to work – identification of the factors affecting positive and negative indicators

If you would be willing to offer your internal parental programme as a case study for research, we'd be delighted to hear from you.

We invite you to get in touch with us:

nicki@theparentmentor.co.uk or david@davidclutterbuckpartnership.com

In conclusion

Having a baby obviously brought different experiences and changed the way I was and who I am. My mentor was able to create a space for me where I felt completely safe to say how I was feeling. I was able to go into that room and know with utter confidence I could say "today was a good day", or "today I didn't really want to leave my son." She was able to help me work through what those feeling were and order them.

I think sometimes women think they can have it all and what I've learned is that it's not easy. You have to work really hard at it and you have to switch between being mother and being professional and career driven. What I did in the first instance was beat myself up, that on day one I didn't walk back into the office being ready for my next promotion. Given time and given the space to understand myself, and the process and everything I was going through, you can do it. I think the whole mentoring process sped up my return and was a catalyst for getting me back to being myself in the workplace. I'm in a much better place now and looking for the next challenge whatever that might be.

(Manager, Royal Society of Chemistry)

With increasing numbers of women returning to work post maternity, fathers taking shared parental leave, same-sex parenting and adoption, the transition associated with leaving work and subsequent collision of career and parenting we know is not confined to one or two individuals. The story is repeated time in and time out, and if we take a moment to notice, it is happening in front of us right now. It is a story of change, of multiple endings and new beginnings, new experiences, questions, choices, challenges and at the heart a new life. We have Sheehy's words (p. xxi) in mind when we reflect on the unique potential that mentoring offers in flexing to meet the needs of the individual, yet taking comfort from the fact that there is a place for generalisations that may be helpful to plan for effective support.

Employees will continue to become parents – our challenge as employers is to engage in that journey, using the talent and experience from within the organisation, supporting the transition to working parenthood and, in doing so, ultimately the organisation becomes supported too.

References

Amabile, T., Kranes, S. (2011) *The Power of Small Wins*. www.hbr.org/2011/05/the-power-of-small-wins. Accessed November 2015.

Bachkirova, T., Jackson, P., and Clutterbuck, D. (2011) *Coaching and Mentoring Supervision: Theory and Practice*. Open University Press, McGraw-Hill, England.

Batista, E. (2014) The Art of Saying a Professional Goodbye. *Harvard Business Review*. www.hbr.org/2014/05/the-art-of-saying-a-professional-goodbye. Accessed August 2015.

Bussell, J. (2008) Great expectations: Can maternity coaching affect the retention of professional women? *International Journal of Evidence Based Coaching and Mentoring*. Special Issue No. 2, 14–26.

Chivers, J. (2011) *Mothers Work! How To Get A Grip On Guilt and Make A Smooth Return To Work*. Hay House UK Ltd.

Clutterbuck, D. (2004) *Everyone Needs A Mentor*. 4th ed. CIPD Chartered Institute of Personnel and Development, London, England.

Clutterbuck, D. (2011) *Mentoring and the Gender Agenda*. www.general physics.co.uk/downloads/Mentoring-and-the-gender-agenda-v1.0-Oct-2011(216).pdf. Accessed May 21, 2012.

Clutterbuck, D. (2014) *Everyone Needs A Mentor*. 5th ed. CIPD Chartered Institute of Personnel and Development, London, England.

Clutterbuck, D. and Lane, G. (2004) *The Situational Mentor: An International Review of Competences and Capabilities in Mentoring*. Gower, Aldershot.

Cox, E., Bachkirova, T., and Clutterbuck, D. (2010) *The Complete Handbook of Coaching*. SAGE, Los Angeles, CA.

Cranwell-Ward, J., Bossons, P., and Gover, S. (2004) *Mentoring: A Henley Review of Best Practice*. Palgrave Macmillan, New York, NY.

Daloz, L. (1999) *Mentor: Guiding the Journey of Adult Learners*. Jossey-Bass, San Francisco, CA.

DeHaan, E. (2012) *Supervision in Action. A Relational Approach to Coaching and Consulting Supervision*. Open University Press, McGraw-Hill Education, England.

EMCC. (2004). *Guidelines on Supervision: An Interim Statement*. www.emccouncil.org. Accessed June 29, 2012.

Figes, K. (2008) *Life After Birth*. Virago Press, London, England.

Filsinger, C. (2012) How can maternity coaching influence women's re-engagement with their career development: a case study of a maternity coaching programme in UK-based private law firms. *International Journal of Evidence Based Coaching and Mentoring*. Special Issue No. 6. http://ijebcm.brookes.ac.uk/documents/special6-paper-04.pdf (Accessed September 2015).

Flanagan, C. (2015) *Baby Proof Your Career*. Rethink Press, Great Britain.

Freeman, L. (2008) *Maternity Leave Coaching Scheme: Keeping Mum*. www.personneltoday.com/articles. Accessed May 30, 2012.

Hall, L. (2013) *Mindful Coaching: How Mindfulness Can Transform Coaching Practice*. Kogan Page, London, England.

Harrison, N. (2008) Benefits case study: Clifford Chance: Maternity plan delivers the goods, *HRMagazine.* http://www.hrmagazine.co.uk/article-details/benefits-case-study-clifford-chance-maternity-plan-delivers-the. Accessed October 2015.

Hawkins, P., and Shoet, R. (2000) *Supervision in the Helping Professions.* McGraw-Hill, Open University Press, Maidenhead, Berkshire, England.

Hawkins, P., and Smith, N. (2006) *Coaching, Mentoring and Organizational Consultancy: Supervision and Development.* McGraw-Hill, Open University Press, Maidenhead, Berkshire, England.

Hewlett, S.A., and Luce, C.B. (2005), Off-ramps and on-ramps: keeping talented women on the road to success, *Harvard Business Review,* 83(3), 43.

Hilpern, K. (2007) 'Watching with Auntie,' *Coaching at Work.* January 2007 (p. 35–39). www.coaching-at-work.com/2007/03/01/watch-with-auntie/. Accessed May 2012 and August 2015.

Kirkpatrick, D.L. (1959) Evaluation of training, in Craig, R.L. and Bittel, L.R. (eds.). *Training and Evaluation Handbook.* McGraw-Hill, New York, NY.

Klasen, N., and Clutterbuck, D. (2002) *Implementing Mentoring Schemes: A Practical Guide to Successful Programs.* Butterworth-Heinemann, Oxford, England.

Kline, N. (2002) *Time to Think: Listening to Ignite the Human Mind.* Ward Lock, Cassell Illustrated, London, England.

Kline, N. (2015) *More Time to Think: The Power of Independent Thinking.* Cassell, Octopus Publishing Ltd., London, England.

Kram, K.E. (1983) Phases of the mentor relationship, *The Academy of Management Journal,* 26(4), 608–625.

Leimon, A., Moscovici, F., and Goodier, H. (2011) *Coaching Women to Lead.* Routledge, Hove East Sussex and New York.

Liston-Smith, J. (2011) Supervising maternity coaches, in *Coaching and Mentoring Supervision: Theory and Practice.* Bachkirova, T., Jackson, P., and Clutterbuck, D. (eds.). Open University Press, McGraw-Hill Education, Maidenhead, Berkshire, England.

Mainiero, L. A. and Sullivan, S.E. (2005) Kaleidoscope careers: An alternate explanation for the "opt-out" revolution. *The Academy of Management Executive (1993–2005),* 19(1), 106–123.

Maltz, M. (1960). *Psycho-Cybernetics.* Bantam Books, New York, NY.

McKinsey. (2012) *Women Matter 2012. Making the Breakthrough 2007, 2012.* http://www.mckinsey.com/Features/Women_Matter. Accessed May 2012 and July 2015.

McKinsey. (2015) *Diversity Matters 2015,* Full Report (pdf). www.mckinsey.com/insights/organization/why_diversity_matters. Accessed October 2015.

Megginson, D., Clutterbuck, B., Garvey, B., Stokes, P., and Garrett-Harris, R. (2006) *Mentoring in Action: A Practical Guide.* 2nd ed. Kogan-Page, London, England.

Megginson, D. and Clutterbuck, C. (1995) *Mentoring In Action.* Kogan Page, London, England.

Megginson, D. and Clutterbuck, D. (2005) *Techniques for Coaching and Mentoring.* Butterworth-Heinemann, Oxford, England.

Megginson, D. and Clutterbuck, D. (2009) *Further Techniques for Coaching and Mentoring.* Butterworth-Heinemann, Oxford, England.

Merrick, L. and Stokes, P. (2011) Supervision in mentoring programmes, in *Coaching and Mentoring Supervision: Theory and Practice.* Bachkirova, T., Jackson, P., and Clutterbuck, D. (eds.). Open University Press, McGraw-Hill Education, Maidenhead, Berkshire, England.

O'Neil, D. A. and Bilimoria, D. (2005) Women's career development phases, *Career Development International,* 10(3), 168–189.

Concise Oxford English Dictionary. (2004) 11th ed., Oxford University Press, Oxford, England.

Ridler Report. (2013), www.ridlerandco.com/ridler-report. Accessed July 2013.

6th Ridler Report. (2016) Strategic Trends in the Use of Executive Coaching. Webinar Presentation to AoC (Association for Coaching), ICF (International Coach Federation), and EMCC (European Mentoring and Coaching Council) December 1, 2015. Clive Mann, author and principle researcher (unpublished).

Sheehy, G. (1977) *Passages: Predictable Crises of Adult Life.* Bantam Books, New York, NY.

Sparrow, S. (2009) Maternity coaching: Back to work without a bump. *Personnel Today.* www.personneltoday.com/hr/maternity-coaching-back-to-work-without-a-bump/. Accessed October 2015.

Whitmore, J. (2009) *Coaching for Performance: GROWing Human Potential and Purpose: The Principles and Practice of Coaching and Leadership.* 4th ed. Nicholas Brearley, London, England.

Whittington, J. (2010) *Systemic Coaching and Constellations.* Kogan Page, London, England.

Wittenberg-Cox, A. (2010) *How Women Mean Business. A Step by Step Guide to Profiting from Gender Balanced Business,* Wiley, Chicester, West Sussex, United Kingdom.

Index